# Victorian Bathing and Bathing Suits

## The Culture of the Two-Piece Bathing Dress from 1837 – 1901

Compiled from Original Sources

Edited by Deb Salisbury

Editor of
*Elephant's Breath & London Smoke: Historic Colour Names, Definitions & Uses*
and
*Fabric à la Romantic Regency:*
*A Glossary of Fabrics from Original Sources 1795 – 1836*

Published by
The Mantua-Maker Historical Sewing Patterns
Abbott, Texas
2013

First Edition 2013

Published by
The Mantua-Maker Historical Sewing Patterns
100 PR 232
Abbott, TX 76621
deb@mantua-maker.com
http://www.Mantua-Maker.com

Cover arranged by Deb Salisbury
Cover photos from *Peterson's Magazine*, 1870 and *The Delineator*, 1894

This book is dedicated to SuZ Miller, with my greatest affection.

Deb Salisbury

# Table of Contents

# Introduction

When I decided to create a new bathing suit pattern, I searched for a modern book documenting Victorian bathing suits. To my surprise, I couldn't find one. Yet I had quite a few period magazines with engravings of bathing dresses in my collection. While I was doing more research, I fell in love with the traditions and ethics surrounding American, English, and French bathing.

This book focuses on the culture of bathing, swimming, and sea bathing across the decades, and on women's bathing suits, noting their styles, variations, and evolution, all quoted from the original writers of that time, and includes over 125 illustrations. I've included descriptions and engravings of men's and children's suits whenever I found them, but their clothing was not as well documented as the ladies' dresses.

The culture and proper dress of bathing changed radically during Queen Victoria's reign, led, of course, by the French. The accepted ladies' one-piece bathing gown gave way to the two-piece bathing suit, and bathing went from a medical treatment to a social event.

Around 1845, the classic Victorian bathing suit for American and English ladies came into existence, but even into the 1870s some women wore a long shirt-like garment, which billowed and floated while in the water, and clung to the figure when out of the water. This gown was no end embarrassing – to British and American eyes.

Men wore as little as they could get away with, which usually meant nothing at all until the ladies discovered the fun of playing in the water.

Bathing was not for the faint of heart. It was supposed to promote health, and presumably beauty, but from the descriptions many sea bathers must have felt half drowned. The following letter, written in 1820, describes a routine that was repeated for the next fifty years – until bathing for fun became fashionable.

October 25. [1820, Sidmouth, Devon] ... Our cottage overlooks the beach, and I have been surprised to find that, cold as it is, the ladies have not yet given up bathing; every morning I see from my window, while I am dressing, several of them braving the element; but not a single man. The way in which they bathe is as follows: the lady enters one of the bathing machines which stand along the beach – little wooden houses upon high wheels – and it is moved down to the water's edge. After undressing, she puts on a long loose gown, and descends from the machine, by a step-ladder, upon the sand. There she is met by a couple of old fishermen's wives, called guides, each of whom takes an arm, and, turning her back to the water, wait for the next wave. It comes dashing on; and, just as it curls and breaks on the shore, they plunge her backward, and she is completely overwhelmed. This is repeated as often as desired, and the lady then returns to the machine and dresses.

Miscellaneous Writings of F. W. P. Greenwood, 1846

The earliest reference to a lady's suit with trousers I've found was in 1838, and the wearer was mocked. Even the French bathing dress was not admired in its early days. It was plain, usually black, and, at best, boring.

Once fashion got hold of the bathing suit, the dress evolved rapidly. By 1870, many bathing suits were simply gorgeous. Fashion magazines began to include descriptions and engravings on a regular basis, vying to provide the most up-to-date styles. Bathing went from a quick, unpleasant dip in the ocean to an enjoyable social event, and swimming became popular.

# 1837

O DREAD and magnificent ocean! ... Much in this way did I apostrophise the gentle bracing waves, as they played invitingly for me to leap to their bosom from the steps of one of the excellent bathing machines on Southsea beach, where I had sat for a moment looking at the duck-like *sit* on the water of the American razee, the "Independence," lying at Spithead (on her way to the Baltic). If I did not like the look of her, it was because we had nothing at Spithead at the moment to vie with such taunt spars. Why reflect upon it? So I plunged outright, and revelled in the luxury of the most delicious exercise – swimming out just far enough to avoid the current setting along shore, which is often dangerous, from its drawing off. Fatigued at last with pleasure, pure and exquisite, I regained my dressing-room. With the door open, I sat some time wrapt in the soothing influence of the beautiful view before me – the boats, ships, steamers, wherries, gave animation to the waters; and the lovely landscape of the Isle of Wight (gay Ryde, laughing at the water's edge,) completed the charm. ...

The slow-and-sure ships of our fleet were always as good as the best! At the word "best" I awoke, and found my feet getting wet by the splashing of the coming-in tide. The lad that runs the machines down in the water, and draws them up by a windlass, knocked at the door to know what I was about. I was ashamed to say I had been asleep; for really a bathing-machine on Southsea, or on any other beach, is no place to "caulk " in

*The United Service Journal*, August 1837

At Coney Island, which is three miles from Bath, and is joined to Long Island by a bridge across a narrow inlet, is a fine beach for bathing, with a public house, and other conveniences. A rail-road is attached to the establishment, with cars leaving the hotel for the beach, a distance of eighty rods, every few minutes, during the summer season. The bathing at this place is not surpassed by any in the United States., The beach is white and hard.

New York as it is, 1837

As to the police of the town, that, too, is admirably like that of the west-end of London; with only this considerable difference in favour of that of Brighton, that in the whole town you will not in a week be pestered by a tithe portion of the sturdy beggars by whom you would be pestered in walking from Berkeley Square to Boodle's. The most timid ladies can walk by the sea-side at any hour of the day without running the slightest risk of insult, being either directly or indirectly offered to their feelings. Very different, indeed, was the case thirty years agone! We were about to say, that at that time the police of the town was execrable; we should have given the town more credit than it deserved, for, in truth, it could boast of no police regulations at all that were worthy of any community in a higher state of civilization than Hottentots or Esquimaux. When the place was only resorted to by a few invalids, the long line of cliffs afforded abundance of convenience for decorous bathing. But as the number of visitors increased, so their character altered. It was no longer the invalid alone, with an anxious friend or a staid attendant, who arrived; but the gay, the idle, the dissipated, and in many cases the dissolute, also resorted there; and to use the quaint expression of a writer of the time, "the limits of male and female bathing got strangely confounded; both sexes might be seen bathing within a few yards of each other, while spectators of both sexes lounged up and down the beach, neither bathers nor spectators seeming to dream that there could be the least possible harm in such a scene! Fancy such a scene at Brighton now! Both bathers and spectators would, we opine, very soon find themselves on terms far more intimate than agreeable with that able, and active magistrate, Sir David Scott.

The Guide to Knowledge, 1837

# 1838

And Mrs. Matthews Shuffle, with her pretty arch attendant Olympe, is vulgarising even the poet's sacred mine of similes, the "azure bosom of the deep:" the waves, like crested warriors, bow before her: could they do otherwise, when she came forth in a bathing dress of green with full trousers and a bathing wig?

Let not incredulity hazard a smile. To their shame be it spoken, many loungers made it a morning's amusement to look at the bathers; and Mrs. Matthews Shuffle thought that, were she seen going into the water with her long black hair dishevelled, no doubt could ever arise as to its being her own; while a dry wig being in readiness in the machine, no great inconvenience would ensue.

Fitzherbert, 1838

BATHING GOWN.
PLATE 8. FIG. 25.

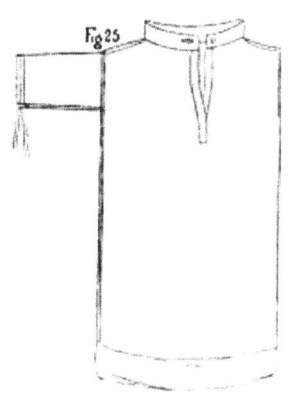

Bathing gowns are made of blue or white flannel, stuff, calimanco, or blue linen. As it is especially desirable that the water should have free access to the person, and yet that the dress should not cling to, or weigh down the bather, stuff or calimanco are preferred to most other materials; the dark coloured gowns are the best for several reasons, but chiefly because they do not show the figure, and make the bather less conspicuous than she would be in a white dress.

As the width of the materials, of which a bathing gown is made, varies, it is impossible to say of how many breadths it should consist. The width at the bottom, when the gown is doubled, should be about 15 nails: fold it like a pinafore, slope 3 1/2 nails for the shoulders, cut or open slits of 3 1/2 nails long for the arm-holes; set in plain sleeves 41 nails long, 3 1/2 nails wide, and make a slit in front 5 nails long.

In making up, delicacy is the great object to be attended to. Hem the gown at the bottom, gather it into a band at the top, and run in strings; hem the opening and the bottom of the sleeves, and put in strings. A broad band should be sewed in about half a yard from the top, to button round the waist. ...

BATHING CAP.

These are made of oil-silk, and are worn, when bathing, by ladies who have long hair. Cut a piece of oil-silk, 4 nails long and 8 nails wide; double it so as to make a square; let the doubled part be the back of the cap, and slope off the corner at the top, towards the back, in a curve, so as to shape it to the form of the back of the head. Sew up along the top of the bathing cap, binding it with tape at the seam, both at the top and in the front. Lay on a tape behind to form a hem, making oylet-holes at the ears, and passing a string through each oylet-hole, which is fastened down at the opposite side; these strings draw up the cap, when worn, to the size required.

It is advisable, however, for those who have not long hair, to bathe in plain linen caps, so as to admit the water without the sand or grit, and thus the bather, unless prohibited on account of health, enjoys all the benefit of the shock without injuring the hair.

These caps are often worn by children when the head is shaved, if subject to diseases in the head, as ring-worm, scald head, &c.

The Workwoman's Guide, 1838

We were amused a few days since with an account in a newspaper, of a meeting at some large town – we think in Yorkshire – convened for the purpose of raising a subscription for building baths; where, in reply to an oration in favour of bathing, an old gentleman of known robust health "arose to reply," and told the assembly that the custom might be very salubrious, but he was certain that, judging from experience, it was not essential to health, for he had never been into water for *sixty-five years*.

Now we so far agree with this hydrophobist, that many strong constitutions remain strong, *notwithstanding* that the act of ablution to the whole surface is never performed; but we think that persons of more weakly habit would be benefited by the use of the bath; while those again of very delicate health would find it alarming to commence, and difficult to continue, the practice on the approach of winter.

Very confident we are, that much injury has resulted from the injudicious use of cold bathing; many a delicate girl has been hastened to her grave by the ignorance of those in authority over her. "Let her go to the sea-side and bathe, it will brace her system, and restore her bloom;" she is accordingly taken to the coast, probably to Broadstairs, Ramsgate, or some other watering place on the eastern shore, to be pierced through with bleak winds; instead of inhaling the soft breezes of Devonshire, on the south side of one of its downs. Early in the morning she goes shivering to the beach, and if a "*machine*" be ready, she is quickly among the breakers, with a keen north-easterly wind flapping the canvass, and piping in at the crevices of the frail tenement. Chilled in body, depressed in spirits, she reluctantly undresses, puts on a cold clammy bathing dress; and with dabbled feet, as white and cold as marble, stands quaking and shrinking on the steps, till the guide's impatience urges her to the hated plunge. She regains the sodden floor, redresses herself, and returns to her home to curl her hair, – more cold, more dispirited than before she left it. Head-ache, languor, chilliness ensue; and too frequently a fit of illness closes the scene. Such ill-managed bathing is, alas! *we know,* of no rare occurrence. The most robust constitution could not sustain it with impunity; how then can the fragile bear it, and not suffer! It is well known to medical men, and all mothers ought to be aware, that cold bathing is highly injurious when any sensation of chill is experienced. A brisk walk of short duration, that is, to circulate the blood, raise the spirits, invigorate the frame – *but never to heat or fatigue it,* – is indispensable: and the bath ought to be taken immediately afterwards; no standing about till the genial glow has subsided: – briskness, mirth, a rapid plunge overhead – another – and out again, quick and forcible friction with coarse and dry towels, rapid redressing, another immediate and hilarious though short walk, should be enforced, and then home for adornment, if needed, but not to breakfast – that meal ought always to be taken above an hour before the bath. Few are able to encounter the shock until they have been fortified by a meal, yet that meal should have ceased its first demands upon the digestive powers ere fresh calls are made on the frame. Attention to the above directions will obviate some of the objections to the use of cold-bathing for the very delicate.

*The Magazine of Domestic Economy*, February 1838

# 1839

As the beach at Southwold partakes of the advantages enjoyed by other sea-port towns for sea-bathing, it naturally induces many strangers to sojourn among us during the summer season for that purpose. Three convenient bathing-machines are kept on the beach for their accommodation, which are attended by strong and careful persons, and afford the temptation of bathing in the sea without the possibility of observation. These consist of a commodious wooden chamber, which is closely jointed against every wind – is ascended by a safe-stepping board at one end – and terminated towards the sea at the other end by an impervious curtain or awning of thick tent-like canvass, which forms a covering, strongly secured on all sides, over a kind of wooden cradle or well-fenced crib beneath it, floored with open boards, in which, firmly secured to the frame-work of the machine, the most timid bather may enjoy the watery element without the slightest cause of apprehension or molestation. The cradle is terminated by a door into the sea for the ingress or egress of swimmers. This is a great improvement. For persons in sound health, who are not subject to chill from a longer stay in the water, and who may therefore enjoy it safely, would be little content with the boxed-up limits of a sea-water imprisonment.

<u>Southwold</u>, 1839

[at Ramsgate] "Why, I'm blessed if there a'nt some ladies a-going in!" exclaimed Mr. Joseph Tuggs, with intense astonishment.

"Lor, pa!" exclaimed Miss Charlotta.

"There *is*! my dear," said Mr. Joseph Tuggs. And, sure enough, four young ladies, each furnished with a towel, tripped up the steps of a bathing machine; in went the horse, floundering about in the water: round turned the machine, down sat the driver, and presently out burst the young ladies aforesaid, with four distinct splashes.

"Well, that's sing'ler too," ejaculated Mr. Joseph Tuggs after an awkward pause. Mr. Cymon coughed slightly.

"Why, here's some gentlemen a-going in on this side," exclaimed Mrs. Tuggs, in a tone of horror.

Three machines – three horses – three flounderings – three turnings round – three splashes – three gentlemen, disporting themselves in the water, like so many dolphins.

"Well, that's sing'ler," said Mr. Joseph Tuggs again. Miss Charlotta coughed this time, and another pause ensued. It was agreeably broken.

"How d'ye do, dear? We have been looking for you all the morning," said a voice to Miss Charlotta Tuggs. Mrs. Captain Waters was the owner of it.

"How d'ye do?" said Captain Walter Waters, all suavity; and a most cordial interchange of greetings ensued.

"Belinda, my love," said Captain Walter Waters, applying his glass to his eye, and looking in the direction of the sea.

"Yes, my dear," replied Mrs. Captain Waters.

"There's Harry Thompson."

"Where?" said Belinda, applying her glass to her eye.

"Bathing."

"Lor, so it is! He don't see us, does he?"

"No, I don't think he does," replied the captain. – "Bless my soul, how very singular!"

"What?" inquired Belinda.

"There's Mary Golding, too."

"Lor! – where?" (Up went the glass again.)

"There," said the captain, pointing to one of the young ladies before noticed, who, in her bathing costume, looked as if she were enveloped in a patent Mackintosh, of scanty dimensions.

"So it is, I declare!" exclaimed Mrs. Captain Waters. – "How very curious we should see them both!"

"Very," said the captain, with perfect coolness.

"It's the reg'lar thing here, you see," whispered Mr. Cymon Tuggs to his father.

Sketches, by Boz, 1839

# 1840

Bathing abroad is a very different operation to the mode as practised in England. At Havre I was amused observing the process. You enter a canvass box and undress, putting on, as a bathing costume, a blouse pantaloons, and oil-skin cap, and being thus equipped, as if for exhibition on a tight rope, with the addition of a pair of sabots to preserve the feet, you follow the path, indicated by planks, along the shingles for some hundred yards, in the face of all the world, followed by a man, also in a bathing dress. Arrived at the edge of the water you present your hand to your companion, and enter the wide expanse together. Thus, hand-in-hand, like lovers resolved to dare fate in each other's company, the pair commence a promenade, getting deeper and deeper amongst the waves, till they reach the hips. This lasts as long as you please; half-an-hour, or for hours, as it may happen, and according to the *society* which may arrive – as a French person must have society everywhere – and then you return to your canvass box in your wet garments.

A Summer Amongst the Bocages and the Vines, 1840

Deb Salisbury

# 1841

[Margate] Bathing. – The bathing-machine, as now used, was the invention of a Quaker, named Beale, an inhabitant of Margate, and an engraving of the first vehicle of the kind may be seen in the bathing house, at the back of the harbour, for many years kept by him and his descendant, and now occupied by Mr. Hill. This is the original line of bathing houses, having galleries at the back, from which the bather steps into a machine, and assembly-rooms in front, in which the concerts used to be given. The price of bathing is as at other places. The subscription to the rooms is but 3s. 6d. for the season, which entitles the party to read the daily papers, and a piano-forte is furnished for the use of the ladies. Here are also warm, shower, or sulphur baths, and baths *en douche*. Machine bathing may likewise be had on the shore under Buenos Ayres, towards the Infirmary; and in the Fort there is an extraordinary erection, or perhaps, excavation would be a more correct term, called

The Clifton Baths, being built in the solid chalk, rising in a circular form, surmounted with a dome 33 feet high. Two chimneys, to represent pyramids, crown the structure. The buildings consist of a waiting or subscription-room, 40 feet long, fronting the sea, opening on to a terrace 100 feet in length, in which alcoves and seats are introduced at convenient distances. Twenty bathing-machines stand under the former, 10 feet above high-water mark, whence there is an easy access to the sands. There is also a horse road from the cliffs, that reaches the sands by a gentle declivity. There is a plunging bath, 80 feet by 40, for females and children, and all kinds of medicinal baths, as elsewhere. The place is altogether well deserving of a visit, and is a singular and indisputable evidence of the enterprising spirit of its projector and proprietor, Mr. Boys, a solicitor at Margate. Upwards of 12,000 persons have visited the Clifton Baths in a single season.
...

[Ramsgate] Bathing. – One of the many advantages afforded to the town of Ramsgate from the building of the pier has been the improvement of its sand, which, from being narrow and of small extent, is become very considerable, and affords every possible facility for the accommodation of the numerous machines which crowd it during the season ; and many hundred yards of a space formerly rocky and rugged has, since the erection of its extensive harbour, been made level and sandy, affording a delightful parade for the company upon leaving the machines after bathing. Upwards of thirty machines are employed every morning during the season, and several convenient waiting-rooms have been built where the company resort, to take, in their turns the benefit of the invigorating bath. The proprietors pay every possible attention to those visitors who honour them with their support, – providing for their use cleanly and comfortable machines, with careful and experienced guides, under whose protection the most delicate and timid may bathe in safety.

Direction-posts are placed on the sands, and constables stationed to prevent persons bathing openly from approaching the machines, or offending the decency of those who use them, and to ensure a certain extent of promenade for them after bathing.

The hours of bathing are from six till twelve o'clock; on Sundays till ten.

| *Terms of Bathing.* | *s.* | *d.* |
|---|---|---|
| A lady taking a machine, guide included. . . . . . . . . . | 1 | 3 |
| Two, or more ladies, guide included, each . . . . . . . . | 1 | 0 |
| A child taking a machine, guide included . . . . . . . . . | 1 | 3 |
| Two, or more young children, guide included, each | 0 | 9 |
| A gentleman taking a machine, guide included . . . . | 1 | 6 |
| A gentleman bathing himself . . . . . . . . . . . . . . . . . . | 1 | 0 |
| Two, or more gentlemen, guide included, each . . . . | 1 | 3 |
| Two, or more gentlemen, bathing themselves, each | 0 | 9 |

The Visitor's Guide to the Watering Places, 1841

Ladies fond of sea-bathing as a luxury, and a pleasant bracer of the whole animal economy, should never exceed a couple of good dips. Rubbing the whole surface of the skin during several minutes, should immediately succeed in the bathing machine, and be followed by a brisk walk home. Ladies always fear to wet their hair, from the difficulty of drying it. But I think that if they bathed without the oilskin cap, and the water were allowed to wet the head twice a week, the action of the salt water would prove very beneficial, and prevent the hair from falling off. After the bath, the hair should be wrung and wiped as dry as possible with towels. On the fair bather's return home, she should have her head and hair rubbed with a couple of yolks of egg beaten up with a spoonful of lemon juice, and immediately after well washed with abundance of either cold or lukewarm soft water, until the head and hair are quite clean. ...

BATHING OF INVALIDS.

Sea-bathing, as a remedy for specific disease, as well as a protection against the dangers of weak and unsettled health, requires to be conducted with much more care than that intended only for luxury, or the preservation of an already robust condition of body. ... And yet in watering-places generally, all bathers are put upon the same footing by the ignorant individuals who earn their subsistence as attendants upon them. The coarse brutality of the bathing-women, in dipping the bathers, is sometimes productive of considerable evil; and where nervous timidity has existed in a bather, this sort of conduct has sometimes raised an alarm in the patient fraught with a thousand times more mischief than the amount of benefit yielded by the bath itself, unattended with such a circumstance. During my experience, I have known many a poor girl and boy, weak, sickly, nervous – starting at a sound or a shadow – when seated trembling on the steps of the bathing-machine, afraid either to advance or recede, suddenly and unexpectedly pulled down head foremost by the brutal female attendant, and soused in the water with just as much unconcern and absence of tenderness, as if she were dipping a whelp. I have frequently seen a fit of illness the consequence, and the impossibility of ever inducing the frightened child to try a second bath without employing force, and thereby creating an injury much greater than the one sought to be removed by the bathing.

The women who attend upon ordinary female bathers in the machines, should be persons of kind, soothing, and persuasive manners. That there is no lack of such persons, is proved by the nurses in every hospital throughout the country. These are obtained so qualified, because, the office of nurse being elective in establishments supported by voluntary contribution, such qualifications are looked for, and those candidates who have them not, are rejected. If, then, ordinary bathers, in good health, require in their bathing attendants the qualities I have mentioned, what must be the case with invalid bathers, to whom the least oversight is a vehicle of mischief, the least roughness a cause of pain and alarm, and to whom a word or a look skilfully applied often brings relief! For such persons, the bathing-women should possess all the qualities of the best hospital nurses: blandness, kindness of manner, gentleness, persuasiveness, a knowledge of the mischief that may result from mismanagement, either before, pending, or after the bath, and, above all, a great deal of tact, or, in plainer words, of "mother wit." As the earnings of the bathing-women are by no means inconsiderable, females possessing such qualifications should, by a proper encouragement held out by proprietors of bathing-machines, be induced to embrace this calling, instead of leaving it to be exercised only by ignorant, often by dram-drinking fisherwomen. A woman known to the bathers as being thus gifted would obtain such preference, that she would soon realise an humble fortune.

The Hand-book of Bathing, 1841

# 1842

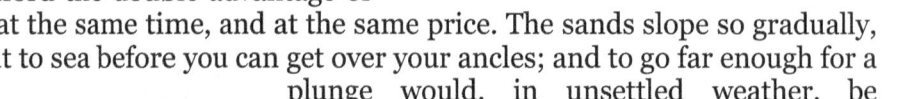

MARGATE COSTUMES. ...

The Baths hold a very conspicuous position. Their interior economy is also admirable. Hot bath and towel, three shillings; which, with the usual gratuity, makes hot sea-bathing at Ramsgate just six dips to the pound. ...

[Worthing] The grand attraction to this place is the bathing-machines; which afford the double advantage of a carriage airing, and a dip at the same time, and at the same price. The sands slope so gradually, that you have to be taken out to sea before you can get over your ancles; and to go far enough for a plunge would, in unsettled weather, be positively dangerous, lest a storm should burst and overwhelm yourself and the bathing-cart before you have time to return.

A WATER EXCURSION.

Punch, 1842

BATHS & BATHING.

The Beach at Hastings is proverbially excellent. The bathing machines have, however, no hoods, and are, therefore, not so private as those used at Margate; they stand upon the beach below the Parades, both at Hastings and St. Leonards: the charge is 1s., or less, in proportion, for a number of attendencies.

The Bathing establishments are two in number, viz; the Pelham Baths, Pelham Place, one of the handsomest establishments of the kind in the kingdom, and the Marine Baths, on the Parade, near the Library; they are much frequented. Portable baths and invalid chairs are let upon hire, and a person will attend from the bathing establishments when shampooing is required.

Picturesque Excursions, 1842

The effect of the cold sea bath is to give tone to the system, and it is well suited to all cases of debility when there yet remains sufficient vigour of the system, to induce reaction after the patient comes out of the water. As a general rule, cold sea-bathing is never useful unless a glow is experienced over the entire surface of the body after the immersion. It is always advisable that persons who are very delicate should commence with a tepid bath, repeating it two or three times, and lowering the temperature each time; or such persons, if they have not been in the habit of adopting the practice previously recommended, of sponging the body over every morning, should do so for two or three previous mornings, before they venture into the sea. Those who have followed this excellent plan will require no other preparation whatever.

The best time of year for bathing is doubtless the summer and autumn, although I have known persons bathe in the sea the whole year, with evident advantage. Assuredly no one ought to commence a course of sea-bathing except in the seasons above named, at which period the temperature of the sea varies from 55° to 70° Fahrenheit. The hour for sea-bathing must, in some measure, depend upon the state of the tide; but, generally speaking, it will be found most serviceable as near the hour of noon as possible; this will be a sufficient time after breakfast for the invalid to have taken exercise, a circumstance which, if not carried so far as to produce great languor and excessive perspiration, will be highly serviceable to the patient, as it renders the circulation more vigorous. If there be a little moisture on the skin, it should always be wiped off before going into the bath, this of itself will not be injurious, as long as the surface of the body is not chilled, nor the circulation enfeebled by over fatigue.

Hastings Considered as a Resort for Invalid, 1842

# 1843

BATHING GOWN. – The materials employed are various, flannels, stuff, or calamanca, are the most preferable, giving free ingress to the water. The length must be determined by the height of the wearer, and the width at the bottom should be about fifteen nails. It should be folded as you would a pinafore, and to be sloped three and three-quarters nails for the shoulder. The slits for the arm-holes must be three nails and three-quarters long, and the sleeves are to be set in plain: the length of the latter is not material. It is useful to have a slit of three inches, in front of each. The gown is to have a broad hem at the bottom, and to be gathered into a band at the top, which is to be drawn tight with strings; the sleeves are to be hemmed and sewn round the arm or wrist, in a similar manner.

The Ladies' Work-Table Book, 1843

Both sexes here promiscuously commingle; it is true that both Gentlemen and Ladies are compelled by the police to wear bathing dresses; yet, to the English eye, unaccustomed to such scenes, it must, indeed, seem strange to see males and females in flannel robes, saturated with water, clinging so closely to their limbs as to expose the exact form and proportions of each bather, dancing, romping, and sporting together; chatting, swimming, or floating, in close vicinity, apparently wholly unconscious of the impropriety they are committing: nor will he feel less disgust, than astonishment, when he sees some ten or twelve stout peasants, of both sexes issue, from the same bathing machine. I have myself counted sixteen males and females entering the same vehicle, seemingly without the least idea of the indecency they were about to be guilty of. Nor even in the higher ranks, is it an uncommon sight to see a man and his wife dressing and undressing in the same bathing machine. When our countrymen first see these strange indelicacies, they feel shocked, and turn away feeling sure that they would die, rather than be guilty of following such a bad example: in a few months afterwards, they not only look on with a careless and unastonished gaze, but readily join the party who thus promiscuously gambol amidst the waves. A stranger to Ostend may fancy I am too severe, that such an assertion is censorious. For the confirmation or denial of ray statement, I beg to refer him to any old resident in Ostend, or the still better test of his own future practical experience.

Belgium, 1843

# 1844

The sea is the best place for swimming in; running rivers, and the "brook that brawls along" are next to be chosen; and the still, dull pond, the last. In either case, the bottom ought to be of gravel, or smooth stones, but quite free from holes, so that there may be no danger of hurting the feet, or sinking in the mud. Weeds must be carefully avoided, lest the feet get entangled amongst them. The swimmer should ascertain that the bottom of the stream be not beyond his depth; and if he has no one with him who is acquainted with the spot, he should endeavour to fathom it before venturing in. Bathing is best performed when entirely naked: but, if this be unsuitable, short drawers may be worn; and sometimes in jackets and trousers: the bathing-dress may be made of calico.

The Boy's Treasury of Sports, Pastimes, and Recreations, 1844

*Rules for Sea-bathing.*

(1). Sea-bathing should be continued for at least five or six weeks, at two periods in the year, making June a part of the one period, and September of the other. By thus allowing an interval between the two courses of bathing, a more salutary change may be effected in the fluids and solids, than if it had been persisted in for many months without intermission.

(2). *The young and delicate* ought gradually to prepare themselves for sea-bathing, by previously using *the tepid bath,* at a temperature commencing at 90°, lowered five degrees each time, and terminating at 65°.

(3). Bathing ought not to be commenced until two or three days after arriving on the sea-coast; during which, it may be advisable to take a moderate dose of salts, or a tea-cupful of sea-water, every morning before breakfast. Sea-bathing is attended with risk after great fatigue, as on coming from a long journey; and after the body has been long engaged in any exertion, which has produced lassitude, debility, or chilliness; and when there is any marked determination of blood to the head or lungs. It is an indispensable rule, never to bathe after having taken medicine, or while under its influence, or with a full stomach.

(4). The robust and healthy may bathe early in the morning before breakfast; but persons of a delicate or feeble constitution, or who are in the habit of dining late, and indulging in the luxuries of the table, ought rather to bathe about two hours before dinner. It is better for such persons, to bathe on alternate days, than for many days consecutively. Daily bathing frequently produces lassitude, accompanied by a manifest wasting of the body.

(5). It is now a rule in bathing, to avoid going into the water when the body is cold, so that even infirm persons should not use the cold bath, without having previously taken some moderate exercise. This doctrine cannot be too strongly inculcated. Dr Currie justly observes, that bathers ought not to wait on the edge of a bath, or of the sea, until they are perfectly cool; for if they plunge into the water in that state, a sudden and alarming chilliness may supervene, which would not have been felt, had they been moderately warm when they went into the water.

(6). Attention should be paid to the nature of the bathing place. A bottom of clear sand is to be preferred. Sea weeds are to be avoided; for they frequently contain pointed shells, which are apt to inflict dangerous wounds.

(7). It has long been considered a useful rule, to have the head first wetted, and indeed many think it necessary to plunge head foremost into the water. It is asserted, that a rush of blood to the head, with all its direful consequences, may take place, if this precaution be neglected. This practice however, has of late been objected to. A sudden plunge is a violent and unnatural exertion, which ought not to be insisted upon *with delicate people;* and several of the bad effects which are ascribed to cold bathing, and which have forced many who were anxious to persevere in its use, to abandon it, are supposed to have originated from the effects of this very practice. Plunging headlong into the water, with most people, occasions unpleasant sensations, affecting both the eyes and the ears; and no one should do so, who suffers inconvenience from it. Those however, who feel no bad effects from the practice, may persevere in it.

(8). The time spent in the water, should not exceed a minute or two. If longer immersed, the body should be kept during the whole time under the surface of the water, and in action, in order to promote the circulation of the blood. It is much better to remain completely immersed in deep, than to take repeated plunges in shallow water.

(9). Upon coming out of the water, the body should be wiped dry, with a rough cloth, and the ordinary dress quickly resumed. It is more necessary to replace the usual vestments quickly, than to be extremely anxious to have the surface of the body perfectly dry, as wetness from salt water is not likely to be prejudicial.

(10). After bathing, moderate exercise is necessary to promote the return of the heat of the body, care being taken that it is not violent, nor too long continued.

(11). If bathing occasion chilliness, a meal should be taken soon after the bath; breakfast in the morning, in the forenoon, some warm soup. Indeed if immersion, instead of being succeeded by a glow on the surface of the skin, be followed by chilliness, languor, or headach, bathing should by no means be persisted in.

(12). During a course of sea-bathing, and when even the warm sea-water bath is used, friction with a flesh-brush, or coarse woollen gloves, ought not to be omitted. It may enable a patient to continue the course, when otherwise he must have given it up.

3.

Bathing-machines are exceedingly useful, and ought to be established at every bathing station. When properly managed, and in good repair, they afford a means of bathing in almost all weathers. They preserve the clothes, and save the bather from injurious exposure to cold winds while undressed.

4.

Bathing-dresses should be made of a very open texture, so as freely to admit water. They prevent the temperature of the body from being so much reduced, as to render bathing in cold weather hazardous. To strong and healthy men, bathing dresses are not necessary; but to sickly males, such dresses may prove useful. At any rate, until completely undressed the body should be wrapt in a large dry flannel gown, which should not be laid aside till the very moment of going into the water; by this means, any chill previous to immersion will be avoided, and that salutary glow, which ought always to succeed bathing, will in general be insured.

The Code of Health and Longevity, 1844

# 1845

*Bathing in the Douro.* – It is an amusing sight, and enlivened withal, to look at the rows of white tents, the beautiful girls and their elegant dresses, the crowds of spectators, each sheltered by a bright-coloured umbrella, and some thirty or forty ladies and gentlemen, fat and thin, tall and short, old and young, in the water together, dipping and spluttering, shouting and shrieking, as the white-crested wave rolls towards them – some attempting to swim, others, fearful of being carried out to sea, clinging to their attendants' arms, and endeavouring to make their escape to *terra firma.* Here an old woman bearing aloft a little cherub, independent of any costume, to dip it a due number of times – there a bathing-girl encouraging a stout old gentleman to venture into the water, alter he has received the first souse on the head from the contents of a basin, to prevent his feeling the effect of the shock to his feet. Sometimes three or four young ladies will go in together, or a gentleman may be seen leading gallantly some fair one of his acquaintance: but everything is conducted with the strictest propriety and decorum; so that, however extraordinary the style may appear at first to the stranger, he soon becomes accustomed to it.

*The Penny Magazine,* November 29, 1845

There had long existed in this country a prejudice against bathing, or at least a degree of apathy rather surprising, indicated by the almost entire neglect of providing means for public bathing. Bathing was in the last century considered rather as a time and luxury than with a view to the improvement of health; but at present this is considerably altered; medical writers point out its value, and the public is beginning to be awakened to its importance to all, and particularly to the working classes. Still we are far behind in those conveniences which are essential to its general practice; and the expense and trouble attending bathing prevents its being so much employed as it might be. In France, advantages are placed within the reach of the poor to which the rich alone can aspire in other countries. The number of gratuitous baths which in' given at the hospitals of St. Louis and La Charité is truly prodigious; in 1822 it amounted to 127,752 for the out-patients only of the hospital of St. Louis. In Paris the habit of bathing is so general that the public baths are extremely numerous and cheap. We are only beginning to imitate what has been long established in that way in other countries. Bathing machines at the seaside, which are but of late origin, have diminished the difficulty at the various watering-places; but the use of baths is not yet of sufficiently easy accomplishment except to the wealthy, who can have them in their own houses.

An Encyclopædia of Domestic Economy, 1845

# 1846

[in 1846] For several years past, the town of Newport in Rhode Island has been the most fashionable sea-bathing place in the country. I once spent a fortnight there during the season. The very first day I was there, whilst strolling with a friend on the beach, we met a party of ladies and gentlemen with whom he was acquainted, and to whom he immediately introduced me. After conversing for a short time, I was surprised at a proposition made to us by one of the young ladies to go and bathe with them. I afterwards found that this was no uncommon occurrence at Newport – the ladies and gentlemen having different accommodations, in which they provided themselves with suitable bathing dresses, habited in which, they dash out, hand in hand, sometimes forty of them together, into the surf upon the beach. I confess I thought this more in accordance with the social habits of Paris and Vienna than with those of the United States. There was in it a latitude

which was no more typical of the general habits of the people than is the prudery, which is, in some instances, carried to an excess.

The Western World, 1849

*Consequences of Want of Accommodation for Summer Bathing. – The Daily News* has collected and published a whole column of cases of drowning which have occurred from bathing in rivers during this hot weather. These cases appear in the Provincial Newspapers in every part of England, and strikingly point out the great public neglect in this country of the very necessary means of bathing in summer. The establishment of the baths for the people in London and the large towns of late, shows that a perception of our deficiency in this means of health and cleanliness is diffusing itself in the public mind. Of all people in the world, perhaps the English are the most cleanly in their general habits, and the most defective in the use of the bath. There is scarcely a hamlet in Germany, much less a town, which has not its public baths, where, at any season of the year, and at a very slight cost you may enjoy a warm and cold bath. Again, in almost every river or stream running past towns, at the commencement of summer, wooden baths are erected, more or less extensive, according to the population of the place. Here, at the cost of five shillings for the whole summer, you may, as often as you please, have the advantage of a capacious swimming bath open to the sky, with sheds round for dressing, or of private ones connected with it. There are boarded floors at all sorts of depths, so as to accommodate children of all ages. The utmost decorum is observed, and napkins and bathing drawers are furnished. There is a fine for bathing without drawers. Ladies' baths are also as common. What is the fact in England? In all the fine streams running near our populous towns, there is scarcely such a thing as a summer bath ever seen. People go where they can, and in nine times out of ten are exposed to a charge of indecency, or to drowning. All kinds of obstacles abound to this most necessary and delightful refreshment. The feeling of private property is so strong here; meadows are so fenced and enclosed, that the side of a river is most difficult of access. If you get to it, ten to one but you are threatened with a fine for trespass; or you are warned off, on account of disturbing the fish; or it comes within the chartered limits of some water company, and you see a board offering forty shillings reward for information against you. The consequences are much inconvenience, danger to health, loss of a very healthy enjoyment, and the great loss of life, so laudably pointed out by the *Daily News*. Let us hope that the public will be more stimulated to secure everywhere proper places and accommodation for bathing. Humanity demands it, for the lives as well as the health of the people.

*The People's Journal*, July 4, 1846


THE BATHING-MACHINE HORSE.

This amphibious animal has never been described by naturalists. Buffon jumps over him in a very high manner, and Cuvier does not notice him at all, either under the head of fishes or animals.

The affection of the Bathing-machine Horse for the water is wonderful. It is shown in no other animal so deeply. The Newfoundland Dog will bound into the water, it is true; but is merely a passing plunge, nothing more than a fugitive dip. He rushes in to rescue a sinking stone, or to save some unhappy stick from drowning, but he does not make the sea his home like the Bathing-machine Horse. That quiet animal will stand in the water for hours, and never looks so happy as when he is taking his cold foot-bath. Upon land he looks awkward, and like a fish out of water. As he waddles along, his action betrays his origin. He lifts up his feet as if he were stepping over a number of waves, and when he stops, he will shake himself, fancying he has just come out of the water. The habits of the Bathing-machine Horse are very simple. He generally bathes after breakfast. During the day he is to be met out in the sea; but towards evening he returns to land, where he stops during the night. He has been taught to draw, which he generally does in a straight line, guided by the machine from which he takes his name. His pace is not very rapid, rarely exceeding two miles an hour; but if he is rather slow, at all events he is very sure. He has never been known to run away with, or to upset a bathing-machine. It is lucky he is so tractable, or else bathing might be attended with dangers, for which the cheapness would scarcely compensate. The only instance of viciousness ever heard of in the Bathing-machine Horse was exhibited by one at Ramsgate. As soon as the driver had turned the machine round, he would begin jibbing, which was very awkward for the person inside, who found the machine gradually filling, and his boots and clothes swimming over to France. This propensity, however, was accounted for by the fact of his being a French horse, who had been brought over from Boulogne, and his jibbing, it was explained, was only a desire on his part to back out of England, and return to his native place.

The Bathing-machine Horse, as he stands half hidden in the water, is a fine study for the artist. He is a model of patience. His head hangs downwards, as if it longed to repose itself on the bosom of the ocean – his eye seems to be reading the secrets which are buried at the bottom of the sea – his tail drops gracefully like a lady's back-hair, which has escaped from its oil-skin cap, and burst its comb – whilst his ear is listening to the music of the spheres, as he drinks in the stiff breeze, and looks half-seas-over. The only evidence of life which he gives is when a crab bites his foot, or when an impudent wave comes swaggering up to him for a game of leap-frog, and, without asking his leave, jumps over his back and wets him to the skin, when the Bathing-machine Horse gives a gentle shiver, and resumes his interrupted reflection. The way, however, in which he avoids a wave is rather clever. He generally sees one coming, and lifts up his nose to allow it to pass under him, as if he made a moral compact with himself always to keep his head above water. In this resolve, says Dr. Bushy, many young men of the present day might study him with advantage.

The Bathing-machine Horse is to be met with at all watering-places. I have no recollection of ever seeing one in London. He seems to belong to the breed of night cab-horses, and has an ugly bend in the knee, which certainly looks best when concealed in the sea. The Bathing-machine Horse can be approached without danger, and has very little pride in him, as is shown by his rope-traces, and his collar with its open work of straw.

I never saw a Bathing-machine Horse with a nosebag. I do not recollect ever seeing one eat. What is his natural food – hay, or shell-fish? grass or seaweed? The fact is, the Natural History of this interesting amphibious animal has been very little studied, and is very little known. I am inclined to believe he was the original Triton of which Neptune, when he went out with his state cockle-shell, used to drive a four-in-hand, and I have no doubt that the bathing-women, by whom he is attended and groomed to this present day, are the ancient Nereides, who always swam round him. It is a questionable point, however, whether the Bathing-machine Horse or the bathing-women still retain their wonderful power of swimming. These are only surmises, but, in the absence of facts, surely surmises are better than nothing? I shall be thankful if they only arouse a spirit of inquiry, and induce our *savans* to investigate this long-neglected subject. I feel confident that the Bathing-machine Horse must eventually take his proper stand in this country, and that before long, no Natural History will be complete without him. (Horace Mayhew.)

*The Almanack of the Month*, October 1846

# 1847

Boulogne is a beautiful town, and a cheap place as a residence, remarkably healthy, and during the summer months thousands from England come over to enjoy the luxury of sea-bathing, which cannot be excelled any where. I should suppose one-third of the inhabitants of Boulogne are English, who, on small incomes live in much better style than they could in England, and have more real enjoyment of life. The sea-beach appeared covered with small bathing houses, fixed on wheels; the bathers enter one and lock the door – when ready, a signal is made, and they are backed into the breakers as far as they wish, and then leap out and enjoy themselves as long as they please, for one shilling. ...

The bathing at Boulogne is under the same restriction, as regards the dress of the ladies and gentlemen who bathe in the sea, as at Ostend. The bathing machines, being on wheels are backed into the surf, from which the bathers jump, and both sexes form gay parties, dancing quadrilles, &c., together midst the waves, and play about like so many Naiads in the water; many of the English ladies swim with much more ease and grace than the French, although the French ladies in the water appear more bouyant and elastic – so natural to their nature. Their costume, while in bathing, appears more appropriate and neat than the heavy dress adopted by the English fashionables.

<u>The Tourist's Guide</u>, 1847

Dieppe, however, is much frequented as a watering-place in summer. The *Etablissement des Bains* is situated on the beach, nearly under the castle. There are no proper bathing-machines; and the bottom is a mass of flint shingle, without sand. A series of little huts are erected at the sea-side, from which ladies issue in robes resembling those of nuns, and gentlemen in wide trousers, and thus bathe in public. Ladies are assisted by male dippers appointed for this service, if they require their aid. There are also *hot baths* near the beach.

<u>Hand-book for Travellers in France</u>, 1847

The effects of cold bathing upon the body vary according to the constitution of the bather, and are influenced by the manner in which the bath is enjoyed. If a person, in the full enjoyment of health, plunge into cold water, and continue in it but a short time, the sensation experienced on emerging from the water is highly pleasurable; and when the body is dried, a glow of warmth pervades the whole frame, and the bather becomes refreshed and invigorated. The bather ought, therefore, not to continue for any length of time in the water; else the skin will become pale and contracted, and assume the peculiar appearance termed *goose-skin;* numbness and shivering, and a sensation of weariness, will ensue. To remain in the water after these appearances, is not only to throw away all the benefits of the previous exercise, but to bring about an exhaustion of strength, so great as sometimes to prove fatal.

In proceeding to bathe, certain precautions are necessary. Moderate exercise, accompanied by a general glow upon the surface of the body, is a better preparation for it, than total inactivity. Persons fall into sad mistakes who sit on the banks of a river, or at the seaside, to cool themselves previous to bathing. On no account would it be prudent to plunge into the water when greatly heated, and in a state of profuse perspiration; but, as a general rule, less risk will attend bathing when the body is somewhat heated, than when it is perfectly cooled.

<u>The Boy's Treasury of Sports, Pastimes, and Recreations</u>, 1847

# 1848

Newport stands side by side with Saratoga, whose waters the late M. Purgon, had he known them, would have prescribed to his patients. But, in the eyes of connoisseurs, it possesses an incontestable superiority in its sea-bathing, which will remain a source of perpetual despair to Saratoga. Every morning, clothed in the prescribed garb, wrapped in flannel from head to foot, the young people of both sexes come to seek and receive the surf. The two sexes are separated in distinct groups. But a charming privilege is allowed to those young men, who are so fortunate as to possess, at least, a sister. They are allowed to lend them their services in the place of those hired bathers, who carry them in their arms, and plunge them in the sea. In the confusion of the waves, for a sister that one loves, one can mistake a fair friend that one loves still more. The error is excusable. It is said that certain young men, whom nature has not blessed with a sister, hire, for the season, at Newport, a temporary one, a precious relative, who enables them to join the attractive groups of female bathers.

It is rare that a season at the waters is not crowned by some marriages, which have commenced beneath the wave.

*The United States Democratic Review*, February 1848

Letter XV.

Rochester, N.Y., Aug. 14, 1848. ... Now, it is my opinion that the present fashion of female dress is the cause of so many of us failing to take that outdoor exercise which is absolutely essential to vigorous health. For country walks and climbs, nothing could be so annoyingly inconvenient and unneat as our long dresses, light skirts, thin shoes and fancy bonnets.

This is surely not a right state of things, and I for one would advocate a reform most seriously and earnestly. Why might not we adopt a costume somewhat like the bathing dress we wear on the seashore: loose Turkish trowsers, a tunic or blouse, a black belt, and broad-brimmed straw hat, with the addition of thick boots and a light cane. This, with a tasteful choice of material, might be made a very piquante, picturesque and page-like costume, without infringing greatly on the reserved rights of the other sex. And then look at its infinite advantage over our usual dress, in clambering over rocks, following up trout streams, making way through thick forests and over marshy places, or in braving the sun in the open meadows.

Greenwood Leaves: a Collection of Sketches and Letters, 1850

A lady, not long ago, assured me, that the White Mountains were becoming more *fashionable* every year, and I was about to repeat her remark with regard to Newport, which really seems every year to become a more favorite resort. Ornamental cottages, built in the most perfect taste, are springing up in various parts of the island, and for three or four months in the year they are the residences of some of the most distinguished families in the country, while the transient visitors who come to Newport for a few weeks or days number many thousands. The beach is unrivalled in its hardness and beauty, above all, in its safety, and from ten to twelve o'clock in the morning, it presents a most lively and exciting scene. The bathing costume, which is frightfully unbecoming, is fortunately an effectual disguise, and the gay groups that issue from the bathing-cars, and bound with white feet over the sparkling sands to "wanton with the breakers," seem like unknown genii from the coral caves. A gentleman remarked to me, in view of those who came dripping from the foam of the sea, that hereafter he renounced his belief in the old Greek fable of the origin of Venus.

*The Union Magazine*, December 1848

BATHING IN THE SEA.

In the warm months of July and August, many people, who can spare the money, are very fond of spending a few weeks at the sea-side, for the benefit of their own health and the health of their children; the sea-breezes being very refreshing and invigorating, and bathing in the salt water being very strengthening and healthful.

But most of the young people who read these pages have not perhaps ever seen the sea; they live in villages or towns in, what are called, the midland parts of this island, and have not seen more water than that in the large pool, or the narrow river or wide brook that runs through the valleys.

Children are very fond of seeing waters. What delight they will express on seeing a larger pool of water than they have ever seen before, with swans swimming about on its smooth bosom in stately pride, or a flock of geese paddling their bulky bodies over it, or a whole tribe of noisy ducks playing their frolics in this their favourite element – now diving and then swimming, and sometimes flying just over its surface, and settling again on their liquid resting place. And should there be a boat at hand, what a treat to get into it, and feel themselves sliding along so gently and pleasantly that they can only tell they are moving by looking at the trees on the bank. Very nice this: but young people should be very careful never to get into a boat and go upon deep waters without somebody with them to take care of them. I will tell yon a little tale about some children who got into a boat by and bye.

Well: if children are pleased on seeing pools and rivers of water, how much more delighted are they to see the great sea itself, with its rolling waves and mighty waters. When they stand on the sea-shore for the first time and behold, outstretched before them, nothing but water for miles and miles and miles, they are usually silent with surprise and wonder, and seem as if they could hardly, as the saying is, believe their own eyes! But there it is sure enough – nothing but water, as far as you can see and farther. And there go the ships – some with white sails move gallantly along over the waves, which are like rolling hills of water – and some driven by steam power cut their way through them, regardless alike of wave, or wind, or tide – there they go like living things on the broad bosom of the deep – crossing and re-crossing each other – but no fear, for there is plenty of room for them all on that great world of waters!

Oh I could stand for hours gazing on such a scene! No wonder that children should be almost transported with it, and express their surprise and delight in unmeasured terms, when, for the first time, they behold the great wide sea.

And not only is the sea and the ships passing to and fro a glorious sight, but its shore of fine sand is a delightful place for young people. The sea itself is very deep, but towards the shore it is often shallow and flat in many places, and when the tide has gone down you may walk on the level sands, without any danger, for a great distance. Sea-sand is very fine and quite clean, and so nicely set together that you do not sink in as you walk over it. Children may run about on it and play down to the water's edge without fear, or wander over it seeking for shells, and stones, and other curious things which the waves have left behind them. Only they must mind and watch for the tide coming back again; but of this they need not be in much fear as it always comes very gradually, leaving plenty of time to get out of the way safe on the land.

When these sands are again covered with water, then is the time for bathing. The people who live there and attend to the bathing machines know how deep it is, and what is the right time, and which is the right place. Some do not use a machine at all – I mean some men who are good swimmers – they will go to a distance down the shore and undress, and plunge in, and swim about for a long time just where they please. But women and children are safer and more comfortable to undress and dress in a machine. These are usually attended by women, who assist them in and out of the water. The machine is like a covered market cart with a door, and is sometimes drawn on wheels into the water by a horse, and sometimes, as in the picture, it is fixed on a boat and pulled by a man with oars.

As I have said before, sea-bathing is very healthy, and it is very agreeable too; for sea-water is not so cold as spring or river water, and it is so strong that it will almost bear you up if you lie still, and keep your hands down by the side of your body. Some people will swim and float about on it for a long time without taking any cold.

All this is very nice and pleasant, especially after a hot summer day, or before, for some prefer having a bathe before breakfast, as it gives them a good appetite, and they can eat their bread and butter, and a plate of fine fresh shrimps, with a greater relish after they have been in the water, and had a walk on the shore.

Some of our young readers may be ready to ask if there be any danger from large fish when bathing in the sea. There is off some shores of distant countries, but not off our shores. Sometimes, but very seldom, a shark, which is the most fierce and terrible of all the monsters of the deep, may be seen off the English shores. But this, as I have said, is very seldom, and when one is seen it is considered quite an extraordinary circumstance. During the early part of this summer, 1848, a shark was seen off the Norfolk coast, and a fisherman is said, after a severe

struggle, to have succeeded in capturing it. It was, we are told, longer than the tallest man in England.
The Children's Magazine, 1848

# 1849

Bathing is best performed when quite naked, but, as in the bathing establishments in large towns and cities, and in thickly-settled parts of the country, decency forbids entire nudity, a kind of short drawers is worn, as may be seen in our engravings; and where ladies and gentlemen bathe in company, as is the fashion all along the Atlantic coast, and especially at Rockaway, Coney Island, Long Branch, etc., shirts and trowsers are worn by the men, and flannel bathing dresses, made for the purpose, by the ladies.
The Science of Swimming, 1849

Nothing beyond the regular routine: in summer a few families left their comfortable houses up the mountains, or in the far-off towns, and came to the seaside to enjoy sea air and bathing; and there was always, I am sorry to say, a very unseemly turning of heads on the first or second Sundays of the "bathing seasons," to peep at the strangers as they entered the church. Whether it was from a love of solitude, or habitual pride, Annie did not know, but "the bathers" were seldom visited by the old resident families. They were allowed to see the plantations at Dove Hall, the grotto, the temple, the cottage, and the fine old garden and orchard, if they liked, on stated days; but that was all, unless Annie's grandmamma heard that some one was *very ill;* then she would send the persons afflicted presents of fruit or cream, and lend them the carriage, or the use of "the bathing-box," for there were no bathing-machines along that lonely coast.

Annie's "bathing-box" was very like a sentry-box, with a door to it: it was fastened against the cliff with stakes and ropes, and carted up to the coach-house in November, and down to the strand in April. "The bathers" used to dress and undress in the caves, or under the rocks, so that to be allowed to use the "bathing-box" was considered a great luxury.

Annie had often longed to join the "bathers'" children, who went racing and shouting along the beach; but she knew she must not do so; and so she patted her dog or her pony, or talked to her mamma or her maid, and got rid of the desire.
Grandmamma's Pockets, 1849

# 1850

Being ordered by my medical adviser to bathe, I went to order a gown and cap.
'Madame has forgotten the trousers.'
'No, it was not a forget, for in England we do not wear them; but pray make me a pair.'
'French ladies,' said the couturiere with a look of stern morality, 'would be shocked at the very idea of bathing without them.'
*Chambers' Edinburgh Journal*, May 4, 1850

## SEA-BATHING – ITS DECORUMS.
"Manners" writes to the Leading Journal, complaining, for the hundredth time, that bathers of the softer sex at Brighton are annoyed by the indecent curiosity of men. One person whom, with a wildness of imagination beyond poetry, Manners thinks it possible to find a "gentleman," hired a boat to row up and down where ladies were in the water. That society cannot settle this matter, does not say much either for the intelligence or the moral tone of our day. Were society endowed with a truly healthy feeling, brutes like the "gentleman" would be scouted in every circle, and punished by that most deplorable form of exile the being "sent to Coventry." In America they would promptly settle his curiosity by "lynching" him. In England we have not sufficient force of character to put down this species of brute.

Indeed, the bathing question is one of the greatest opprobriums of our intelligence and cultivation. We are sometimes pestered with complaints against bathers on behalf of perambulating ladies; at another time, bathing men complain that women *will* wander too near; then we have suppression of a most healthful exercise, or its limitation to the most comfortless hours; and now we have a revival of old complaints against such things as this Brighton gentleman. The state of public feeling seems to be a permanent conflict between prudery and prurient coquetry. We suspect that prudery sets the bad example. If bathing, under due regulations as to costume, were more common – as common as healthful considerations would make it – there would not be this wonderment and indecent rush to catch a glance at some wet Godiva. It is shameful that the opportunities afforded by our coasts – especially such a noble beach as that at Brighton – should be rendered unavailing by the brutal impertinence of the few. Why does not a manly association of true gentlemen take the matter in hand, by setting the fashion of bathing in proper style, and by taking possession of the marine frontier so to castigate miserable cowards like Manners' sea-serpent? It would be a chivalrous emprise well suited to the day. The Knights of the Bath would need no harder weapon than the scoop of their own right hand and the good seawater.

*The Living Age*, November 2, 1850

[Southsea, England] By this time we had reached the beach; and finding all the bathing-machines engaged, took refuge beneath the colonnade of the Rooms, till our favourite water-nymph, Peggy Banden, should be at liberty to do her spiriting for us. As bathing-women are a very peculiar and distinct race of feminines, we will amuse ourselves by sketching Peggy, while we wait her leisure. She is Cornish, and comes from Cawsand Bay; her height is some five feet eleven, and she is stout in proportion; her dress a pair of canvas trousers, a canvas petticoat, a jacket, and a black bonnet of no shape in particular.

*Chambers' Edinburgh Journal*, November 23, 1850

* Baldness can be imitated capitally with an oil-silk bathing cap. At a pinch a baby's cap with pink lining might do; but Macassar Rowland himself could not tell the oil silk. ...

SEASHORE.

A CHARADE IN THREE ACTS.

ACT I.

SEA –

DRAMATIS PERSONÆ.

Careful Mother.   Little Children.   Two Bathing Women.

Nervous Old Gentleman.   Visitors.

Scene – *The Sands of Brighton, with the curtains at the end of the room bulged out like the atoning of a Bathing machine.*

Enter Bathing Women, supposed to be wet through. They bow to Careful Mother And Little Children, and express their great love for the darlings. Careful Mother makes signs to them, and they fetch towels and hand the bathing party into the machine.

Enter Visitors, who, by pretending to swim, inform Bathing Women that they wish to bathe; and having each paid a card-counter, they demand towels, and hurry off with them under their arms.

Enter (from behind curtains) one of the Little Children in its night-gown. It screams at the sight of the water, and kicks violently, but is instantly seized by the Bathing Women, who take it by the arms and legs and plunge it into the waves. This is done three times, when the Infant is taken out in a fainting condition, and handed to Careful Mother. When all the "angels" have been dipped, the Mother closes the curtain, and *exeunt* Bathing Women.

Enter Nervous Old Gentleman, swimming in a huge mackintosh for bathing-gown. He wears

spectacles. He expresses that it is very cold, and that he is about to get into his bathing machine, and points to the one which Careful Mother and Little Children have hired. Advancing to the curtains he is surprised to find the door locked, and pushes violently against it. A loud scream is heard within. As Nervous Old Gentleman continues pushing, a parasol is thrust out from the curtains. He is pushed back, and falls head over heels into the water.

Enter Two Bathing Women armed with long sticks. They keep their eyes shut, and drive off Nervous old Gentleman.

The curtains of bathing machine are then drawn aside, when exit Careful Mother and Little Children with very wet hair, and looking so much better for their fainting and screaming.

Bathing Women bow them out.

Acting Charades, 1850

# 1851

[One man's experience] It was in 1765 that a M. Poitevin established, the first. At the present day, between the Pout d'Austerlitz and the Pont de Jena, there are between twenty and thirty; two or three of these are appropriated to women. The price of admission varies from four to fifteen sous, and the baths are thus of very different classes; their general arrangements are, however, the same, and it will suffice, therefore, to describe any one of them. We choose for this purpose the bath on the Quai d'Orsay, a little higher up than the Pont de la Concorde; it bears the name of its founder, Deligny, and also that of National School of Notation.

A wooden staircase leads down to the hank of the river – a narrow strip of land, on which grow some fine poplars. Before you is a gateway, designed in the Moorish style, and approached by a bridge; on either hand, are flowering shrubs and evergreens. You enter, paying the price of admission, and an additional charge for your *caleçon* and *peignoir:* the *caleçon* is a pair of cotton drawers; the *peignoir*, a kind of wrapper of the same material. These secured, you go on, and find yourself under a colonnade; this colonnade surrounds a large oblong basin of water, the surface of which is about six feet below it. Round the colonnade, and opening on it, you see a multitude of little doors; these give access each to a little closet, and each closet has a little bench, a little glass, a little bootjack, and a few little pins to hang your garments on; light is admitted by a little window in the exterior side of the edifice. Above the colonnade is another gallery, and from it enters a second storey of little closets. There are three hundred and forty in all, and, as you have already guessed, they are for undressing and dressing in. ...

But by this time you are undressed; you have put on your *caleçon* and your *peignoir,* find come forth from your closet. Shut the door after you, and take the number of it, that you may find it again; we, too, have donned our drawers, and thrown our wrapper over our shoulders. Let us take a turn round the gallery before we make our plunge; there are some hundreds like ourselves walking about: they are chatting, or smoking, or watching the swimmers. Those men in white trousers, straw hats, and shirts striped with red, are the swimming masters, and they are ready either to give you lessons, if you know nothing of natation, or assistance in your peril, if you have imagined you knew something of it, and find you don't. Those other fellows, with blue stripes instead of red, are the *garçons de cabinet*, and their office is to open the door of your closet for you, to take care of your valuables, and to receive as many sous as you please to give them when you go away. Now we come to the lower end of the bath: you see it is full of boys – a perfect fry – paddling about, or, to use a Scottish word, than which there is not a more expressive in any language, *ploutering* in the water. Two splash a third, and drive him out of the bath half blinded. One lies with his hands on the wooden bottom, kicks out with his legs, and hopes, the hypocrite, to persuade some fool he is swimming. Some of the more experienced instruct the less, supporting them with a hand under the chin, or in the strings of the *caleçon.*

Hogg's Instructor, 1851

Deb Salisbury

# 1852

The watering places are all more or less crowded now: in France the sea-bathing begins much earlier than in England: swimming is very generally taught, and many women swim perfectly; it is certainly a good thing to be able to do so, and as an amusement it adds greatly to the pleasure of bathing: the costume employed is frightful; it consists of a black stuff tunic and trowsers; the latter very loose, all in one. There are all sorts of varieties of oil-skin caps, and some, who value their complexions, wear a wide-brimmed straw hat. I wonder that the French ladies, who think so much of what becomes them, and who, even by the sea-side dress as carefully and as coquettishly as in Paris, have not invented something less ugly than their present bathing costume: it must require some courage to doff their pretty gowns, graceful *mantelets,* and becoming little bonnets, and emerge from the tent where they change their attire, in the oil-skin cap, the tunic and trowsers, and list slippers: it must be confessed, however, this dress is very convenient: after all, it is not unlike the Bloomer, which seems, by-the-bye, to have died a natural death.

*The Ladies' Companion and Monthly Magazine,* August 1852

The bathing periods of the day at the American watering-places present rather a novel feature. The beach, for perhaps a mile, is skirted with small ill-shapen dressing-houses used during the season, and standing all the winter like a row of bleak, gloomy sentinels, as forlorn as Savoyard packmen. At eleven o'clock in the morning, a number of sunburnt women in crumpled old bonnets and careless costume, are hurrying from one house to another with baskets of towels and arm-loads of bathing-dresses, which they distribute with surprising celerity. Soon after, groups of most fancifully-dressed people will be seen emerging and plunging into the white foam of the surf, disporting with the billows, and kicking the waves head-over-heels, in a manner enough to make old Neptune, or Venus, or a select committee of Amphitrites, rise from their dripping mansion, and politely request that such vagaries with the water be instantly discontinued.

The spectacle is really a curious one. There are five hundred bathers dressed in every shade and variety of colour – blue tunics over yellow trousers, crimson coats with mulberry overhauls, moon-tinted pantaloons with jackets of purple. No carnival ever presented so wild and grotesque a medley. Rome! abandon thy laurels; and Venice! hide with shame in thy own gondolas; for ye never produced so bewildering a saturnalia of costume! Keeping, consistency, and harmony are sacrificed. The very fishes must waggle their little speckled tails in curious admiration, and the sun, "the great orb itself," seems to wonder what is going on, that man (and woman) kind have thrown off the garb of commonsense to revel in the motley habiliments of agonised fancy.

To see long troops of fifty and a hundred bathers all plunge in the boiling surf hand in hand is an exciting picture. The waves dash over their bright dresses, and the next moment they appear dripping like sea deities after an elemental Waterloo. This hydro-frolic is immense delight for the young people, especially when a timid companion shows a weak point in the water. How they shriek when their mouths fill with brine, or leap to the rescue if the strong waves should carry one from his feet! Some one's hat is floating yonder on the waters – one moment dancing on the topmost wave, anon sinking into an abyss of spray. Now for a race among the juveniles! Away they go, like a band of young otters – plunging, splashing, and shrieking, in the wildness of the excitement, much to the horror of matrons and governesses on the sands, who are in momentary dread lest they get beyond their depth, to never more be sent to bed on *terra firma.*

Dashes of American Humour, 1852

[In France] The women have also their baths at four sous, at which be it observed to their credit, on their own testimony however, they preserve an exterior decency not to be seen in the corresponding class of bathing houses among the males. The female bathing costume is much the same as that in use at Newport and Cape May. Occasionally are added ruffled night-caps and coifed hair, which are said to have, as can readily be conceived, a horrible effect. The most coquettish embroider their "pantalons" in different colors, and wear in the water their bracelets and necklaces. The advantage of costume, as compared with the male bathers, is decidedly with the female, though even among them, it must be ungallantly confessed, that the modiste's art performs wonders.   *Harper's Magazine,* November 1852

# 1853

Bathing in the surf on the beach is *the* event of a Newport summer's day, and they manage this sea-dipping very differently from the way in which it is done in England. Along the beach, which is, as I said, about a mile in length, and smooth as sand could make it, stood at about thirty feet from the edge of the water, a row of bathing-houses. They were not, as in our country, wheeled into the waves, and superintended by a dreadful old woman, who dip ferociously, but remain fixed, the bathers emerging from them in dresses, and hurrying into the waves, which roll as if to meet them.

From the shelving nature of the almost flat beach one must wade some distance, in order to get into tolerable deep water, but it is glorious to sit down and let the Atlantic waves roll over you. Then the bathing costumes are extraordinary, everyone being attired according to his or her peculiar taste, for ladies and gentlemen bathe together. The fair Naiads are usually attired in a sort of tunic, confined round the waist by a sash or belt, which reaches to the knee, and pantaloons, the head being covered with a chip hat, trimmed with gay ribbons. As these dresses are of all colours, and mostly gaudy ones, it may be easily supposed that on the beach and in the water quite a kaleidescopic [sic] view is obtained. The gentlemen are also fancifully attired, and nothing can be more amusing than the spectacle of three or four hundred ladies and gentlemen bobbing up and down in the surf, leaping with laughter and screams of delight, as great waves roll in, or clumsily paddling to the shore. For two hours this amusement lasts, and during its continuance the beach is thronged with gazers, on foot, horseback, and in carriages. During the time mentioned, a white flag floats from a staff near, indicating that no one must bathe except in costume, and a red. one substituted telling that all dress may be dispensed with.

Transatlantic Tracings, 1853

# 1854

JONATHAN AT THE SEA-SIDE.

Miss Smith, may I have the pleasure of taking a bath with you, or of bathing you? is an invitation which one often hears at this place from a gentleman to a lady, just as at a ball the invitation is to a quadrille or a waltz, and I have never heard the invitation refused. Very various are the scenes which on all sides present themselves in the bathing republic. Here a young, handsome couple, in elegant bathing attire, go dancing out into the wild waves, holding each other by the hand, and, full of joy and courage of life, ready to meet any thing, – the great world's sea and all its billows! There again is an elderly couple in gray garments, holding each other steadily by the two hands, and popping up and down in the waves, just as people dip candles, with solemn aspects, and merely observant to keep their footing, and doing all for the benefit of health. Here is a young smiling mother bearing before her her little beautiful boy, a naked cupid, not a year old, who laughs and claps his hands for joy as the wild waves dash over him. Just by is a fat grandmother with a life preserver round her body, and half sitting on the sands, in evident fear of being drowned for all that, and when the waves come rolling onward, catching hold of some of her leaping and laughing great children and grand-children who dance around her. Here a graceful young girl, who now, for the first time, bathes in the sea, flies before the waves into the arms of father or mother in whose embrace it may dash over her; there is a group of wild young women holding each other by the band, dancing around and screaming aloud every time a wave dashes over their heads; and there in front of them is a yet wilder swarm of young men, who dive and plunge about like fishes, much to the amazement of the porpoises (as I presume,) who, here and there, pop their huge heads out of the billows, but which again disappear as a couple of large dogs rush forward through the water towards them in hope of a good prize.

*The Anglo-American Magazine*, May 1854

Fig. 5 is one of those bathing dresses so necessary to a sea-side excursion or residence, if the invigorating sea-bath is to be enjoyed as it should be. The material is common Scotch plaid, green and red, in alternate checks. It is cut short in the bloomer fashion, which, though very convenient when half veiled in snowy surf, ought to astonish the sharks themselves on dry land. But a bathing dress is only intended for convenience, and the least idea of making it elegant would be preposterous. The dress is made with a loose skirt set to an old fashioned tight yoke, and gathered around the waist with a plaid belt; it is cut short, leaving the feet and ankles free. Long bishop-sleeves, fastened around the wrist and a band, protect the arm. The pantalettes are made loose, and fastened around the ankles with narrow bands.

*The Anglo-American Magazine*, July 1854

# 1855

Fashion has invaded every domain, requiring that even the "sweet neglect" which pleased the bard, should be cut after the most approved Paris pattern, and that the very bathing-dress should have a fanciful air about it. ...

BATHING DRESSES.

Fancy has been allowed its full scope in these garments, and in its various attempts to make a pretty thing out of an ugly thing, has at length manufactured a series of absurd costume, which people the astonished shores of the grand and simple ocean with a motley array of grotesque and ridiculous figures, such as might be imagined to belong to the train of the wild "Abbot of Misrule." Now there is no *becoming* bathing costume – it is useless to seek it – the whole operation, though healthful, and gone through with a view to future beauty, is unbecoming, from the garments to the ungainly struggle with the wild wave, and the blue tinge its embrace leaves on the face and lips. Having established this fact, what next remains, is to find, if not a becoming, an appropriate costume; and here, as in all other things, the simplest is the best. Black serge or the commonest alpaca, costing about twenty-five cents per yard, are either one or other suitable materials. The dress should consist of trowsers, made full and fastened round the ankle with a button – a full waist up to the throat, and a full tunic reaching to the knee, with long sleeves, for the salt sea and the sun together tan the skin. To this, a large thick straw flat, as broad as it can be procured, and the costume will be as complete, comfortable, and unobtrusive as possible; therefore: will it the nearer approach the becoming in more ways than one, for it is morally unbecoming to seek the conspicuous, or to strive to attract in the operation of bathing.

*Graham's Magazine*, August 1855

I was greatly amused, the following morning, observing the ladies bathing; for as they are attired for the double purpose, as I presume, of bathing and being seen, there is no impropriety whatever in looking at the fair creatures in the water. The garments worn on these occasions are of the gayest colours, consisting of a Bloomer kind of costume, in which the upper part contrasts strongly with the lower. The head is generally surmounted by a quaintly-shaped white cap, ...

In truth, it is a strange scene; and does not abate in interest when the ladies emerge from the water, in their gaudy costumes, exhibiting trowsers of all colours, and countless pairs of little white feet, twinkling on the sand. This early bathing must be as conducive to health, as it is an exhilaration of spirits; for, during my travels, I saw no ladies with such glowing complexions as those at Nahant. In the words of an American enthusiast, – "They come down to breakfast after their bath, freshened up, looking as sweet and dewy as an avalanche of roses."

A Vacation Tour in the United States and Canada, 1855

PREPARATION FOR CONQUEST.

At six o'clock the lions deliver themselves into the hands of their hair-dressers and corn-cutters, preparatory to their conquests upon the Boulevards and Champs Elysees, and to dine long and sumptuously at Véfour's, the Trois Frères Provençaux, or the Maison Dorée. The aquatic taste of some of the bathers changes frequently the cafe of the school into a restaurant, and they remain here to dine, gazing without constraint, in their simple costume of drawers, upon the animated scene before them. With the thermometer at 90° in the shade, one can readily conceive the charm of relinquishing broadcloth for the scanty garb of a Tahitian, relieving the tedium of a dinner, and stimulating the appetite by an occasional plunge into the cool river.

The women have also their baths at four sous, at which, be it observed to their credit, on their own testimony, however, they preserve an exterior decency not to be seen in the corresponding class of bathing-houses among the males. The female bathing-costume is much the same as that in use at Newport and Cape May. Occasionally are added ruffled night-caps and coiffed hair, which are said to have, as can readily be conceived, a horrible effect. The most coquettish embroider their "pantalons" in different colors, and wear in the water their bracelets and necklaces. The advantage of costume, as compared with the male bathers, is decidedly with the female, though even among them, it must be ungallantly confessed, that the modiste's art performs wonders. The cafe scenes of the male schools are not rivaled in the female.

EN COSTUME.

NYMPHS OF THE SEINE.

Whatever emulation exists of this nature is confined to the heroines of gallantry and opulent pleasure, who hold their bacchanal revels apart. As I have lifted the veil from the male bathers, impartial justice requires at my hands the same toward the female. Voici! As on the pavement, beauty, grace, and harmony mingle with age, obesity, and ugliness – the most delicious with the most grotesque and amusing image. Forgive me, shade of Mohammed! But 'tis true, and pity – 'tis true.

READY FOR THE PLUNGE.

Parisian Sights and French Principles, 1855

# 1856

Upon reaching the beach, each individual retires for a moment to the interior of one of the myriad board-built bathing-houses erected thereabout, and presently issues forth, dressed from head to foot in red or blue flannel; which arrangement at once entirely obliterates all signs whereby you are enabled to distinguish the lady from her maid, the millionaire merchant from his clerk, or the blackleg from the divine; and in the place of so many personages, of either high or low degree, you have a shame-stricken, woollen-swathed army of 'forked radishes, with heads fantastically carved,' who hasten as quickly as possible to hide their wounded sensibilities in the surf.

*The Knickerbocker*, January 1856

Deb Salisbury

There are no houses built around the beach, as there would be in England, no marquee with its circulating books, and chairs for those who like to pass their morning on the sands, and watch the ebb or rising of the ocean. The reasons for this are various. Firstly, this out-door life is neither suited to an hotel belle, nor to the Marthas of American private life, "much cumbered" with domestic occupation. In the next place, the great power of the sun would make sitting on a beach under his glare entirely impossible; and, lastly, the bathing arrangements are such that no one would desire a family view of the beach during the bathing-hours.

No bathing-machines are used, but along the beach stand rows of little shanties, each a trifle larger than a sentry-box, just capable of accommodating yourself and a colony of spiders, every variety of which may here be found. If you will go with us to the beach at 10 A.m. on a fine day in August (the height of the Newport season), you may see issuing forth from these frail tenements all the beauty and fashion of Newport, the same that floated past you last night in the ball. "Old men and children, young men and maidens," in every variety of fancy tunic. "Women in every description of bathing dress. Old women, young women, thin women, thick women, big feet, little feet, red feet, brown feet, rushing about. Carriages of all kinds. 'Fast' men, fast horses, universal confusion." Such is a description of Newport beach at bathing-time, and every visitor to Newport will bear witness to its accuracy. Young, pretty girls, dressed completely *à la* Bloomer, in scarlet, yellow, blue, or orange serge, immensely full, with double, treble, and quadruple skirts, trimmed with an endless number of yards of worsted galloon, and as coquettishly put on as any cloud of tarletan or *crêpe* in which the owner danced the night before, are running with bare feet into the surf under the heads of hackmen's horses, with screams and shouts of merry laughter. Their partners of the night before escort them into the waves as they did through the mazes of the *cotillon*.

*Bentley's Miscellany*, August 1856

The *baigneuses*, or bathing-women, of Biarritz wear a peculiar costume, of which they are evidently not a little proud. It is certainly becoming. [ ← ]

*The Illustrated London News*, Supplement August 16 1856

We are brought to the verge of a phenomenon which shows more plainly than anything else how strong and universal the impression is that a trip to the sea-side is *pro tanto* a return to savage life. We have been told that at the American watering-places – Newport, in Rhode Island, for example – ladies and gentlemen make appointments over night to walk together into the waves next morning. In the clear rocky pools at the base of the Pyrenees, a bearded beau will sometimes be seen playing dominoes against a fair partner on a floating board. We in England are gradually introducing the same marine fusion of the sexes – only, unfortunately, while in America and France everybody has an appropriate costume, the attire is confined in England to the weaker half of creation. Really, this is a delicate subject, and some excuse must be asked for handling it. We are quite aware that *Paterfamilias,* who writes indignation-letters from Margate to the *Times,* is a bit of a prude; but it is not necessary to go to the crowded Kentish watering-places to convince oneself that in this case he is more than justified. It really does seem as if English ladies, in addition to those curious hats, put on a new set of manners and morals during their annual visit to the sea-side. No doubt, the appearance is worse than the reality, but the scandal to third persons is not the less for that; and surely it is not desirable that these bathing customs should be the first thing to strike an intelligent foreigner on his landing at Newhaven, Folkestone, or Dover. If the corporations of the bathing-towns will not exert themselves to mark out separate localities for bathers, and to enforce the separation, there will be nothing left except for gentlemen to remedy a scandal which is certainly not of *their* creation, and to consent to go into the water in much the same costume which the Prince-consort is said, we believe unjustly, to have devised for the undress of a heavy dragoon.

*The Saturday Review*, August 30, 1856

Deb Salisbury

# 1857

[Biarritz] We pass the twenty cabins for bathers, which form a semicircle at the head of the bay, and take our seat on the white sands which lie between these cabins – "baraques," as they are called – and the sea. And now, I do assure you, that if all you know of sea-bathing is, that you have been rattled into a few feet of salt-water in some crazy old machine, and have there plunged solemnly into a dark hole, to be solaced during your stay by the affrighted screams of children, and the shrieks of women undergoing the same dread ordeal, but with less fortitude and less forbearance than yourself, – if this is all you know, you will be astonished at the scene in the midst of which you find yourself. From one of the "baraques" behind you comes a lady in what might have been the model Bloomer costume: long trowsers of black woollen serge and a frock of the same, full and short, reaching the knees, confined at the waist by a leathern girdle, and fitting close to the throat.

This is the costume "de rigueur," without which no creature of woman-kind may go into the sea. Of course it is open to additions and improvements. Of the former class are list shoes, almost essential in walking over the sands to and from the "baraque" to the sea; and there is the little oilskin cap, trimmed with quillings of scarlet or blue worsted-braid, and of very bewitching effect; and the large oilskin cape, reaching to the knees, which is taken off at the water's edge, and put on as soon as the bather leaves the sea.

Among the improvements we may class the trimming of dress, &c., with some bright-coloured worsted-braid. But what excuse can be offered for the adoption of lace sleeves and collars and coral bracelets in the sea, and the like pretty imbecilities?

Lest fathers, brothers, and husbands should here unduly exult, let me give notice that the man's costume is more susceptible of ornament than that of the woman; a fact which has not been lost sight of by the "lords of the creation," as we shall see. At present we will accompany our young lady to the bath. As soon as she leaves the "baraque," she is joined by a "baigneur" or "baigneuse," holding in his or her hand a pair of gourds; they walk over the sands together, and if she does not know how to swim, the gourds are tied round her waist before she steps into the sea. Be sure, that if she dips her head or takes three or four plunges, she is an Englishwoman; the French do not think this at all essential; and a Frenchwoman walks into the water, lies down on her back, and floats out to the rope stretched across the mouth of the bay, or strikes out to swim, taking the greatest possible care to keep her head out of the water. The number of good swimmers – men, women, and children – whom you will see in one day will astonish you; and all those who cannot swim and float are learning to do so: very easy with the help of gourds, and very pleasant in this deliciously warm water.

The costume for mankind – also "de rigueur" – is a pair of loose cotton or woollen trowsers and a tunic fastened round the waist by a band, and mostly with very short sleeves. But whereas the woman's dress is invariably black, that of the man may be chosen of any colour or shade of colour. Light blue, pink, lilac, red, &c. are in great vogue, and being in cotton, are worn without ornament. But the "great swells" have costumes of dark woollen stuff, purple or crimson; and these are trimmed with large pearl buttons, each as big as a half-crown, placed in a row down the outside of the trowsers, and the tunic in a like manner elaborately ornamented.

*Littell's Living Age*, January 17, 1857

They had been in the surf; and the young lady's cheeks were as red as roses; and her hair had come down, and the wet had made it part into a thousand little shining curls; and her little bare feet were as delicate as sea-shells. I saw Mr. Noall's eyes following her until she disappeared. I thought the full Turkish trousers, and all that, were very romantic; and I secretly longed to see myself attired in them, and feel the delicious sensation of the sea breaking over me in the arms of Mr. Noall. But I shall have to wait until we are married (oh, Miranda, how that sounds I) for I've discretion enough to know that the water would wash every trace of the rose-pink from my cheeks, and that, instead of making my hair curl like Miss Stanley's, it would straighten it out into anything but beautiful locks; and, as for my feet, dear, you know, confidentially, that they never were as plump as pin-cushions, nor as soft as lily-leaves.

*Godey's Lady's Book*, August 1857

Deb Salisbury

*Hints on Bathing.*

To a good swimmer even, a dress, however light in texture, is a serious impediment to free action, while to the ordinary swimmer it is a dangerous clog, and in its use by such, life is very easily endangered. Firstly: beware while so clothed venturing into water deeper than is necessary for the actual purpose of swimming. Secondly: beware of plunging into water the temperature of which you have not ascertained. Thirdly: beware of bathing in the heat of the day, or with the body over-heated. Fourthly: beware of bathing immediately after any meal, when the digestive organs are in full activity; and lastly, when you use the bathing-dress, let it be light in texture and white in colour, or a near approach to it. If you observe the first caution, you will, in case of accident, not be beyond the reach of the sight of any person at the surface, even if the water be muddy. If you attend to the second and third, your system will not be paralysed by a sudden cold shock; if you heed the fourth, you avoid (the moral certainty of a contrary course) cramps and their result, death by drowning and apoplexy. And if you heed the last, you, in one way, lessen your danger, as your garments will then absorb but little water; while, at the same time, you have the strongest chance of rescue in case of accident, as the colour of your drawers will be the readiest clue to your whereabouts, and your probable resuscitation.

<u>How to Make Home Happy</u>, 1857

# 1858

The Port Vieux is the favourite resort both of the bathing and non-bathing visitors at Biarritz. Around the concavity of the amphitheatre, facing the sea as the boxes of a theatre face the stage, are a number of small cabins, built on piles, about four feet from the ground. Those on the one side are devoted to the ladies, and those on the other to the gentlemen bathers. Their back entrances abut on the cliffs, which rise abruptly to a considerable elevation. On the beach, between the cabins and the sea, – in the pit, as it were, – are placed chairs, which are occupied in the morning by nursery-maids and children, and in the middle and latter part of the day by the most fashionable of the visitors, who congregate to chat in the continental way, and to look on the aquatic appearance and performances of their friends and acquaintances and of the public generally. Both ladies and gentlemen wear a "bathing costume." With the former it consists of loose, black woollen drawers, which descend to the ankles, and of a black blouse or tunic, descending below the knees, and fastened at the waist by a leathern girdle. On leaving their cabins, they put on also a wide waterproof cape, which they keep on until they reach the water's edge, and which is then taken off by the bathing attendant. This costume, like all picturesque costumes, makes the young and the pretty look younger and prettier, but certainly does not set off to the same degree the more matronly of the lady bathers. All, however, young and old, seem totally indifferent on the subject, and pass smilingly before their friends and the spectators, appearing to enjoy every stage of the performance. Most ladies have an attendant, male or female, and many are, or speedily become very tolerable swimmers. They are to be seen daily swimming, with or without assistance, at a considerable distance from the shore. The gentlemen's dress is a kind of sailor's costume, and, as custom gives them more latitude with respect to colour, material, and make, great varieties are observed. The exquisites of the place seem to take a pride in showing themselves off thus prepared for their marine gymnastics; and I have often seen them, cap in hand, feet and ankles naked, talking to their lady friends sitting around, previous to taking their first plunge. Once in the water, all the bathers, male and female, mingle together; the timid remaining near the beach, and the bold and learned in the art of swimming striking out into deep water. The utmost decorum, however, prevails. The husband assists his wife, the father his young daughters; but strangers keep at a respectful distance in the water, as they would on dry land.

At first, this aquatic mingling of the sexes strikes the English beholder as an infringement of the laws of propriety and decorum, but a more close scrutiny brings the conviction that such is really not the case, – indeed, that this mode of bathing is infinitely more decorous and decent than that which is pursued on our own shores. The bathers are, to all intents and purposes, dressed; and there is, in reality, no more impropriety in their witnessing each other's marine sports than there is in the members of a masquerade mingling in the streets during the carnival at Rome or Naples. A few days after my return to England I was at Brighton, and on opening my

bedroom window, at an hotel which is situated in the most crowded part of the town, the first sight that greeted me, immediately in front of the hotel, was half a dozen men, perfectly naked, wading about, with the water not much higher than their knees. I was involuntarily reminded of Biarritz and of its bathing community, and could not but mentally confess that decency was not on the side of the *modus operandi* which was then illustrated before my eyes. I may add that, once in the water, a light woollen or cotton dress is not felt, and in no way interferes with liberty of movements and with the pleasure of bathing. Indeed, to a modest man it is a great comfort to feel that one can raise one's shoulders out of the water without being a bugbear to all beholders.
    *The Lancet*, January 1858

If we were writing for the fashions of the month, we should thus describe the costumes: –
No. 1: Ladies' bathing dress, *a la Venus Anadyomene.* Body fitting tight when wet, no sleeves, skirt long or short, according to taste; trousers *a la grand Turc.* Material, *escol* or merino – pink, green, or other colour – tastefully braided; straw hat or parasol, and white kid gloves! It is expected that crinoline will be much worn, of course as a protection against sharks, crabs, and other feminine antipathies.
No. 2: Gentlemen's dress, *a l'acrobat, caleçons, de rigeur*; the rest according to taste and complexion; straw hat, kid gloves, and a cigar or meerschaum to smoke while floating on the back.    *The Ladies Companion*, April?, 1858

A BATHING DRESS may at first sight appear to lie beyond the domain of fashion. Still there is no reason why this should not be pretty as well as appropriate. The one which we illustrate may be made of delaine flannel, or any similar material, edged with a darker shade of the same; or of bambazet, with a fringe of buckshot, covered with the material of the dress, with pellets of lead in the lower skirt. This latter material will be found quite available. [ ← ]
*Harper's New Monthly Magazine*, June 1858

Another fault is a habit of overdressing, or attiring in a way not suitable to the occasion. It used to be a subject of remark with travellers that American ladies knew not how to dress on a journey. Frequently their most expensive silks, their handsomest shawls, the gayest bonnets, and all the jewellery they could muster would be brought into requisition. The more generally correct idea of taste would not permit this now, but many foolish persons still load themselves with finery at every possible opportunity, whether the circumstances demand it or not. A bathing-dress, for instance, which ought to be perfectly simple and capable of easy and ready adjustment, is sometimes transformed into a ridiculously elaborate toilette, which we are astonished the water is not afraid to touch. Under the proper heads our lady readers will find descriptions of sensible and modest bathing-dresses, which they will do well to take as models. ...

This illustrated model of a bathing-dress is one of the most simple, and at the same time one of the most convenient and becoming in the world. It is made of any dark thick material, and consists of a tunic and trowsers gathered into a narrow band, which buttons round the ankle. The tunic is confined by a belt at the waist, gathered into a yoke and buttoned in front. It is completed by a narrow band at the throat. Straight sleeves slightly full, and also gathered into a band at the wrist.    *Frank Leslie's New Family Magazine*, August 1858

*Sea-bathing* possesses so many advantages in regard to health that we need not enlarge upon the subject. We will merely offer a few hints. The periods of the year best suited for this delightful object are the summer and autumn, when the temperature of the water on our shores varies from 55° to 70°. The time of day for bathing in the sea must depend upon the locality and the state of the tide. In general, however, the best period is about noon, or two or three hours after breakfast, if the sun is not too powerful. A great addition to the comfort of the patient would be a knowledge of the art of *swimming,* which is unfortunately too rare among the fair sex. Much of the enjoyment of the sea-bath is lost by a lady being reduced to undress and dress in a confined bathing-machine, and then to be driven out to sea in a manner calculated to create terror and dismay. Any person can learn swimming in a short time by taking a lesson from a frog or a dog that may be floating about in the water. A little observation will show that our arms and legs should be moved in the same way, and practice will prove how easy and delightful are such movements. One rule is enough – never to raise the hands above the ear, and there will be no dread of sinking. What greatly retards a woman in such exercise is the description of *bathing-dress* generally adopted in our country, viz., that of common thick blue or grey flannel, which in the space of a few minutes becomes so saturated with water as to weigh down the body and impede progress greatly. We would, therefore, advise all ladies who are inclined to learn swimming to adopt the dress worn by Frenchwomen for this purpose, consisting of drawers and a short dress over, made of grey or brown serge, and, after practice has rendered our fair friends perfect, we are sure they will liberate themselves from such trammels as bathing-machines, and freely enjoy the element God has given for our use.

After undressing, the body, as quickly as possible, should be thoroughly wrapped in a large dry flannel gown, which should not be laid aside till the very moment previously to going into the water. By this means the shock of immersion will be avoided, and that salutary glow which ought always to succeed bathing may in general be insured. Before bathing in the sea it is an excellent precaution in the young and delicate gradually to prepare themselves by previously using the *tepid bath,* at a temperature commencing at 90°, lowering 5° each time, and terminating at 65°.

<u>Health for the Million</u>, 1858

# 1859

BATHING DRESS.

The material is common Scotch plaid, green and red, in alternate checks. It is cut short, in the bloomer fashion, which, though very convenient when half veiled in snowy surf, ought to astonish the sharks themselves on dry land. But a bathing dress is only intended for convenience, and the least idea of making it elegant would be preposterous. The dress is made with a loose skirt set to an old fashioned tight yoke, and gathered around the waist with a plaid belt; it is cut short, leaving the feet and ankles free. Long bishop-sleeves, fastened around the wrist and a band, protect the arm. The pantalettes are made loose, and fastened around the ankles with narrow bands.

*Arthur's Home Magazine*, July, 1859 (Note: copied from a 1854 article with identical engraving)

The bathing dresses are now very frequently made into quite a pretty costume. Full loose pants are fastened round the ankles, leaving a frill of the same material to fail over the instep, and a blouse, coming about half way down to the knees with sleeves close at the wrists and finished with a ruffle, completes the costume, which is fastened by a leather girdle, or a belt of the material of the dress, round the waist. The material should always be woollen, which is much better adapted for the water, and more durable than any linen or cotton fabric. We have seen some very pretty bathing dresses of dark blue, bound with crimson, others of brown finished with scarlet. Either of these would both look and wear well.

*Frank Leslie's New Family Magazine*, August 1859

JULY 14th, 1859, was a gala-day at Niagara Falls. ...

The "Cave of the Winds," at Niagara Falls, is situated at the foot of the rock, between Goat and Luna Islands, and is one of the most terrific sights on the American side. Near the entrance to the Cave, is a dressing-room, in which we exchanged our ordinary clothing for a cotton bathing suit, coarse shoes, waterproof bonnet, &c., in which uncouth garb we were prepared to get a sound ducking. The gentlemanly guide gave us much valuable information in regard to the Cave, its dimensions, phenomena, and associations, before we entered.

This wonderful cavern has been formed by the constant action of the water upon the soft substratum of the precipice behind the Fall, leaving a dense vault beneath the limestone rock which hangs overhead, thirty feet beyond the base. In front, the transparent falling waters form a mammoth, moving curtain. On account of the tremendous pressure on the atmosphere beneath this arch, the Cave is filled with perpetual, yet ever-varying and raging storms. The war of elements in this watery abyss is fierce and overwhelmingly sublime. Out through the spray, when the sun shines, quivers a beautiful rain-bow.

The Cave is one hundred feet wide, one hundred and thirty feet high, and nearly forty feet deep. Along the rocky and uneven floor of this wild cavern, the spray is hurled violently backward, until it strikes the rough walls of the precipice, then curls upward to the ceiling, thus causing the constant turmoil which gives it the name of the "Cave of the Winds." A hand-railing has been erected across all the most perilous places, to which the visitor may firmly cling, while the mad waters are driven in his face. I descended this foaming, roaring abyss, with feelings of indescribable awe. The louder than ten-thousand-thunder music of dread Niagara roared with the rolling waters from the hights [sic] above. Sometimes, as I journeyed downward into the gulfs of spray, the wind and water would dash in my face, almost beating my breath away, and threatening to hurl me from the rocky pathway to the fearful depths below! Then a flash of sunlight would dart through the spray, revealing rainbows of beauty and brilliance beyond the power of description. To the right were the dark and rugged rocks – to the left the snow-white torrents of Niagara's mighty river, rolling overward to the gulf beneath our feet.

I was informed by the guide, after we came out from the Cave, that but few have the nerve to pass under the Fall. Occasionally ladies have gone through. Indeed, thrilling as is the experience, I remember it as one of peculiar interest. It makes an impression upon the soul never to be forgotten.

The Old Log Schoolhouse, 1864

Deb Salisbury

# 1860

*First Impressions of the New World,* anonymous, but from the Pen of a lady... We will give our authoress's description of the bathing parties at Newport, as – like oyster-eating – it is considered one or the institutions of the country: –

'There are three beaches formed round a succession of points, the whole forming a lovely drive on dry hard sand; and such a sun as we gazed on yesterday, setting over these distant sands, passes description. On the first of these beaches are arranged more than one hundred bathing machines, at about one hundred yards above high-water mark, looking like sentry-boxes on a large scale, with line dry sand between them and the sea. We went down on Saturday to see the bathing, which is here quite a public affair; and having fixed our eyes on a machine about a dozen yards off, we saw two damsels enter it, while a young gentleman who accompanied them went into an adjoining one. In a few minutes he came out attired in his bathing dress, and knocked at the ladies' door. As the damsels were apparently not ready, he went into the water to wait their coming, and in due time they sallied forth, dressed in thick red baize trousers, and a short dress of the same material, drawn in at the waist by a girdle. The gentleman's toilet was coloured trousers, and a tight flannel jacket without sleeves. He wore no hat, but the ladies had on very piquante straw hats, trimmed with velvet – very like the Nice ones – to preserve them from a *coup de soleil.* They joined each other in the water, where they amused themselves for a long time. A gentleman friend's presence on these occasions is essential, from the Atlantic surf being sometimes very heavy,' &c.

*Fraser's Magazine,* February, 1860

# 1861

The period of the year best suited for sea-bathing is summer and autumn, September and October being, when the temperature of the water does not fall below 50 degrees, the best months in the year. The time of day for sea-bathing in general depends on the state of the tide, either before breakfast, or two or three hours afterwards, being the best periods: remembering always that to bathe when the stomach is full, or when the sun is very powerful is neither productive of health nor comfort.

Before bathing in the sea, it is wise, particularly in the young and delicate, gradually to prepare themselves by having one or two tepid baths, and the first time a person bathes in the sea, they should on no account, remain in the water longer than five minutes.

Upon entering the machine the body should be wiped dry and the ordinary clothing being quickly resumed, a little exercise should be taken at once; remembering, however, that the replacing of the clothing is more important than that the surface of body should be completely dry.

We hope our fair readers will not be shocked if we say a few words on swimming. No one can experience the real pleasure of bathing unless they possess this, to some persons, unfeminine accomplishment. Those, however, who have acquired this healthy art, should always practice it when in the water, as the muscular action required in swimming keeps the blood in motion, and by keeping up the temperature of the body causes the reaction to be more complete.

The chief draw-back to ladies swimming is the bathing-dress used in this country. The most commodious, and at the same time the most pleasant to the wearer, is a garment, consisting of a dress and drawers in one, made of grey serge, and having a band to confine the waist. They are also far preferable, in all cases, to the common blue flannel, which, when saturated with water, becomes very heavy and inconvenient.

The What-not; or Ladies' Handy-Book, 1861

Mincing carried a large basket. Mrs. Green Brown, who was very liberal and openhanded, was surrounded by those most uncouth of naiads, bathing women, directly she appeared on the beach. One amphibious creature, with a very red face, a huge black bonnet, a blue serge dress, and black cloth trowsers, with a resolute expression, a very broad back, short waist, and bony frame, (guiltless of crinoline,) claimed her at once as her "own dear lady," and laid her huge hand also on

Lucy, whom she called "a pretty dear."

Mrs. Green Brown, desiring Mincing to give Mrs. Blair her bathing dress and cap, clambered up into one machine, followed by her maid, Lucy Blair tripped up the stairs of another, and both were fairly launched and sent out to the sands by the means of ropes and pulleys. Lucy had scarcely had time to put on the smart bathing dress, consisting of a tunic and trowsers of grey serge with broad green and scarlet stripes, and trimmed with a great amount of green and scarlet braid, when a hoarse voice and a thump at the back of her machine announced the bathing woman.

"Come, my pretty dear," said the woman, standing up to her waist in water, "give me your hand. It's your own precious Betsy, she'll take care of you! One, two, three, and away!" and before Lucy was the least aware of her intention, the marine she-Hercules had ducked her repeatedly, as easily as if she had been a baby; she then fastened a rope round Lucy's waist, secured it to the machine, and told her to "float, wash, splash, and duck, and dive, and swim if she could, while she went and dipped the other pretty dears as was all waiting for their own precious Betsy."

Lucy, recovering from the first shock, and feeling confidence as she grew used to the water, soon ventured out the whole length of the rope, and her spirits exhilarated as she had seldom felt them before, by the vivifying effect of the sea-water, the fresh morning breeze, and the amusing scenes around her, thoroughly enjoyed her young existence; everything looked *couleur de rose*. ...

No marine coquette at Dieppe or at Biarritz, could have surpassed Mrs. Green Brown. A white and scarlet tunic, and a pair of full trowsers of the same material, made her a very showy object; but the most remarkable thing about her was the profusion of long golden hair, that fell in silken ripples from under a scarlet netted cap, glistening with coral beads. Her neck and arms, very white, very fat, and a good deal exposed, were also hung with coral. Eyebrows and paint she had not ventured on; but her face was a good deal concealed by the hair that hung over it, and no one but Mincing and herself was aware that the golden torrents that shone so brightly in the morning sun, were nothing more nor less than Mrs. Green Brown's bathing wig!

The Daily Governess, a novel, 1861

# 1862

There is excellent bathing for those who like bathing on shelving sand. I don't. The spot is about half a mile from the hotels, and to this the bathers are carried in omnibuses. Till one o'clock ladies bathe; – which operation, however, does not at all militate against the bathing of men, but rather necessitates it as regards those men who have ladies with them. For here ladies and gentlemen bathe in decorous dresses, and are very polite to each other. I must say, that I think the ladies have the best of it. My idea of sea-bathing for my own gratification is not compatible with a full suit of clothing. I own that my tastes are vulgar and perhaps indecent; but I love to jump into the deep clear sea from off a rock, and I love to be hampered by no outward impediments as I do so. For ordinary bathers, for all ladies, and for men less savage in their instincts than I am, the bathing at Newport is very good.

North America, 1862

The depth of the water, in the place chosen for swimming, should, if possible, be not less than eight feet, and the clearest and calmest water possible should be selected. The pupil wears drawers, fastened by a string above the hips, and covering about half the thighs. They must be made loose, so as to allow the freest, action of the legs. ... When the pupil can swim about ten strokes in succession, he is released from the pole, but not from the rope. When he can swim about fifty strokes, he is released from the rope too; but the teacher remains near him with a long pole, until he can swim 150 strokes in succession, so that, should he sink, the pole is immediately held out to him. After this, he may swim in the area of the school under the superintendence of the teacher, until he proves that he can swim half an hour in succession, when he is considered fit to be left to himself, and, in some swimming schools, receives a particular mark on the drawers, that the proficient may be distinguished from the unskilful. Before this degree of progress is reached, pupils are not allowed to take part in long excursions.

The Popular Encyclopedia, 1862

# 1863

BATHING ABROAD AND AT HOME.

It is by trifles that national character is most distinctly shown. All the more elaborate and important institutions of nations have a tendency to assimilate to each other. The results of reasoning and reflection will be the same in all countries; and the arrangements which are the result of them cannot, in the end, differ very much. But in the smaller matters of life, the subjects of mere caprice and taste, a nation's cutaneous tendencies make themselves very plainly seen. Bathing – a subject with which, as actors or spectators, a considerable number of our readers will be familiar just now curiously illustrates the difference of the two nations which, in more important matters, are gradually drawing more close together. The two systems are much valued by the two nations; and the plan of one is wholly intolerable to the other. The Englishman cannot endure the restraints of the French system, and the Frenchman boldly sets down all our talk about morality as humbug when our laws and customs tolerate such outrages upon decency as are witnessed at an English watering-place. To an Englishman the charm of his system is its independence. His bathing-machine is his castle. The little bit of sea it encloses is his peculiar property. No one can encroach upon the few cubic feet of water he has appropriated for the time. If he likes to sally forth for a swim, he comes and goes regardless of the existence of any one else. It is not necessary for him to take any notice of his most intimate acquaintance who may be bathing in the next machine. He adopts precisely that amount of clothing or nudity which comports best with his own idea of what is comfortable or decent. He need take heed of no regulations, and recognise no public opinion in his proceedings. The sea and he have it entirely to themselves. That mixture of freedom and seclusion which constitutes an Englishman's chief happiness finds its highest ideal in an English bathing-machine. To carve out for the time being a private property even in the sea, and to have contrived a movable house for the enjoyment of a luxury in which seclusion seemed impossible, is quite a triumph of the national peculiarities. In France, the whole spirit of the scene is changed. The pastime ceases to be the isolated, surly, exclusive affair which it is upon the English coast. But, at the same time, it loses its characteristic freedom. Like every other action in the life of a French citizen, it is tremendously regulated by the Government, and it is as much made the opportunity for the display of a Frenchman's gregarious tastes as any other part of the day's employment. There is no period of the twenty-four hours at which the beach looks so gay, so full, so picturesque, as during the bathing time, and at the place which a paternal Administration has selected as the most suitable. Perhaps what makes it the liveliest is the curious costume in which many of the figures upon it appear. The Government has taken the observance of decency under its own protection, and prescribes with accuracy the apparel to be worn. It looks a comical kind of decency to English eyes. The men are dressed in a sort of trowsers and jersey all in one, which differs from ordinary garments of that description chiefly in being much too short in the legs and arms. This arrangement seems to be a compromise between the Government's appreciation of decency and the natural human desire to be as naked as possible in the water. But, to a stranger, it looks as if all the male population of the place had been seized with a sudden fancy or dressing in the clothes of their little boys. But they are not the oddest figures of the scene. The Government, having ascertained the minimum of clothing that is respectable for men, appears to have come, by a kind of mechanical logic, to the conclusion that a similar quantity is abundant for women. The result is, that the beach is peopled with a number of nondescript-looking figures, bearing very much the appearance of short, ill-made men, scantily dressed in chocolate-coloured serge – a sort of forked radish turned brown from keeping – which it requires some effort of reasoning, on the part of people who are not habituated to this Paradisiacal innocence of costume, to believe may possibly be ladies. All these figures wander about in the aimless dilatory way which appears to be an integral portion of the amusement. Some are approaching the water with lazy steps, wondering whether it is not rather cold, and, in the agonies of deliberation, displaying the beauties of their costume to considerable advantage. Others, who have had their dip, are picking their steps wearily over the shingle, looking in vain for the *cabane* where they may relieve themselves of the dripping garments which cling to their figures with a tenacity which gives rather a statuesque effect. All this time, by way of contrast, the beach is full of non-bathers – women dressed as only French women can dress – who are come to enjoy the spectacle. The contrast between the well-distended cones of gorgeous drapery which sweep along to and fro across the beach, and the poor brown, dripping, bifurcated spectres who are creeping over the pebbles up to their *cabanes*, may give a philosopher food for reflection upon the distinction between accidents and substance. If any anxious parents wish to provide a cure for some love-stricken youth, let them take him to see the mistress of his affections bathing at a French sea-place. Romance itself could not survive the sight of the fair one, associated in his mind with graceful movements and flowing lines and harmonious colouring, emerging from the water in the similitude of a magnified brown rat on its hind legs, which has narrowly escaped from drowning. Few who have not witnessed it can imagine how much of feminine beauty can be left behind by its owner in a *cabane*. But the scene in the water is stranger still to English eyes. It looks like some mythological picture representing the Tritons carrying off the Nereids, or the Satyrs pursuing the Nymphs. The first thing that meets the spectator's eye is several couples in the water, holding each others' wrists, and to all appearance struggling violently. One of each of these couples is one of the brown rats we have described, and whom, by this time, the spectator has learned to speak of in the feminine gender. The other is a very muscular broad-shouldered Frenchman in a sailor's dress, who appears to look upon the brown rat as his own peculiar property. Generally, he seems to be shaking her violently by the wrists, and taking the opportunity of each successive wave that passes to duck her under its crest. Sometimes he is grasping her round the waist; sometimes he is tugging at one arm; sometimes she seems to have been just cast ashore by a very violent wave close by him, and to be lying in a suppliant attitude at his feet. At one end of the *cabane*, for the better display of manly and feminine forms, is erected a spring board, from which these strangely clothed beings, of either sex, are projected into the sea. Sometimes they take "headers," sometimes they take "footers," but the fairer portion of creation, unaccustomed to these athletic feats, is very apt to take that compromise between the two to which Etonians were in the habit of assigning an uneuphonious name. It is fair to say that all these pastimes are not invariably conducted under the rough manipulation of the muscular French *baigneurs*. Ladies who are fastidious prefer that the male hand in whose guardianship they struggle with the waves shall be one with which they are not wholly unfamiliar. Such an arrangement may be more correct, but it is not nearly so comfortable. Uninitiated males are much more apt to be upset by the waves themselves than to be able to give much assistance in the critical moment to their tottering charges. Husband and wife may often be seen entering the water affectionately hand-in-hand, and returning more speedily than they had intended, clutching each other in an involuntary embrace as they are tumbled over by some unusually large wave. Brothers, or even casual friends, are put to the same use by ladies who shrink from the *baigneur's* sinewy arm; and it is quite the proper thing for a lady to make an appointment with her male friends for a swimming party, always assuming that her accomplishments enable her to bear her part in it. But experienced bathers do not trust to such a frail support. It is no consolation to the fair one who is let go at the critical moment, and washed up by the surf in admired disorder, that the arm which played her false was a conjugal or fraternal limb. And after all, it is a pity, when you have gone so far, to distress yourself with any remnants of English decorum. When you have once persuaded yourself to run the ordeal of walking in the comical tights, into which your dress is converted by the water, across a large open place, in presence of crowds of well-dressed gentlemen and ladies, any further display of fastidiousness is an unnecessary injury to your comfort.

Englishmen, at least, will never be very partial to this system of bathing. They gain nothing by it except the very questionable privilege of being allowed to swim about among their female friends, both parties disguised, *par ordre superieur*, in a dress of exquisite absurdity. Though all opportunities in which the sexes are allowed to mingle freely are of course valued by young men on their promotion, still it can hardly be said that the French plan of bathing adds anything to their opportunities in that respect. It would hardly be possible to commence an eligible acquaintance in the sea, or to pursue a promising flirtation at the moment that both parties were wading out dripping wet upon the shingle. A neighbouring *cabane* might give an opportunity for a Pyramus and Thisbe adventure, if unfortunately the *cabanes* of the two sexes were not generally kept apart. On the other hand, it is an utter destruction of the comfort of bathing. It is not bathing

– it is only getting wet through in a rather elaborate manner. Moreover, it requires more courage than a good many English people of either sex possess, to face an admiring assemblage of well-dressed and scrutinizing spectators in such a costume. But the fact that the system exists in France, and has been carefully arranged by the authorities as a model of decency and decorum according to their ideas, may teach us a lesson as to the conventional character of those terms, and the danger of censuring an apparent breach of them in the customs of other nations. It is difficult for an Englishman to conceive a method of proceeding less consistent with his ideas of strict decorum; and yet it is adopted by a people who unanimously agree to censure him for his outrageous disregard of decency in respect to the same subject-matter.

*The Saturday Review*, September 5, 1863

[Dieppe, France] The ladies bathe under one end of the esplanade, and the gentlemen under the other, while the fashionable crowd leans over, or sits by the low esplanade wall, inspecting the proceedings. This contiguity is, no doubt, the cause of the wonderful toilettes, *specialités des bains*, which fill the shops here, and are used by all the ladies and many of the men. They consist of large loose trousers and a jacket with skirts, made of fine flannel or serge, of all shades of colour according to taste, and of waterproof bathing caps, all of which garments are trimmed with blue, or pink, or red bows and streamers. Over all the *baigneurs comme il faut* throw a large cloak, also tastefully trimmed. Thus habited the lady walks out of her hut attended by a maid, to whom when she reaches the water's edge she hands her cloak, and, taking the hand of one of the male *baigneurs*, proceeds with such plunges and dancings as she has a fancy for, and then returns to the shore, is enveloped in her cloak by her maid, and re-enters her hut. These male *baigneurs* are a necessary accompaniment of the performance. I have only heard of one case of resistance to the custom, which ended comically enough. A young Englishman, well known in foreign society, was here with his wife, who insisted on bathing, but vowed she would go into the water with no man but her husband. He consented, and in due course appeared on the ladies side with his pretty wife, in most discreet apparel, went through the office of *baigneur*, and returned to his own side. This raised a storm among the lady bathers, and the authorities interfered. The next day the lady went to the gentlemen's side; but this was even more scandalous, and was also forbidden. The persecuted couple then took to bathing at six in the morning; but, alas on the second morning the esplanade was lined even at that untimely hour by young Frenchmen, who, though by no means early risers, had made a point of being out to assist at the bath of their eccentric friends, and as these last did not appreciate the *éclat* of performing alone, for the amusement of their friends, the lawless efforts of *ces Anglais* came to an end. In England, where dress for the water is not properly attended to by either sex, one quite understands the rule of absolute separation; but here, where every lady is accompanied by a man in any case, where she is more covered than she is in a ballroom, and where all her acquaintance are looking on, it does not occur to one why she should not be accompanied by her husband.

*The Spectator*, September 26, 1863

We will begin with the bathing-woman. She was the terror of my infancy, a baleful blue spectre, who poisoned by anticipation the pure pleasures of crab-catching and sand-digging. Clad in garments of indigo-coloured serge, with a complexion like that of a boiled shrimp, with a harsh sou'wester voice, which she strove to disguise under an utterance of honeyed sweetness, she waded through the water in quest of her victim. I, that luckless little wight, was probably standing on the top step of the machine, timorously essaying the temperature of the marine fluid by crooking my great toe. Approaching with wheedling words, she seized me in her ruthless grasp, and plunged me thrice beneath the briny wave. Oh, the anguish of those moments! I used to come up blue, blubbering and shivering; and can scarcely believe that now I take to the water as kindly as a Newfoundland dog. ...

Talking of France, I like their compulsory adoption of a bathing costume. The great majority of bathers cannot travel far from their residences, and consequently must take their watery amusement in close juxtaposition. Is it not better to wear a dress which enables a man to ask a lady to bathe, as he would ask her to take a walk, than to skulk apart on the separate system, as we do in England? With regard to ladies' bathing attire, however, the British dress clings too closely to the figure, while the French is a really fashionable garment, which would not excite especial remark if worn on *terra firma*.

But there is one point in which I don't like the French system, and that is the pertinacious manner in which they seek to prevent you from drowning yourself. I know it is not from love and admiration for me, John Bullock, Esq.; it is because the mayor and townsfolk of the watering-place in question fear that an accident will bring their *bains de mer* into disrepute.

*Chamber's Journal of Popular Literature*, October 17, 1863

# 1864

The Seine baths are a type of the whole. They are far more convenient than this ladies' bath in London; indeed, this was not built for ladies, it is only set apart for their special use upon the day I have named. The water is that of the Seine; it flows into the large inclosed space built in the river. There is a platform nearest the landing-place, making the depth suitable for children; that is a great advantage. Beyond this the water is deep enough for diving, and there is a clear length for swimming of about 40 or 45 yards. The ladies wear very tasteful dresses, fitting close at the neck, with a girdle round the waist, and a kind of Turkish trousers tied in at the ankle; everywhere else the garments are loose. English ladies, about half a century ago, were wont to adopt a dress something after that fashion when they gossiped away with the dandies of the period up to their necks in the vaunted waters of the 'Queen of the West.' How does it happen that in these modern days they have substituted the far less ornamental and convenient shirt? ...

As a rule, society in the sea – that is, the English sea – is of a very limited character. Here and there a few ladies staying in one town and bathing at the same hour, fraternize – can ladies be said to fraternize? – and agree to hold on to their ropes and fling their arms about in that peculiarly ungraceful manner which excites such intense derision in French women who have been taught better, and that is all. The gentlemen are far away if they are bathing, and if not they are lounging on the beach making critical comments – which are impertinent.

What a remarkably uncomfortable, inconvenient dress English ladies adopt for bathing! They are prone enough to follow French taste in bonnets and shawls. Why not go a little further, and adopt their really capital bathing costume? It would not, when they rose, Venus-like, from the waves, cling to them, producing that statuesque effect, which I may suppose it is their object to avoid. But this is only a minor advantage. It would only remain for gentlemen, as is the case at the best French watering-places where the use of full costume by both gentlemen and ladies is compulsory, to adopt a similar dress, for us to have real society in the sea; and when this takes place, ladies will soon be swimmers. At Biarritz, a gentleman asks a lady to swim with him in the morning just as readily as he would invite her to waltz at night. Why not in England? – at Brighton as at Boulogne, in Devonshire as at Dieppe. The ladies have everything to gain by it, the gentlemen nothing to lose.

*London Society*, June 1864

# 1865

THE *ton* who patronize Newport, Long Branch, Cape May, and the other sea-side resorts, will be interested in knowing what is worn in *the water* on the other side of the Atlantic. A fashion writer remarks: – " I have not mentioned bathing costumes in any of my recent letters, and still it is a subject which deserves the attention of your readers, as, during this warm weather, all the world either is, or will be, meditating bathing. The two colors preferred, this season, by lady bathers, are poppy-red and white. Black, or rather dark blue, is only worn by those who are indifferent to the effects of their *toilette* at all seasons and on all occasions. The white bathing costumes are made of flannel, sometimes twilled and sometimes plain, assording [sic] to taste, and are ornamented with either blue or scarlet braid. They effect the form of a *chemise russe*, with a small sailor-collar turned back from the throat; a moderately-wide scarlet waistband separates the *chemise russe* from a short petticoat, underneath which can be seen the wide straight trousers, which descend as low as the ankles. Scarlet worsted braid is sewn round the petticoat, and down the outside seam of the trousers. Formerly, bathing attire reminded us of the dress worn by the *debardeuses,* and which was always a very favorite costume at fancy balls. But now it is altered, and the most fashionable style is what I have just described. To protect the head from the sun, a small sailor hat, made either of straw or of black wax-cloth, is worn. It proves altogether a very becoming costume to young ladies when it is made in scarlet and white. White, striped with black, has also a good effect, and it is also a very general style to make the *chemise russe* different from the trousers. The hair is encased in a coral worsted net, and three coral worsted bandelets are bound round the head; the hair is worn as high as it is possible to arrange it, in order to prevent it from getting wet. The head-dress, although simplicity itself, is very charming, as it recalls the Greek style; so, when the features are classical and regular, few ornaments are found more decoming [sic]. When modified and made of silk braid, instead of worsted, and with velvet bandelets, instead of woolen ones, it is very pretty for home wear."

*The Ladies' Repository*, August 1865

Little boy's bathing-dress of striped flannel, edged with the same colour as the stripe. Scarf of the same round the waist. [ ← ]

*Le Follet*, September 1865

#### The Proper Bathing-dress.

I must now say a word or two respecting the costume most appropriate for the little bathers. A short pair of pantaloons, with a little blouse, fastened together by a strap at the waist, will be found to be the best; or the two garments may be made all in one piece. The material should be composed of wool, thin, porous, and light. If the dress be made to button in front, children will be able to dress and undress themselves.

It has been objected to this style of dress that it prevents the free exercise of the limbs in the water, and particularly swimming, and it has been proposed to use in place of it simple drawers. It is further urged that this woollen material, however light and thin it may be, prevents the direct contact of the water with the body, and so destroys the effect which the immediate contact of the water produces, viz., the kind of tonic friction which is owing to the *shock* of the waves, and which these objectors regard as the most beneficial of the effects of the sea-water. One physician, Dr. Dutrouleau,* has strongly advocated the views just mentioned, and has even gone so far as to say that the costume for the bath should be reduced to the most slender dimensions; and that it would be better were there none at all, inasmuch as the water ought, during the whole time of immersion, to be in direct contact with the child's skin.

If the bathers, and women especially, who frequent the shores of Dieppe, were to follow literally the recommendations of the learned inspector of that station, by adopting the very primitive, or rather *negative,* costume which he advises, it must be admitted that the beach at that place would present a very singular *coup-d'œil,* and one which would suggest the question whether the advantages in point of health were not being gained at the expense of decency and propriety. Certainly, I admit all the advantage which is derived from the stimulating action of the shock of the waves upon the child's skin, and I look upon the kind of stinging which is occasioned by it as productive of a wholesome action upon the cellular and muscular tissues of his frame. But is there any good ground for saying that the light woolly tissue I have named is able to prevent these good results, or even to lessen them? I think not. Moreover, it is well known to every medical practitioner that those abnormal congestions, or local engorgements of blood in various organs, for the removal of which sea-bathing is so eminently serviceable, are almost always situated in parts of the body, as the neck, or upper or lower parts of the body, which the kind of dress I have recommended leaves uncovered.

I may go further and declare my conviction that, apart from those ideas of decency and propriety which ought to govern the habits which prevail at our bathing-places, far from being productive of any inconvenience, such as the objectors bring forward, this light tissue of wool has the double advantage of protecting the skin from the burning rays of the sun and from the painful impression which the air and the water produce at the moment of immersion and of emersion from the bath. This statement, I take it, is justified by the habits of all those people who are habitually exposed to be wetted by saltwater; such as fishermen and sailors, who constantly wear some kind of woollen dress in order to prevent the too rapid evaporation of the water, which would otherwise become a cause of incessant chilling of the surface of the body.

A little straw-hat, or a handkerchief tied round the temples, will serve to protect the head of the little bathers from the fierce rays of the sun, which are felt to be so powerful when the body is immersed in the water. Children may also wear very thin shoes. Where the beach is composed of close fine sand, they will be unnecessary; but if the ground be covered with loose pebbles, little children often wound their feet if not protected by some kind of covering.

Sea-Air and Sea-Bathing for Children and Invalids, 1865

# 1866

This is not a difficult task for you, my young brother, for it is a right conceded you, not only by nature but by society everywhere, to have your garments, pants, coat and vest, constructed with reference to practical action of the chest, upper and lower extremities, as the highway to fame, all-absorbing to Young America, and to your young heart already foreshadowed in bright hopes and dreams, is paved by practicality. But for once lay aside your long coat, your vest also, and instead substitute the knit-woollen jacket, which is equally loose, lighter and more expedient. You are now ready to commence your pilgrimage; wait a little for your sister. More laborious, my blue-eyed maiden, is your preparation, for in accordance with long stereotyped public opinion and prejudice, your garments, long and closely fitting, oblige you to be impractical, inefficient and in active, all of your movements being within a constrained, prescribed limit. In your early childhood, when first you began to use those tiny feet, your mamma, as good common sense would suggest, laid aside your long swaddling clothes and wisely adapted your garments to the more perfect freedom of muscle and limb. But you are a young lady now, and prefer to sacrifice wisdom, convenience, and even gracefulness, which you almost worship, rather than be thought eccentric, and endure the unpleasant, wearying gaze of both acquaintances and strangers. With this I do not find fault, while you sit quietly with your books, piano or needle, or recline upon the sofa; but now, as we attempt something by way of practical physical culture, these garments must be laid aside, and a dress adapted to the free exercise of the entire body be donned.

Let me guide you in this, lest you mistake in its preparation. It is best made of flannel or merino (the color as suits your taste and complexion), which curls closely to the form, and which will prevent too rapid evaporation from the surface of the system when heated from exercise, and also the sudden check of perspiration. A yard or two less than you require for the ordinary dress will be sufficient.

Make the waist loose, of Garibaldi form, save short upon the shoulder, reaching only to the point where is placed the union of the arm with the body, a little above which should be the entire fullness of both the back and front part of the waist in two plaits of an inch each in depth. The waist should be made long, so that when the arm hangs by the side it falls over a couple of inches. This gives freedom in raising the arms without lifting the skirt. The belt into which this fullness is gathered should be so loose that when the lungs are fully inflated the abdomen will of course then protrude; it can be brought round the body and lap one inch.

Well would it be for both the present and future generations if this rule was observed by all mantua-makers. We would not then need to fear the extinction of the American people. The sleeves are best made straight, and gathered into the arm-size, also into a band about the wrist. The skirt, in which the especial eccentricity of the dress consists, needs to be about two-thirds as wide as the ordinary dress, and, in length, should come just below the knee, so as not to restrict in the least the free movements of the feet and limbs.

The pants of the same material as the dress, very loose and long about the body, the lower part twenty-seven inches in width, and gathered into a ruffled band about the ankle, else into an elastic band around the calf of the leg, the surplus length drooping according to the Turkish style of pant. The latter is more artistic in style, and will not be objectionable in the mind of your brother as too nearly approaching his mode of dress.

You can make the costume still more attractive by trimming the band upon the shoulder, the skirt, the outer side of the pants, and other parts of it as suits your taste and convenience. Now, with your standing collar and plain linen cuffs, your costume is complete, and adapted to dancing, skating, bathing, gardening, climbing of mountains, fishing excursions, etc.
*The Herald of Health and Journal of Physical Culture*, June 1866

Fancy bathing costumes are introduced, and serges in all colours manufactured for the purpose. The form that is now almost universal is the complete and modest, yet incommoding covering of a pair of loose trousers and a tunic fastened by a band. Worsted braid is employed to trim them. A deep invisible blue serge, with scarlet trimming looks pretty and not too showy. The sleeves are short, the neck cut quite high, but square, and rouched round by scarlet braid. The breast should be double, to insure its keeping well closed, and the tunic and trousers should be attached so that they can be thrown off together. Sky blue, magenta, orange, yellow, green, and French grey, as well as more sober browns, violets, and maroons are made up. Very nice felt bathing shoes and boots are now produced, of becoming shapes, pretty colours, and at low prices, so that the untidy and uncomfortable fashion of wearing old shoes tied with string will hardly be long retained. The felt shoe being soft, can be wrung out easily. An excellent seaside shoe made of Russian leather is to be used this year. It is shaped like an Oxonian, ties on the instep, and is stout and strong; and with a wafer-proof sole will probably wear a couple of seasons. Russia leather never absorbs wet or dirt, and can be perfectly cleaned daily by using a dump sponge. The price is about twice that of the ordinary seaside sand shoe, but, in addition to a superior appearance, its durability is about sixfold, and the hose is also preserved by it. We can recommend the new shoe to the use of the economical. A new bathing and swimming dress is made with a plain-fitting bodice top ending in trousers, all in one piece.
*The Family Friend*, August 1866

The principal of these bathing-places are called the Côte des Basques, the Port Vieux, and the Côte Napoleon. The Port Vieux is a narrow inlet much frequented by swimmers, while the bay known as the Côte Napoleon, is patronized more by those whose powers of natation are limited, but who yet desire to enjoy the pleasure of a dip in the salt sea or a plunge amongst the waves of the Bay of Biscay, which in that spot they can do with perfect safety. At one extremity of the Côte Napoleon stands the villa Eugenie, while facing it at the other is the white-faced casino. Down upon the sand near to the casino is the bathing establishment, – a long, low, somewhat gaudily-painted building of a mock Moorish pattern, and into this imposing edifice enter, at opposite ends, ladies and gentlemen dressed in the very extreme of fashion, to emerge in a short time more plainly than elegantly clad for the water. The ladies' attire consists of tunic and trousers, sometimes fancifully and tastefully embroidered and decorated; while the gentlemen make their appearance in somewhat similar articles, of a stripy, faded, washed-out hose, and incongruous nature.

It requires at first no little *sangfroid* to walk thus attired for two or three hundred yards, through a crowd of lounging belles and beaux seated or strolling on the sands, who congregate together and make critical remarks concerning you as you pass; but it is an ordeal to which all bathers, both male and female, must submit before they can take the water at Biarritz; and as use is second nature, the novelty speedily wears off, and the promenade is treated as a matter of course, and stare is returned for stare, and criticism for criticism.

The various methods in which different bathers choose to enter the sea are well worthy of note by all who desire to enjoy a hearty laugh. The smooth sandy shore slopes very gradually, and bathers may proceed to a considerable distance without being out of their depth, though even on a calm day the waves roll in at times with considerable force. In entering the water the favorite style with young France is a skip and a jump, a run, a leap over two or three ripples, a splash, and a retreat, then a cautious advance and a species of wild dance, as if the bather were performing the can-can with a wave for a partner, and finally, a terrific plunge into three feet of water; middle-aged France, conscious of the buoyant nature of fat, walks with elephantine tread some little distance into the sea, throws himself upon his back, and floats placidly and contentedly till a wave washes him up amongst the promenaders on the shore, and leaves him there prostrate, high and dry, when he rises and repeats the performance. Ladies trip lightly down the shore to the water's edge, throw aside the dainty little slippers they have worn over the loose, dry, gritty sand, which, fine and soft though it be, irritates bare feet not a little, and then not unfrequently stand while an attendant empties a bucketful of water over their heads preparatory to their crossing the boundary of king Neptune's domains. A favorite amusement amongst the bathers at the Côte Napoleon is, to form into line, ladies and gentlemen holding each other's hands, and then advance boldly towards the rolling waves. Just as the white crest towers above them, all spring upwards and are borne in by the advancing tide. Naturally some are unfortunate and do not make their leap in time, but the great object is to keep the chain of linked hands unbroken, and those who first regain their feet on the soft, firm sand, assist in righting their less fortunate companions; but should a second wave follow close upon the heels of the first, probably the whole party are rolled ignominiously over, and after a few seconds come panting and dripping to their feet. This pastime is attended with no danger, for the water is shallow and the beach shelving, while, moreover, a boat is stationed throughout the day at a certain distance from the shore, to prevent even good swimmers going beyond a particular point, ready at a moment's notice to proceed to the assistance of any bather who may have imprudently ventured out of his depth.  *Every Saturday*, August 25, 1866

Women must and will trim, as spiders spin webs, and bees make honeycombs. They even trim bathing-dresses: one would think that nothing could redeem them from their hideousness. But they obey a law of their being.
*The Atlantic Monthly*, October 1866

# 1867

Fig. 1. – Dress of scarlet flannel, trimmed with a plaiting of black flannel, bound with white braid. The pants are full, and have elastic bands on the edge in order to confine them to the leg. The dress is made with a yoke, and perfectly loose, being caught into the waist by means of a scarlet belt. The cap is of oiled silk, trimmed with scarlet and black.

Fig. 2. – Dress of scarlet and black bathing cloth. The long gored *paletot* is turned up with scarlet flannel cut in scallops and edged with black braid. The hair is covered with an oiled silk cap, trimmed with scarlet. The hat is of black glazed cloth, trimmed with scarlet.
*Godey's Lady's Book*, July 1867

### A WORD ABOUT BATHING DRESSES.

The bathing season has now arrived, and to those of our number who will visit the seaside for summer recreation and enjoyment, a few words may not be amiss upon the subject of bathing dresses. I think nothing can be uglier than the water costumes one often sees at the shore, and it is not until within a year or two that ladies have commenced to consult grace and effect in the construction of these suits, any garment or garments being made to *do* which should simply conceal the person of the wearer. What a queer outfit one gets who is dependent upon those who loan garments at the shore.

We dropped down at Cape May last summer and spent a day or two, enjoying the sea-bathing of that famous locality. As the trip was unexpected and somewhat hurried, we took no bathing dresses with us, but trusted to our luck to hire them at the shore. The best thing I could secure was a long, scanty, blue flannel gown, into which I could only squeeze myself with the greatest difficulty. When at length I was fairly inside, and had belted it down with a shoe-string in place of the original girdle, which was missing, I stepped out upon the beach to await the coming of my liege lord. Presently a strange-looking being, something between a Sandwich Islander and a circus clown, approached and touched me on the shoulder. I was about to resent this familiarity, when the queer object spoke my name, and I found it was my own husband, robed in a full suit of striped bedticking. We enjoyed a hearty laugh, each at the other's expense, but soon forgot our appearance in the luxury of the surf; and as we came out, all dripping, remarked that the water was indeed a great leveller – in this plight we were as good-looking as most of our fellow bathers.

The best bathing dress, for convenience as well as looks, is cut similar to the Dio Lewis gymnasium suit, consisting of loose Garibaldi waist, with short tunic or skirt fastening at the left side. This is worn over full trousers, gathered in at the ankle. The whole suit should be of the same material. Flannel or serge are most commonly in use. These, when soaked with water, become very heavy, and also cling to the form. We have lately seen recommended brown holland, which, it is said, possesses neither of these disadvantages. For trimming, either white or scarlet braid should be used. Other colors change at once when put into water. It may be put on in various ways, to suit the taste of the wearer. Short sleeves are preferable to long ones, as they give freer use of the arms for swimming, or in case of danger.

*Arthur's Home Magazine*, July 1867

[St. Malo, France] This is a quaint and rather dirty town, built upon an island, that has been converted into a peninsula. It does not offer much to detain the traveller; though he will propably [sic] find a bathe refreshing, and may amuse himself by watching how they do these things in France. The coast is not adapted to machines, so you enter one of a series of canvas sentry-boxes on wheels, wherein you disrobe and then clothe yourself in costume resembling that of young France in the present day; that is, from the knee upwards – below is nature unadorned. The females are dressed in a sort of bloomer attire. Thus habited, you calmly walk through an admiring crowd to the sea, wherein both sexes disport themselves in company. Very little swimming seems to be done, for which the dress is rather unfavourable, being heavy when wet; paddling about knee-deep seems the staple amusement. When you have finished, you either walk back as you came, or, for a small fee, have your box brought to the water's edge.

*Once a Week*, August 3, 1867

There is a simple style of bathing dress, which may be recommended to English ladies, as preferable to those hideous blue gowns which form the sole bathing costumes on certain points of the coast. It is made of striped blue and white serge, and trimmed with blue of a darker shade. The 'bottines' are of canvas bordered at the tops with blue, and have flexible leather soles. At the back of the cap, to which a couple of blue streamers are generally attached, is an oilskin-bag designed to hold the bather's back-hair. [ ➔ ]

*Tinsley's Magazine*, August 1867

## 1868

WE take the following from the "Englishwoman's Domestic Magazine," a periodical which, we believe, is now recognised as the best authority on all details of dress: –

"All the world," to translate a French phrase, is thinking of sea-bathing just now, and quite a new series of bathing costumes are being prepared for the season. Some of these will appear a little extraordinary, perhaps, to some of our English readers. Here they are, such as we have seen them: –

The Parisian costume – a *pantalon,* very wide and gathered round the ankle; a full jacket, with a round basquine, fitted to the waist with a belt, and short sleeves; a Parisian cap, trimmed with a ruching of red braid, with a large rosette on one side.

The Swiss costume – double skirt, very short, and low square bodice, trimmed with red braid; waistband, fastened with a rosette; Swiss hat of black oil-cloth, with a red rosette on one side, and a net of red soutache to fasten up the hair.

The Marin costume – a straight loose pantalon and tight jacket, grey, with blue facings; marin hat and blue net.

And the Russian costume – wide pantalon and blouse, fastened slantwise, trimmed with braid and large buttons; Russian cap, edged with a thick ruche, and finished off by a tassel.

All these costumes are completed by high boots of soft leather, lined with cork, bound and laced with braid of the colour of the trimming: they are with or without heels.

*The Country Gentleman's Magazine*, July 1868

BATHING COSTUMES. ...

Fig. 1. – Costume of purple flannel, with trimmings of white flannel. The bodice is fastened with white buttons and a white band and buckle. Bathing-cap of oil-skin, trimmed with red worsted braid.

Fig. 2. – Blouse and trowsers of red flannel, trimmed with white. The blouse is ornamented with a ruche of white cashmere, and a scarf of the same is tied round the waist and falls in long ends at the back. Bathing-cap of oil-skin.

Fig. 3. – Costume of white and lilac striped flannel. The blouse is trimmed round the bottom with a border of white flannel, and caught up on each side with a tab of the same material. The collar, wrist, and waistbands are also white. Bathing-cap of oilskin, with a pinked-out ruche of the same material as the costume.

Fig. 4. – Costume of a darkish gray flannel, trimmed with strips of lighter gray flannel; waistband to match the trimming. Round oil-skin bathing-cap, edged with a ruche of red worsted braid.

Fig. 6. – Bathing-dress of red flannel, trimmed with strips of white flannel, and fastened round the waist with a red and white cord and tassels.

*Godey's Lady's Book*, July 1868

SEA-BATHING.

It cannot be too forcibly impressed upon the visitor at the seashore, that this pre-eminent feature of our watering-place is a ready means for *good* or for *harm,* according to the manner in which it is used. Those who emerge from the luxury of a bath and soon suffer the enervating effect of reaction, often conclude that sea-bathing "does not agree with them," and envy the apparently peculiar organization of others who become vastly strengthened and built up in a regular, systematic use of the same remedial agent. In nearly every such instance, the fault lies with the (individual) bather, *not in the bath.*

A few simple directions will be very serviceable and render surf-bathing highly beneficial as well as luxurious and fascinating, IF they be adhered to, not occasionally, but *constantly.*

It should be premised that the effects of sea bathing on the system may be either stimulating or depressing, as already intimated; when properly indulged, as a gentle stimulus, invigorating the prostrate system and increasing cutaneous circulation, also, in cases of disease, removing the same by chemical action, in the absorption of the salts found in solution in the sea water.

1st. *Provide a suitable bathing suit.* The transient guest may prefer hiring a dress at the bathing ground, which can be done at from thirty-five to fifty cents. The regular guest will prefer buying a few yards of material and making up the garment, trimming according to taste, or they can be bought at reasonable prices on the shore. Mohair, or, next to that, flannel, is the best material; cotton or linen stuff adheres unpleasantly, in the water, and is uncomfortable. They should be made pretty full – ordinary shirt and pants for gents, and a sack, belted in over the pants, for ladies; a broad-rimmed chip straw, secured under the chin, protects the head from the sun, and a few, use bathing shoes. The latter are unnecessary, however, and are liable to fill with sand. An oil-silk cap is worn by many ladies.

A Complete Descriptive Guide of Long Branch, N.J., 1868

# 1869

87.107. – Ozias Morse, Concord, Maas. – *Bathing-Dress.* – February 23, 1869.

*Claim.* – Constructing a bathing or swimming-dress in one garment, having the opening for putting it on extending from the neck to the waist, and being whole below the waist, substantially as described.

*Annual Report of the Commissioner of Patents for the Year 1869*, 1871

Nos. 1 and 2. BATHING DRESSES. – Blue flannel is the best material for bathing dresses, because the color is moderately cheerful and does not fade. Black, red and white are used, according to taste. No. 1 is trimmed with buttons, and a ruche of pleated worsted braid, black, white or red. No. 2 is of more simple make than the polonaise style of buttoning on one side. The bodice given is for a slight figure, and is intended to fit loosely about the shoulders, and be just a little full at the waist. Both it and the tunic are to be sewn into the same waistband, and buttoned down the entire length of the front (it will be found more convenient to sew it up part way, leaving only a slit to button). It is trimmed with worsted braid, laid on flat, two or three rows. Both these tunics are rather shorter than are generally worn, except by young girls. Long sleeves are almost universally seen.

*The Ladies' Friend*, June 1869

TOO BAD OF THE FRENCH. – At Dieppe, in France, the following notice has been issued by the police:– "The bathing police are requested, when a lady is in danger of drowning, to seize her by the dress and not by the hair, which oftentimes remains in their grasp."

*Good Health*, June 1869

The bathers come from the little white houses that form a row upon the shore. How bright with anticipation is every face! It is so good to dash into the surf and fling the cool drops about. The women are in all colors, of flannel, and serge, and moreen, and coarse poplin; white, gray, blue, striped, and plaid. They wear trowsers, full at the hips, buttoned at the sides, and loose at the ankles. A short skirt reaches to the knees, and a pretty little jacket, zouave, with mock vest, or a blouse completes the dress. An oil silk bag cap with elastic string protects the hair, and a broad straw hat shields from the sun. Half high Polish boots of white flannel loosely made, with rubber soles, and tied at the ankles with a worsted. cord and tassel are better than the heavy wooden clogs. The dresses are trimmed with bright worsted braid, either quilled at the edge of the garments, or binding them in scallops. Sashes of plaid worsted, fringed at the ends, are very tasteful, instead of belts. An oil silk bag, or one of Manilla twine is useful to hold the dresses as you go to and from the shore.

Gentlemen's bathing suits are made similar to those for ladies, excepting that they are not so full, and the yoke to the blouse is smaller, and the collar wider. The Navy blue flannel is a favorite material.

*Mother's Journal*, August 1869

LADIES' BATHING DRESSES.

GREAT reforms have been made within the last few years in the bathing dresses worn by ladies. Great reform was needed – for the preservation of modesty as well as of health and comfort. The long, loose gown, formerly worn, was apt to dab wet and flabby against the bather as she left the water, and cause a chill. Swimming in such a garment was very nearly something miraculous. Even in dipping in and out of the water, it would cling round the legs and impede freedom of motion. The very greatest objection of all was, that occasionally the air filled it, or the wind caught it, as the bather rose above the surface of the waves, and bore it up above the crest of the water like a balloon. The dress now in vogue amongst ladies of the highest rank, becoming more general every season, and which we hope will soon be universal, is of French origin.

At many of the French watering-places, machines are not known. A row of buildings on the shore serves bathers to undress and dress. From these they run across the sands to the water. Perhaps it is to this circumstance that the pretty and modest dresses now in vogue owed their origin. To swimmers such clothing is indispensable. The bathing garments consist of a pair of trousers and a blouse belted at the waist, with or without sleeves. There are a good many different ways and fashions for making these. Some are very plain, some piquant. A lady, not young, or ill-shaped, should choose a plain garment; as also will those of retiring disposition and delicate sentiment. A very stout woman, on the wrong side of forty, attired as a jaunty young sailor, would be ludicrous. Equally absurd would a tall, angular, very thin lady seem in like adornments. But young and pretty girls may be allowed to give some scope to the lightness of their hearts, which will express itself in fanciful costume. There is no reason why bathing garments should not be made with taste and some ornament; but by ladies of good character, what is remarkable and "loud" will be decidedly avoided. They will not desire to call any particular attention to themselves in the water by conspicuousness, though they may naturally and properly desire not to look unsightly objects, but rather pleasing ones, to their companions, or to any one who inadvertently sees them, in addition to securing their own comfort and protection.

The French bathing dress is cut like a boy's tunic or larger. The pattern of a boy's brown Holland pinafore enlarged will prove a good guide. Fig. 1 shows the shape. It is cut open at the throat, sits plain on the shoulders, from which it is sloped straight away; the armholes afterwards are hollowed out. It should be long enough to reach the knees, when finished, in front, and two, or even three 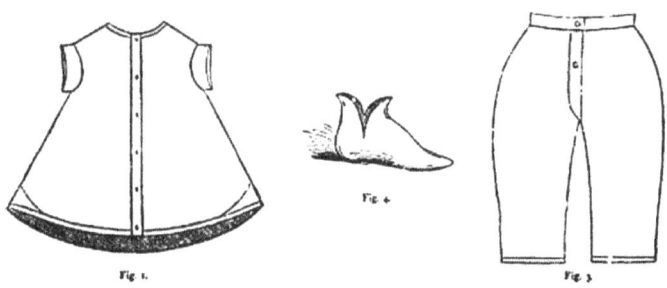 inches longer behind. The sleeves are from two to three inches deep. The waist-band is made of the material doubled, and hooks over the blouse, reducing all the figure. Down the front there is a two-inch wide hem on one side only; the other is simply bound with braid. Large buttons fasten it down the front. Before cutting the front out, pin a fold down the centre of four inches wide. This allows sufficient for the two-inch hem to be made, and to lap over under side. The trousers can be cut from any pattern of white ones that fit (see Fig. 2). They are joined behind, turning in an inch at one side and a little way up in front. An inch-wide false hem is put on the rest of the front and sloped away to the join. This will be observed in Fig. 3. It buttons an inch over the inner side, which is the one that has an inch turned in. Stitch this across a little below the join, and cut off the superfluous turning at the back. Pleat the trousers into an easy waistband two inches wide, double. Do not make them fuller than is absolutely necessary, for the less material used the better; the more there is employed, the heavier the gown will be when saturated with water. The serge used should be of a very light fine make. The French have an excellent serge for the purpose, and are partial to black suits. Many of these are trimmed with cross-cut bands of tartan, wide on the skirt, and narrow on the body, sleeves, and trousers. A pretty variety of patterns is made by rounding off the corners of the skirt of the blouse at the dotted lines in Fig. 1, making the round come to a marked point where the side-seams meet.

Serge costs about half-a-crown a yard, and is very wide. A costume will take about five yards. A width is required to cut each leg, and a width each for the front and back of the blouse. The sleeves, bands, &c, can be cut out of the pieces. Bathing caps are made of oil-silk, covered with coloured chenille nets.

Join the skirt to the band of the body. The sleeves may be mere epaulettes, deep under the arm, and scalloped quite away to the top; or square, short sleeves, or long ones. Long sleeves are of the coat shape, with very open cuffs. The band is made of the material, and hooks on. It should be quite loose, to allow perfect freedom of action to the bather or swimmer. The natural movements of the body in the water are far more graceful than the wholly imaginary excellence of a braced-in waist, the artificial smallness of which is as strikingly marked and ugly, as rouge cheeks compared to the real bloom of health and beauty. The trousers should be cut from the pattern of a boy's knickers, if the lady making them has got a suitable pattern. Of course, they must be considerably larger than a boy's, and half as wide again at the upper part. Pleat them into a band. They are entirely joined. Put them on first; then the blouse; and, lastly, the band.

Coloured flannel is a good material for bathing gowns, but serge is better, and also dearer – perhaps not dearer in the end, because wider. It can now be purchased in every colour. Messrs. Howell and James, of Regent Street, have a great variety of serges for the purpose, such as grey, lavender, light blue, magenta, green, white, &c. Nothing is more suitable than a dark blue. This may be trimmed with scarlet military braid, without being remarkably conspicuous. A date brown is not a bad colour for bathing dresses, and may be trimmed with white braid. White, trimmed with blue, is pretty, but a little conspicuous, unless at a bathing-place where such gay articles are commonly worn.

Fig. 7 is a dress of dark blue serge, trimmed with a broad scarlet military braid between two narrow ones. It opens on the cross down the front, and fastens with long hooks and eyes. There is a rosette of braid on the shoulder. The trimming is carried round the skirt. The waistband of serge has a row of wide braid in the centre and a rosette. There are no sleeves; the arms are trimmed round with a ruche of scarlet braid. The neck is cut square just round the throat, and niched. The trousers open above the ankle with a curve, and braided. The hair is brushed off the face and tied back with a ribbon.

A brown serge costume may be made with a two inch wide outside hem all down the dress, very neatly trimmed each side with half-inch wide white military braid. There are two plain rows also on each side of this. Round the neck are points piped with white and rising from a band of white braid. There are short square leaves, waved at the edge and bound with white braid. The edge of the blouse is also waved and bound. The trousers are cut open outside at the ankle, waved and bound round. A rosette fastens the waistband.

Fig. 6 is a dress for a child. A couple of plain breadths are joined, the shoulders sloped, the top hollowed at the neck a little, and pleated in a band, which is afterwards covered by a ruche. A waistband of the material is hooked over it, to keep it to the figure. The sleeves are little puffs, edged with a ruche. The trousers may be cut by any drawers the child wears, and left untrimmed. Children should be supplied with gowns, and many who now refuse to go in the water, would then gladly do so. The child's gown may be filled up with a plain piece to the throat, if desired.

Fig. 8 is a purple gown. It is nearly close round the throat, and is trimmed down the front and skirt with four or five inches of a woollen material, striped purple and white, and cut on the cross, to make a slanting ornament. This looks well with short or with long sleeves and cuffs ornamented. The lower part of the trousers is also bound with trimming.

Fig. 1.    Fig. 8.    Fig. 7.    Fig. 5.    Fig. 6.

A plain costume with one row of broad braid all round looks neat. The neck is square, edged with a ruche of scarlet braid round it.

Fig. 5 is a very stylish costume in the sailor-fashion, fit for a swimming dress. It is of blue, trimmed with white.

Materials of mixed wool and cotton are unfit for the sea, because they pucker in water. The serge or flannel used should be shrunk before cutting it out. Linen and brown holland, which some persons recommend for bathing costumes, are not desirable; they are much too chilly.

Sandals are greatly worn by bathers, especially on stony coasts. There is also another useful invention for bathers by Mr. Norman, bootmaker, Westminster Bridge Road, London. It is a loose boot, of coloured felted flannel, of a mediaeval cut, like Fig. 4, with a double sole of the same, and easily slipped on or off. It can be had in any colour, and is very inexpensive.

Long hair may be left floating, tied back by a ribbon, as it looks prettiest, but is inconvenient (see Fig. 5). Or it may be twisted into a coil on the crown of the head, and secured by a hair-pin each way; or placed in an oilskin cap, edged with scarlet.

On re-entering the machine, after a sea bath, the dress worn in the water should be immediately thrown aside, and the bather should wrap round her a flannel gown, large enough to envelop her person entirely; this is necessary to avoid a chill. Over the gown she should rub herself well in every limb till the skin glows and becomes dry. A loose, coarse flannel is the best for this; and the Welsh make will be found decidedly preferable to Lancashire or any other English kind. However, still better by far is a gown made of *house-flannel,* sold at the oilshops. Its powers of friction, and thereby exciting a healthy and agreeable glow, are greater than those of any better-looking sort. The flannel used in India by the fakirs has the merit of excelling any other for powers of friction, warmth, and almost endless durability; but it is not every one who would be able to procure this.

Such a flannel gown may readily be cut from shrunk flannel by the pattern of a lady's waterproof. It may be made the same size, or a little less full in the skirt and towards the lower part, because a waterproof is worn over the dress, and the flannel gown has no dress to take up its fulness. Very loose coat-sleeves may be put in, and down the front it should wrap over considerably, and be fastened by several large buttons. Keep these buttons up the skirt and slip the gown over the head. A couple of buttons will then in a second close the throat and body. If the arms are in the sleeves, rub the limbs and body vigorously. Those who are not capable of much active exertion may leave the gown unbuttoned, and not use the sleeves, but cast it round them like a cloak, and drag it round and round, and see-saw it from side to side, to dry and warm every part of the skin. The sandals or bathing-boots should have been cast off directly after the flannel gown was slipped on. The boots come off most quickly. A square of coarse flannel, folded two or three times, should be placed in a dry part of the machine for the bather to stand upon whilst rubbing and drying.

Cassell's Household Guide, Volume II, 1869

But the truth is, that it is almost impossible at Dieppe to enjoy one's bath quietly, or wholly to escape from the publicity which, until one becomes hardened in the matter, is decidedly embarrassing. And this brings me to a point at which the French system of sea bathing seems to be conspicuously inferior to our own. I am told that irregularities occasionally take place along on our coasts, and one might wish, as indeed I do heartily, that drawers were the rule and not the exception in England; in France no man or boy is permitted under any circumstances to bathe without them; and it is not to be disputed that the bathing dresses of our English ladies admit of improvement, to avoid that saturated, statuesque appearance which the wearers exhibit as they leave the water or stand above the receding waves. But never in England have I had to make my way in a state of nudity (drawers excepted) down a long beach thick with ladies, many of whom bring their work, which I fancy makes little progress, and their books, which I misdoubt their reading, and take up their positions as nearly as may be to the edge of the water, in which some scores of naked men are disporting, themselves. The distance that one has to walk in this condition depends upon the state of the tide, for bathing machines appear to be unknown at Dieppe, and the little canvas cabins in which one performs one's toilette are stationary, so that at low water the stretch of beach which has to be traversed, and which is thickly dotted with ladies (not often, it is fair to observe, our own countrywomen), presents a sufficiently formidable appearance for a man of ordinary modesty. I question if an Englishman ever feels quite comfortable under the circumstances. With the average Frenchman I am disposed to think it is otherwise, and that the homage of admiring eyes, as he struts leisurely in his nudity before them, is as incense to his vanity. But it is, at any rate, certain that, whether from habit or from some other more deep-seated cause, the Frenchman generally bears the exposure better than we do, and appears to relish the beach part of the performance quite as much, to say the least, as the bath proper. He walks erect, he strokes his sleek skin, he adjusts his caleçons, he "puts on side," he pleasantly recognizes his acquaintances among the crowd, he pauses composedly to talk to some one – nay, sometimes he is accompanied by a lady, who will even, if he be so minded, await his return at the edge of the water with his peignoir on her arm, when she will envelope him in its white folds, pat him approvingly on the back, and walk happily back with him until he retires into his dressing place. The Englishman generally runs down or proceeds by a series of awkward hops, skips, and jumps —he is not always erect; he cannot find the time or the face to swagger under the circumstances, and he gets into and out of the water as quickly as he can. But whether one likes it or not, whether one hurries or loiters, swaggers or is abashed, there can, I think, be no question that the system is really immodest and objectionable. Of the bathing of the ladies there is, perhaps, not so much to complain. They are all clad in a tidy little suit, which consists generally of a black serge tunic loose like a Norfolk blouse, and drawn in at the waist, and a pair of short trousers of the same stuff, or else a jacket and trousers in one. The sleeves of the tunic are more or less short, reaching generally to the elbow; the trousers usually cover the knees. The dress is relieved with little tags of coloured ribbon and trimming here and there, and a bright belt, while a finish and a touch of coquetry are given by a jaunty little hat or cap lined with an oil-silk bag to protect the hair. Sometimes the dresses are of brighter colours, red and blue, more or less trimmed; and in some cases a diaphanous white material is worn by the less modest spirits in place of the sterner serge stuff of which the dresses are for the most part made. There is also considerable licence [sic] allowed in the matter of the shortness of the sleeves and trousers, of which full advantage (if that be the proper word to use) is occasionally taken. But, on the whole, the costumes are about as modest and unobjectionable as bathing costumes can easily be made; and, despite the smart little caps and the bright patches of trimming and ribbon, they certainly fall short of being becoming. But if the costumes are unobjectionable enough and superior to our own for the actual operation of bathing, I question if they should be so regarded for the purpose of promenading the beach – which use they are largely applied. I do not mean to say that when a lady at Dieppe wishes to go for a walk on the beach she dons her bathing costume; but I do mean to say that more time is consumed by many of the bathers between their little bathing cabins and the sea than they spend in the water itself. And I may say further that the instincts of most modest women would revolt from the idea of exhibiting themselves in open air in trousers, and with bare legs and arms, before a number of gentlemen – especially when the saturation of the costume gives a sharpness of definition of the form which, not to put it more forcibly, emphasizes the absence of underclothing. But the absence of bathing machines necessitates to some extent this exposure on the part of ladies who would bathe at Dieppe. The exposure maybe modified or prolonged according to taste. A lady, may, if she chooses, wear a peignoir until she gets into the water, and don it again the moment she comes out; in which case she will have the gratification of presenting the appearance of walking about in her nightgown; or she may bathe at high tide only, or at the "petits bains" to the left of the Etablissement, where there are not so many spectators, or, at least, she may pass as quickly as possible from her cabin to the sea and back. Most English ladies adopt one or more of these expedients. But with the generality of the bathers it is otherwise. The beach for many hours of the day immediately under the terrace of the Etablissement is thick with forms clad as above, and apparently in no hurry to reach the water on the one hand, or the dressing-room on the other; while all along the terrace are rows of chairs, each with an occupant, who has not often forgotten to bring his opera glasses. In front, small bathing canoes, paddled each by a male bather in the costume which nature and the caleçons which the French Administration have given him, pass leisurely to and fro; while the ladies are also taken on the right flank by a considerable body of naked men who are bathing in the space set apart for them. Some few of the men wear complete costumes, and then are permitted to make raids into the female territory, and to mix with the female bathers. The latter are, meanwhile, dancing in circles, some few are swimming, and others are clinging with an abandon which I am told is due to terror, but which looks like something else, round the neck of one of those favoured mortals whose life is spent in bearing lovely burdens into the waves, in calming their fears, and in dipping and ducking them as they may desire. And in order that all may be in harmony in the bathing system at

Dieppe, the Administration has considerately provided for this delicate and delightful duty men instead of women.
*Littell's Living Age*, September 25, 1869

As is appropriate for this time of year, therefore, we give a pretty bathing-dress and some appropriate watering-place toilets. A pretty bathing-dress is very rare, but the one we give is really elegant. It is made of striped blue-and-white serge, and trimmed with blue of a darker shade. The "bottines" are of canvas, bordered at the tops with blue, and have flexible soles. At the back of the cap, to which a couple of streamers are generally attached, is an oilskin-bag designed to hold the bather's back-hair.
*Peterson's Magazine*, July 1869

LADIES' BATHING SUITS,
$4 and upward.
Gentlemen's Plaid Flannel Bathing Suits,
$5 and upward.

*Appletons' Journal*, August 14, 1869

# 1870

As this is the month when most persons that go to the sea-shore take their annual trip, we give, as appropriate for the occasion, several patterns for bathing-dresses, caps, shoes, etc. Most of these are in the front of the number, and are described in the usual fashion department; but we add here engravings of two bathing-dresses, one for a lady and the other for a little girl, which will be found less expensive than the others.

The best materials used for bathing-dresses are gray or dark-blue flannel, being the lightest in texture, cheapest in price, but moreen or tweed; and some persons recommend common bed-ticking as being better than anything else. Of flannel, from eight to ten yards will be required for a lady, for or five for a little girl. The bathing-dress for the lady consists of drawers made open at the ankle, and a loose sacque coming almost to the knee before it is belted, as that takes it up. It is a great mistake to make the upper-garment too long, as it holds too much water, and consequently is very heavy after being in the bath. Our model is trimmed with black worsted braid on gray flannel: white looks better on blue: and either blue or gray bears the action of salt water better than anything else. Blue and white, probably, look well the longest.

The child's upper garment is fulled into a yoke, and is trimmed with black or red worsted braid, quilled in the middle, and only short sleeves. We recommend a common handkerchief, tied round the throat, to protect it against the sun, as being better than the collar, only not so neat-looking. However, a collar of white muslin can be made permanently upon the dress, and the handkerchief used in addition. The cap is of oiled silk, and should entirely cover the hair. With these hints any lady can make up a bathing-costume for herself, much better and cheaper that those made at the stores. Close, tight sewing is of the utmost importance.
*Peterson's Magazine*, August 1870

Fig. IX. – Sea-Bathing Costume of Black Serge. – Trousers fastened at the knee, with leglets of striped wollen [sic] material. Tight-fitting tunic, buttoned at the side, and fitted to the waist with a leather belt.

Fig. X. – Bathing-Costume of White Flannel. – Trousers fastened at the knee by a cross strip braided with a Grecian pattern in black wool. Peplum blouse, with short sleeves, with a braided Grecian pattern, buttoned on each side and on the shoulders.

Fig. XI. – Costume of Black Merino. – Trousers fastened at the knee, and trimmed with a band and cross strip of blue cashmere. Small skirt, with facings of cashmere.

*Peterson's Magazine*, August 1870

# 1871

We now give, here, an illustration of a bathing-dress for a young lady, which we shall describe more at large. This dress is made of black and white plaid flannel, and trimmed with scarlet worsted braid. It consists of drawers, which are fastened to an under-body. These drawers are trimmed up the outside, as seen in the design. The over-dress is cut in a deep, loose sack, coming half way to the knee, or longer, if preferred, and is cut double-breasted, like a boy's blouse, with slightly open sleeves, all trimmed to match, to which is added a worsted fringe, two inches deep. This sack is belted in at the waist with a leather belt. The cap is of oiled-silk, bound with scarlet braid. By making the over-sack lo come below the knee, this could easily be converted into a very pretty "boating costume," with the addition of a sailor's hat. Six to seven yards of plaid flannel, and one piece of scarlet alpaca braid, and six yards of fringe will make this dress.

[ → ] We give, next, an illustration of a bathing, or boating dress, for a little girl. It consists of drawers, which are fastened to an under-waist, and made of gray flannel, bound with scarlet flannel. The bottoms of the drawers are trimmed with a

band of the scarlet, two inches wide. The upper part is a loose sack, with a piece of the scarlet flannel put on heart-shape upon the waist, and continued in the same shape upon the skirt. Pointed cuffs of scarlet at the bottom of the

tight coat-sleeve. This sack is belted in at the waist with a scarf of the scarlet flannel, pointed at the ends. Four yards of gray flannel, and two yards of scarlet, will be required for the dress for a girl of eight or ten years.
*Peterson's Magazine*, July 1871

Fig. IV. – Bathing-suit of Maize-Colored Woolen, trimmed with a red worsted braid, put on in a Greek pattern. The trousers are made full below the knee; the tunic is a little shorter, and the low basque is belted in at the waist. The bathing-cap is silk oil-cloth, trimmed with red worsted braid. [ → ]
*Peterson's Magazine*, July 1871

[Classified Ad] New holland, trimmed bathing costume, 7s.; sea-side hat, trimmed, 4s. 6d., useless to owner.
*The Exchange and Mart*, August 16, 1871

# 1872

*Fig.* 1 – BATHING TOILETTES.
1st Fig. – A Little Girl's Toilette: Composed of white baize flannel. The knickerbocker drawers drawn in below the knee, and edged with a vandyke trimming of blue flannel, the same placed up each side of them. The tunic square-cut in its bodice, and the sleeves short. The whole bordered with a vandyking of blue.
2nd Fig. – A Young Lady's Toilette: Composed of knickbockers [sic] and tunic, with cape of scarlet baize flannel, the escallop trimming worked upon it with white wool, in well-raised button-hole stitch. The tunic and cape is buttoned with white flannel. The sleeves are loose, and the waistband is fastened at the side with a large bow of scarlet flannel.
3rd Fig. – A Young Lady's Toilette: Composed of blue baize flannel, the knickerbockers being drawn in it the ankles with a band of scarlet. The tunic bordered with a band of scarlet, as also the sash. Sailor's collar, and the front, together with the sleeves. This bathing toilette is exceedingly neat and will doubtless become a favourite.
*Bow Bells*, July 3, 1872

SEC. 21. No person shall bathe in the waters of the Bay of San Francisco, within the limits of the city and county, between the hours of seven and one-half o'clock A. M. and sunset, without wearing a suitable bathing dress; and no person shall bathe on Sunday within three hundred yards of the shore, or off any pier or wharf, between the hours of seven and one-half o'clock A. M. and sunset. Any person who shall violate any of the provisions of this section shall be deemed guilty of a misdemeanor; and upon conviction thereof, shall be punished by a fine of not less than five dollars nor more than thirty dollars, or by imprisonment in the county jail not less than two days nor wore than fifteen days.
San Francisco Municipal Reports, 1872

# 1873

1521. – Bathing Suit – gives better satisfaction than any former combination. The demand for something that will not cling to the form upon leaving the water, is supplied in this style: the pleat in the back will not flatten, and the hood may be worn on the head or not at pleasure. Dark blue or purple serge waterproof, or flannel trimmed with black woolen braid, makes the most desirable suits. Requires two yards of fifty four-inch goods for medium-size. All sizes. Pattern, with cloth model, 50 cents.

770. – Bathing Suit – is the popular style for children. Requires two and a half yards of flannel for eight years. Pattern, with cloth model, 25 cents.

*Smith's Illustrated Pattern Bazar*, Spring, 1873

Next we give a bathing costume, with the cap for the protection of the hair. It is made of dark blue, or grey flannel. The drawers are fastened to the waist, which is plain on the shoulders, and fulled into a band at the waist, where the drawers are buttoned on after the fashion of a little boy's Knickerbocker suit. Then the skirt is made separate, and plaited onto another waistband, which also buttons on to the under-waist. The whole is trimmed with two rows of white worsted braid, as wide as can be procured. Large bone or pearl buttons on the front. The cap is of oil silk, bound with scarlet braid, finished with an elastic. In the water it can be pulled entirely over the hair, and should be made sufficiently large to do so, and the elastic tight. Six yards of flannel, at thirty-one cents per yard will be required, and half a yard of oiled silk for the cap, and twelve yards of worsted braid. ...

We give another bathing suit, somewhat different in design. Here the drawers are fastened to an under-waist, and the outside is complete and fits close to the figure. Moreen would be better for this design, as it does not cling so closely as flannel when wet. If white is used, with white. The short sleeves and open neck we don't advise, on account of burning the skin under the sun; but it is certainly more pleasant while in the bath. Here the hat, or cap, seems more fitted for ornament than use; but ladies who bathe much will undoubtedly protect the hair from the salt water, and the face from the blistering rays of the sun.

*Peterson's Magazine*, July 1873

FIG. 1. – BOY'S BATHING TOILETTE.

Composed of blue woollen serge. The trousers and blouse trimmed with white woollen braid, and the devices worked with white wool, as seen. The paper pattern, 2s. 6d. ...

FIG. 3. – A LITTLE GIRL'S BATHING TOILETTE.

Composed of two shades of blue flannel; the tunic and drawers of the light shade, and the bias fold, of which the trimming is composed, should be in the dark blue. A bow of the dark blue, with two small wool tassels, is placed at each side of the apron front. The pelerine or collar is trimmed to match the rest of the toilette. The paper pattern, 2s. 8d.

*Bow Bells*, September 17, 1873

# 1874

NEW YORK FASHIONS. BATHING SUITS.

With the thermometer among the eighties, sea baths are the most enjoyable recreation, and bathing suits are in demand. There is very little novelty among these dresses as seen at the furnishing stores. The suit of which a cut paper pattern was published last summer in the *Bazar* is in the shape that meets with approval. This has a yoke blouse fitting plainly over the shoulders, with the fullness of the waist and skirt in one, and pleated to the yoke; the skirt reaches to the knee or lower, and is confined around the waist by a belt. The Turkish trousers are full, and are buttoned around the ankle. Gray twilled wiry serges are much used for these suits, because they "shed" water instead of retaining it and clinging heavily to the figure. Both plan and striped serges are used, often appearing in one suit, the stripes being set on the pleats, collar, and belt, and forming frills for the neck, wrists, and ankles. Suits of striped

gray serge, made with a deep sailor collar, and otherwise prettily finished, are $8 to $8.50. There are also good suits of striped flannel for $7.50.

Twilled flannel suits are considered very handsome for bathing and swimming, and are made with some attention to nautical style. For instance, they are of dark navy blue flannel, trimmed with wide white Hercules braid on the sailor collar, sleeves, belt, and skirt, and sometimes anchors or stars are wrought upon them. White flannel suits are trimmed with blue in the same way, and the popular blue-gray flannels are gay with crimson or bright blue braid set on in many parallel rows, or scalloped and bound, or else with narrow ruffles edged with a line of color. The ordinary worsted braid used for binding skirts is suitable for this. Such costumes, made in the best manner, cost from $10 to $12; other suits, more simply made and trimmed, are from $7.50 to $10. Swimmers' suits are made without sleeves, and have but one garment, the blouse and trowsers being cut all in one, like the sleeping garments worn by small children. Made of blue or white flannel, trimmed with white or blue braid, they cost $6. Gentlemen wear striped gray and brown flannels and Cheviot suits shaped like those worn by ladies, but with shorter blouses. The best bathing cap is the oil-silk crown of bag shape, large enough to hold all the hair and protect it from getting wet, as salt-water is considered injurious by some, while others find it beneficial, promoting its growth; the difficulty about drying it, however, the greatest trouble. Striped oil-silk caps cost 50 or 60 cents; others, bound with gay-colored braids, are $1. The bathing shoe most used is the Spanish sandal of sail-cloth with Manilla soles, or else entirely of the cloth. Coarse, wide-brimmed straw hats are tied down over the ears for protecting the face from the sun.

BATHING CLOAKS.

Bathing cloaks, to be put on dry when leaving the water, and worn across the beach to conceal the moist figure, are welcomed by ladies who spend the season at the sea-side. They are made of white or brown Turkish toweling, trimmed with brilliant Oriental braiding. In shape they are merely long loose sacques, or else they have yokes with fullness pleated in, ample sleeves, and are always provided with a hood. They cost from $12 to $15 each, and must be long and large enough to cover the whole figure from head to foot. Bathing slippers of this material are made and trimmed to match the cloak.

*Harper's Bazar,* July 25, 1874

Deb Salisbury

No. IV. Light Gray Flannel Bathing Suit. ...

This suit consists of a waist and trousers, cut in one piece, and a blouse, and is trimmed with folds of dark flannel and buttons. Bathing cloak of white and gray striped flannel. For the trowsers join on the pieces turned down in Supplement on Figs 28ᵃ and 28ᵇ, and set these parts together along the line cut across according to the corresponding letters (see diagram of Figs. 28ᵃ and 28ᵇ, reduced to one-sixteenth of full size). Then cut from this pattern two pieces, sew up each part from 1 to 2, and face the under edge with a strip of material an inch and a quarter wide. Sew both parts together from 2 to 3 and from 2 to 4, and join each half of the garment on the shoulder from 5 to 6. Bind the neck narrow, face the armholes and the slit with a narrow strip of the material, an put on buttons and button-holes for closing. The trimming is set on as shown by the illustration. For the blouse cut two pieces from Figs. 29 and 32 and one piece each from Figs. 30 and 31. Having sewed up the seam in the back from 9 to 10, cut the slit along the double line, and pleat the back at the bottom of the waist, bringing X on ●. Sew up the darts in the frons, face the front edge of the right front with a strip of the material an inch and three-quarters wide, and furnish it with button-holes. The front edge of the left front is joined with a fly an inch and a quarter wide, on which the corresponding buttons are fastened. Join the back and fronts according to the corresponding figures, trim the blouse as shown by the illustration, and set the neck on the collar, trimmed with a fold, according to the corresponding figures. Sew up the sleeves from 14 to 15, trim them as shown in the illustration, and set them into the corded armholes, bring 15 on 15 of the fronts.

Bathing Suit for Girl from 10 to 12 Years old.

See Illustration, Fig. 2, on first page.

The trowsers and frock are made of white flannel, and trimmed with red worsted braid. Red cashmere sash, into which fringe is knotted.

No. V. Blue Flannel Bathing Suit.

See Illustration, Fig. 3, on first page. ...

This blue flannel suit consists of trowsers and a frock. The latter is trimmed with white worsted braid and buttons. Bathing cloak of white flannel and bathing cap of oiled silk, bound with blue worsted braid. ... To make the cap cut out of oiled silk one piece each from Figs. 35 and 36, cutting Fig. 35 of double material, however. Sew up the rim on the ends, pleat the crown from 18 to : and from 19 to *, and join it with the rim according to the corresponding figures and signs. Finally, trim the cap with a box-pleated ruche of oiled silk, bound with blue worsted braid, and with a bow.

*Harper's Bazar Supplement*, July 25, 1874

# 1875

Two trim figures, in trim blue bathing-suits, ran hand-in-hand down the shining sands and plunged into the rolling surf – the trimmest, tidiest figures he had ever seen; two young girls they were. Usually, women looked so wretchedly damp and misshapen in bathing-suits.

*Appleton's Journal*, July 31, 1875

I find that ladies, in their bathing dresses, are much more buoyant in the water than persons with nothing on them but bathing drawers. This I account for from the flow of water, more or less, through the bathing dresses, and because they can stand the coldness of the water better than those who have no clothes on, and can remain twice as long in the water as males are able to do. The bathing dress keeps out the repeated cold shocks that the naked body has to incur. Those shocks are caused by the agitation of the water, or by the quick passage of the body through the water. For instance, if you put your feet into water as hot as you can bear it to the bottom of the foot bath, you move your foot around in the bath and agitate the water. You can no longer bear your feet in the water, it becoming too hot; this would be the case in intensely cold water, were you to try it. If you were towed by a fast steamer you would feel the cold much more than if your passage had been slower through the water.

The Art of Swimming in the Eton Style, 1875

## 1876

Very coquettish are the bathing dresses, which affect all sorts of naval forms. Some are sailor in style in blue serge with white facings and embroidered anchors; others are of the Neapolitan type, red and white, with the Masaniello cap. Jockey caps are also worn with fancy bathing dresses. No one presumes to bathe without shoes, and these are strapped on by means of bright-coloured sandals. Cloaks of white woollen edged with colour are provided as a wrap, for the bathing machines are not brought close down to the water. Indeed, coquetry is carried to such an extent in this place of seaside life that many ladies wear flannel corsets underneath their bathing dresses; these are made on purpose so as not to shrink. Another novelty of the kind is the Greek net corset for hot weather, which is a very pleasant wear, and quite firm enough for slight figures.

*Warehousemen and Drapers' Trade Journal*, July 29, 1876

This year's bathing costumes are certainly very pretty. They are of two sorts – the blouse and the cuirasse. The blouse is preferable for the generality of figures, whilst the cuirasse is the specialty for very young, lithesome waists, or for those few elect who may boast of marble busts.

The materials used for bathing costumes are flannel and serge. The colours vary according to the fancy of the wearer. White, grey, or dark blue are the colours most in favour. Scotch tartan, also, is much worn by French ladies for bathing dresses, and looks remarkably well. When not made entirely of tartan, a bathing costume gains effect by being trimmed with tartan. But I will commence by describing a blouse costume of white flannel, trimmed with Scotch tartan. The trousers are pulled in at the knees (like the old knickerbocker) by a band of tartan plaid, and the blouse tunic worn over these trousers is edged round with a deep band of tartan, whilst the collar round the neck and the sleeves is entirely of tartan. The sleeves are as small as an ordinary chemise sleeve. A tartan scarf is tied loosely round the waist, and falls at the side or at the back, according to the taste of the wearer. The cap is of the Scotch-cap shape, and of the same material as the costume. It is lined with oilskin. A tartan band surrounds the head-piece. A water-fowl feather is added (as ornament) in front. The hair may be tucked under this cap, or may be allowed to fall loosely in an oilskin net, covered by another net of silken cord the colour of the wearer's hair.

The bathing-shoes to match this dress are of white linen. They are tied with plaid ribbon, and a little bow of plaid ribbon is placed on the toe-piece.

I can assure you that a lady might almost walk out in this costume, it is so elegant and modest-looking. Many children play all day long in this costume, much to their delight.

One other costume (the cuirasse) is a little more showy. It is closely copied in shape from Joan of Arc's fighting costume. It has trousers to the knees, but almost tightly fitting – not quite, or they could not be taken off easily enough. Over this is a short tunic, also quite tight round the figure; it reaches to about half-way down to the knees. Then over this again is a long and perfectly tightly-fitting cuirasse body, without sleeves. Ladies who bathe in this costume must merely walk through the water; to dance among the waves would be impossible in this tight attire. It is made in dark blue, and is almost covered with white embroidery to imitate chain-work, and thus to complete the illusion.

*Warehousemen and Drapers' Trade Journal*, August 5, 1876

We give next a bathing dress of brown serge, trimmed with bands, cuffs, collar, and sash of white flannel, or muslin. The trousers come about half way below the knee. [ ➜ ]

In the front of the number we give a bathing-suit for a young lady, made of dark-blue flannel or serge. Rather long trousers, trimmed at the bottom with three rows of black or white braid. Blouse, with short or long sleeves, and deep, sailor collar, trimmed with three rows of braid. Belt to correspond. [ ⬇ ]

We also give, in the front of the number, a child's bathing-dress of red serge. Short trousers to the knee, bound with white braid. Blouse, buttoning down the front, with white buttons. Sailor collar, and short sleeves, also bound with white braid. Cotton braid is the best.

We also give, in the front of the number, a bathing-dress for a young girl, of white flannel or delaine. Buttons covered with the same material. The belt, neck-trimming, and sleeve-trimming also of the red. Trousers to correspond with the dress.

*Peterson's Magazine*, August 1876

At the opening of the summer season the shore in front of each hotel at Long Branch is taken possession of by certain men of semi-seafaring appearance, who proceed to setup on the sands, just under the bluff, rows of bathing huts of an architecture so contemptible that even Uncle Tom and Topsy would have turned up their noses at them – shanties, of course, weather-browned boards, unpainted and often even unplaned, rudely nailed together, sides and roof of the same material, as incapable of keeping out wind and rain as so many paper boxes. The same men also set up a shanty of a larger sort, with a roof that is water-tight, which they occupy in company with piles of faded woolen garments which they facetiously denominate "bathing dresses," and which they still more facetiously let to ladies and gentlemen throughout the summer at the rate of half a dollar for each bath. I suppose these men do not really look upon this transaction in the light of being the huge joke it is, but it certainly would not surprise me to learn that a beginner at the business was tortured with mad longings to rush behind the shanty and relieve his pent-up risibles in writhings of laughter after each successive letting of a damp woolen shirt and trowsers tied with a string as a "bathing dress" to a gentleman in the ordinary attire of civilization. Those who pass any considerable time at the Branch, and bathe with regularity, of course provide themselves with bathing suits of their own; but transient visitors do not find it convenient to do this; and how greatly in demand the garments of the bath-keepers are, is shown by the fact that they are often furnished damp and clammy to the new-comer, having had no time to dry since their last tenant paid for their occupancy. If the Witch of Endor had presided at the construction of these miraculous bathing suits, they could scarcely be more ugly and fantastic than they are. That so many Americans are to be found who are willing to put them on, and walk unflinchingly across the stretch of sand between disrobing hut and surf, under the fire of hundreds of glances from the ladies and gentlemen present, is proof that the bravery of the nation should not be lightly impugned. True, they have their reward when the kind ocean covers them with her modest mantle of cool waves. There is no heroism without some guerdon.

Bathing dresses less shabby, and which are scrupulously dried between lettings, to be leased for a sum less absurdly close to their net value, are one item of the reform which is imperatively demanded at Long Branch. If the semi-seafaring Jerseymen who "farm out" these garments can not make a large enough profit – or think they can not – without continuing the existing reproach, the hotel-keepers should take the matter in their own hands. It would certainly be found a wise policy to make the surf bathing a more attractive feature of life at Long Branch than it now is. More people would bathe, and as a consequence – for surf bathing is a passion which grows with indulgence – more people would stay at the hotels, instead of hurrying away, bored, unamused, half disgusted, by the wretched customs of the beach. The very scene would be more attractive to those people – always in considerable force at Long Branch – who do not care to bathe, but like to see the bathers at their frolics. It is a mistake to think that the spectators derive any considerable amusement from the shabby and wretched aspect presented by a bather in an ugly suit. But a group of bathers, such as may sometimes be seen at a French watering-place, where the suits are varied in color and pattern, and fit neatly, is a sight so picturesque that one does not tire of it. There is no good reason why gentlemen who are well dressed in the city should look like scrubbed chimney-sweeps on the bath-ground; nor why ladies should not display coquetry in bath dresses as well as in ball dresses. The idea that a handsome bathing suit "attracts attention" is absurd; nothing attracts so much attention, nor attracts it so unpleasantly, as an ugly and unbecoming bath dress. French ladies realize this, and dress accordingly, selecting their bathing outfit as carefully, with respect to becomingness in color and cut, freshness and fit, as any dress they wear. It is a delicate rose flannel, with pleatings of white; hat trimmed in accordance; pink hose and straw shoes; or it is a navy blue serge, with stripes of yellow, or of white, or of brown merino, or some other tasteful combination. At Long Branch it is almost always a coarse dark flannel, much too large, and crowned with a rough straw hat more fit for a gutter than for a lady's wear. And as for the gentlemen! Ye heathen deities! what scarecrows they usually are! Description could do them no justice. Yet once in a while a handsome or a picturesque costume may be observed among them – a tight-fitting blue *gilet de laine,* with a white star on the breast, or a loose sailor's shirt and trowsers handsomely braided.

There was one tall athlete seen on the sands for a few days last summer who wore while bathing the veritable "togs" of a professional gymnast – hauberk and foot-pieces, tights and trunks. He was really a trapeze performer at a variety show somewhere back in the village, I was told, and so was no true part of the fashionable throng; but he helped to make it picturesque, and his departure left a sombre void.

Another imperative need of the bathers at Long Branch is the hot-water foot-bath, to equalize the circulation after the surf bath is over. This, also, is a feature of French watering-places which we might copy to advantage. So is the provision of better bath-houses. But this, perhaps, is too much to expect; and, after all, it is a minor matter. Not so, however, the matter of safety for the bathers while in the water.

The semi-seafaring Jerseymen who lease the bathing dresses are the only guardians of the beach. Sometimes they are two in number; at the larger hotels, three; but they ought to be a dozen. They loiter on the sands – when not otherwise occupied with their tenancy work – and keep a good-natured eye upon the bathers, ready to go in and help should there be a cry for help. But it is easy to see that when their presence is most needed, when the bathers are most numerous, why, precisely then their garment-letting trade is liveliest, and absorbs all their attention. There should be men to guard the beach, like watchmen, at all hours, with no other duty than to dissuade persons from bathing at unsafe conditions of the tide, and watching those who do bathe, assiduously and unceasingly. Life boats should be constantly plying. This is done in France, and it can be done here. The only protection our bathers have is a rope fastened to stakes on shore and in the water – a great convenience certainly, but puerile indeed when viewed as a measure of safety. When the surf is strong, the rope becomes useless to women and children, whose hands are torn violently from it by the power of the waves.

*Harper's New Monthly Magazine*, September 1876

Some young ladies in bathing-dresses – the hideous bathing gown of coarse woollen has not yet entirely disappeared, but is being rapidly superseded by the natty, commodious, and decorous *costume* of Dieppe and Trouville –

*Belgravia*, Holiday Number, 1876

# 1877

Fashion has greatly improved on the patterns for bathing-suits. They are no longer the hideous things they used to be, but are made with graceful outlines, and are prettily trimmed. The new style is a blouse that is box-plaited, and extends about to the knee. A deep sailor collar finishes the neck, and the cuffs and pockets are ornamented by braids laid on fancifully. The bottom is hemmed and trimmed, and weights made of flat pieces of lead are fastened under at intervals. Scarlet, blue or white bunting is a favorite fabric for these costumes. It is light in quality, but not transparent, and does not hold the water. Flannels, all-wool serges and camlets, are still used, however. They are fancifully striped in Roman colors, or they are of a plain goods made fanciful by bright braids. The hat is a rough, gipsy-shaped straw, trimmed or rather tied on with a scarf like the sash. This passes over the top of the hat, which usually has a pinked ruche made of bias scraps left from the bathing-dress. The slippers of straw or canvas should have ruches of the same, and rosettes. ...

E. Butterick & Co. Patterns...

CHILD'S BATHING COSTUME. No. 4869. – This jaunty costume is made of flannel and neatly trimmed with braid. The pattern is in 7 sizes for children from 2 to 8 years of age, and its price is 25 cents. To make the suit for a child of 5 years, 3 1/4 yards of goods, 27 inches wide, are needed.

MISSES' BATHING COSTUME. No. 4868. [↗ ] – Serge, camlet, flannel and heavy bunting are used for costumes of this description, and bright braids and bands are selected for the trimming. The pattern is in 8 sizes for misses from 8 to 15 years of age. To make the garment for a miss of 12, 4 7/8 yards of goods, 27 inches wide, will be needed. Price of pattern, 30 cents.

LADIES' BATHING COSTUME. No. 4867. – Flannel is the material used for the costume here illustrated, with fancy colored braid for the decorations. The costume consists of drawers and blouse. The blouse has a double box-plait at the back and front, and is weighted with shot or thin slips of lead inserted in the hem. The pattern is in 10 sizes for ladies from 28 to 46 inches, bust measure. To make the costume for a lady of medium size, 7 yards of goods, 27 inches wide, will be needed. Price of pattern, 35 cents.

*Arthur's Illustrated Home Magazine*, July 1877

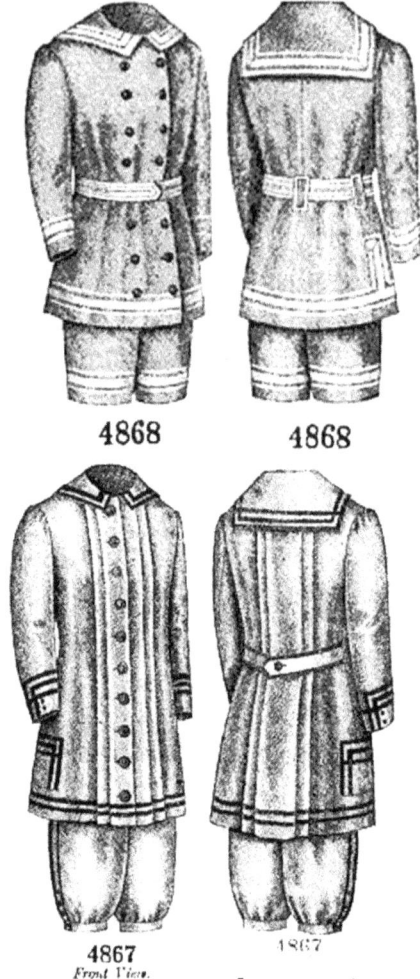

BATHING COSTUMES.

A bathing-dress is best made of flannel. A soft gray tint is                   the prettiest, as it does not so soon fade and grow ugly from contact with the salt water. It may be trimmed with bright worsted braid. The best form is a loose sacque or the yoke waist, both of them to be belted in and falling about midway between the knee and the ankle. Full trowsers gathered into a band at the ankle, an oilskin cap to protect the hair, which becomes harsh in the salt water, and merino socks of the color of the dress complete the costume.

Any other material than flannel becomes limp and unsightly after being worn for a short time.
The Ladies' and Gentlemen's Etiquette, 1877

# 1878

*Dress of the Bather.* – Of the dress adopted by man we can say nothing, as its dimensions offer little room for criticism. That of woman being more complete, a few words may not be amiss concerning the one that will fulfill most completely the conditions required. The bathing dress should be made of a woolen fabric the warp of which is worsted, the woof serge. We particularly insist upon woolen as the material to be worn, as it retains the heat of the body, and therefore prevents a too rapid evaporation. Maroon and blue are the proper colors, as they resist the corrosive and bleaching effects of the salt water. The dress should consist essentially of two parts, a pair of pantaloons and a blouse. The latter should not fit too tightly; the sleeves fastened loosely at the wrist, and slits cut in the garment just below the armpits. A belt of the same woolen stuff is attached to the blouse to retain it at the waist. The pantaloons should be short, upheld by suspenders; they should not be buttoned too tightly to the legs, as circulation would be thereby impeded.

A broad-brimmed straw hat may be worn, but all coverings (such as oil-skin caps so commonly worn by ladies to prevent the hair being wet) preventing a free perspiration on the scalp are injurious, since the secretions from the skin are stopped, and the head has to perform more than its share of the work; and also on account of the increased cerebral circulation, all possible care should be taken to keep that part of the body at its habitual temperature.

Sea-Bathing, 1878

# 1879

*Bathing Costumes.* – A bathing suit, to be comfortable, should be fitted to the neck, shoulders, bust, and armholes just as carefully as the most elegant dress. It need not fit so snugly, but it must follow the curves of the form; and while allowing free motion to the arms, it must not drag about them and excoriate them with every movement.

The most appropriate material is twilled flannel or moreen, as these do not cling to the figure when wet. The trimming should be rows of alpaca braid, either forming the entire garniture or in combination with bands of all-wool delaine of a contrasting color. A bow of black lutestring ribbon, which will not be injured by water, is tied at the neck. Turkish towelling is largely used for this purpose, and trimmed with a bright color looks exceedingly pretty; but all-wool goods is better than any other, as it keeps the body warm. Circulars or cloaks made of Turkish towelling are used by ladies who frequent any of the fashionable resorts. These are made in the "burnous style," or with wide sleeves like the "Hortense." A garment of this kind is only used by those who have a maid or some friend in attendance to relieve them of it as they enter the water, and to have it in readiness as soon as the bath is over, as its use is to shield a dripping figure from currents of air as well as from the gaze of spectators. – *From the N. Y. Herald.*

*The Publishers' Weekly*, June 14, 1879

DESCRIPTION OF OUR CUT-OUT PAPER PATTERN.

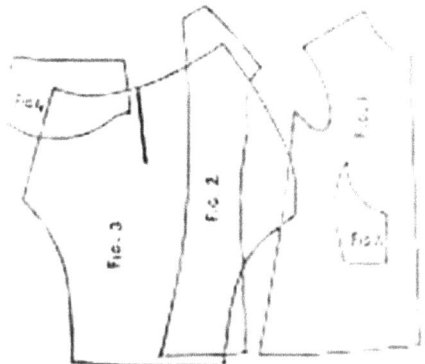

We give for this month's Cut-Out Pattern the shape of a Lady's Bathing Dress.

It is in five pieces.

Fig. 1 – Half of Front.

Fig. 2 – Half of Back.

Fig. 3 – Half of Drawers.

Fig. 4 – Sleeve.

Fig. A – Half of Collar.

The dress being very plain, little description is needed in putting it together; the drawers are made in the ordinary way and trimmed with braid as shown in the illustration. Seven yards of serve will cut the dress the size given.

*Sylvia's Home Journal*, June 1879

No. 2. – Bathing hat of light fancy straw, bordered with a scalloped fluting of the same, on which falls a ball fringe, headed with a band of light-blue silk, surmounted with a box-plaited ruffle. A rosette of blue ribbon loops is placed on the top of the crown.

Nos. 3 and 4 show the front and back of a bathing suit, made of steel-colored Turkish toweling. It consists of trowsers, and a short sleeved frock, fitted with a yoke-neck, cut out square in front. The trowsers are trimmed with an embroidered band and a flounce, plaited, the embroidery being worked with sky-blue linen floss. Similar embroidery trims the frock, the plaited front and back being both confined at the waist

with embroidered straps, fastened at the pointed ends with buttons. A frill of sky-blue cashmere encircles the neck. Large pockets are placed at the sides, and these are ornamented with buttons and imitation button-holes. The quantity of twenty-four-inch wide material required for making is seven yards.

No. 6. – Bathing suit of scarlet pressed flannel. It is made with short trowsers, and frock fitted *à la gabrielle* and belted at the waist behind. The trimmings, disposed on the frock and on the outside portion of the trowsers, are bands of fancy galloon, in colors of black, white and scarlet, and pearl buttons; a frill of white flannel encircles the square-cut neck. The amount of twenty-four-inch wide material required for making is seven yards.

*Frank Leslie's Lady's Magazine*, July 1879

Bathing Dresses.

BATHING is becoming much more of an accomplishment of late years than it was formerly, at least among the feminine part of the pleasure-seekers at the sea-side summer resorts.

Perhaps it is the more general out-door activity among women, and especially among young girls, that has made this change, which is certainly a salutary one. At any rate, that it has really taken place, any visitor to Long Branch, Newport, and the famous metropolitan resorts, Manhattan and Brighton Beaches, can testify. A bathing dress for the summer is almost as much a *sine qua non* as a morning dress, for few ladies like to subject themselves to the chances of such as can be hired from the proprietors of bathing houses, while for those who spend the summer near salt water, the cost of the material would be absorbed in a very few days.

Last year a great innovation was attempted in bathing dresses by cutting them almost close to the form in Princess styles. The clinging dress simply made another skin, which covered the one beneath, but revealed every line and curve of the form. It was the adoption, under very different circumstances, of an exaggerated European style, which, in Europe, has the excuse of being seen by no one, for bathing houses are little wheeled machines which are trundled out into the water to the edge of the sands, and from which the bather steps down into the surf, and which is wheeled out again when she is ready to return.

Here, where women, as well as men, have to walk a distance of perhaps one to three hundred yards, subject to the searching gaze of eyes and opera glasses, such a costume is certainly not suitable or proper, and it is not true to say that it is as decent as the long blue skirt and trousers, for the former, though occasionally disarranged, is easily restored to position on coming out of the water, and gives an appearance of ordinary drapery, which is reassuring at least.

There is no doubt that the less cumbersome the clothing, the more beneficial the bath, and ladies who are fortunate in having private bathing places, will find a flannel dress made with a loose blouse waist, and short closed drawers, very nearly perfection; but for the ordinary bather who has to take her chances with many others, there is no better design than the one which serves also as a gymnastic suit, and consists of a sailor blouse, skirt and trousers. The skirt is plain in

front, and there is no more fullness in either blouse or skirt, than is necessary to its good appearance. This will be obvious from the amount of material required – less than nine yards for the entire suit. Another style of bathing dress is the "Brighton." This has short sleeves and a skirt, which is cut all in one piece with the body, which is plaited into a yoke. This is made with a belt, and is a very pretty style for young ladies, much more dressy and quite as easy to manage as the other, perhaps more so, for it only consists of two pieces and does not require as much material by one or two yards.

[ ← ] An excellent model for misses is the "Undine." The trousers of this design are gathered into a band; the blouse which is less full than the "Brighton," is gathered into a straight yoke at the back but is cut out square in front, and all in one piece in the Princess style.

Twilled flannel, dark blue or Russian gray, is the best

and most serviceable material for bathing dresses, as it does not chill, does not hold water, nor cling to the body so much as other materials. White, black, or red braid are the usual trimmings, put on broad and in clusters, or simply as bindings, according to taste.

It is best not to use shoes when it can be avoided, for the first and natural impulse is to kick them off. But if needed to walk through the sand, plain white duck with cork soles are the simplest and best, as they are easily rinsed off, dried, and pulled into shape.

There are fashions in caps and hats, but nothing has superseded for popular use, the light, coarse, large-crowned straw hat, with deep brim, which is tied gipsy-fashion under the chin. The oiled silk caps are neither so protective from the sun, nor so healthful for wear, and are only desirable for young ladies who wish to preserve under them the crimps that are to make them beautiful for the evening dance.

*Demorest's Monthly Magazine*, July 1879

### TRIMMING FOR BATHING DRESSES.

It has become the fashion to embroider bathing costumes when they are made of white or light-colored flannel. The design, here given, is carried out in coarse fleecy wool of any bright hue, such as scarlet, blue, etc., etc.

*Peterson's Magazine*, August 1879

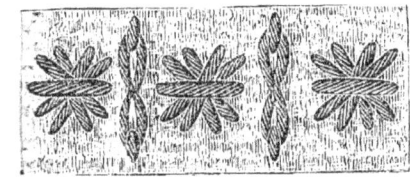

FIG. XII. – BATHING-DRESS OF BLUE FLANNEL, with wide collar; the whole trimmed with yellow braid.

FIG. XIII. – BATHING-DRESS OF WHITE SERGE; kilted front, and coat-shaped back, embroidered in red crewels.

FIG. XIV. – BATHING-DRESS OF BLUE SERGE, trimmed with broad, white woolen braid.

*Peterson's Magazine*, August 1879

Ladies bathe of late years much more than formerly, and a bathing suit is therefore an essential requisite of a summer outfit for the seaside. The "Brighton" is the newest and most approved design for this purpose. It is carefully cut and shaped, so as to admit of perfect freedom, and still preserve neatness and appearance. The sleeves are short, in accordance with the best usage, swimming and healthful exercise in the water being incompatible with the clinging weight of long sleeves about the arms and wrist.

Some daring young women have undertaken to follow continental usage, by adopting a Princess style of bathing dress; but this is rightly considered by many, as an outrage upon good taste, if not decency. In Europe bathing houses are rolled upon the wheel down the sands and into the water, and the bather steps, or throws herself, directly into its partial concealment. When she is ready to come out she is exposed to no running fire of eyes or eye-glasses, but emerges only to be lost on the instant within the privacy of her little house on wheels.

In this country there is no such provision for bathers. Women, young and old, are obliged to run the gauntlet of crowds of spectators, who watch their every movement, until they are surrounded by the friendly waves, and a dress which shall afford a little drapery as well as covering to the limbs, is essential. The fullness of the "Brighton" is laid in three plaits, back and front, and there is no more than is necessary. Navy blue flannel is the best material to use.

*Demorest's Monthly Magazine*, August 1879

Costumes for Bathing.

FIG. 1. – This figure shows the back view of the "Brighton" bathing suit, the front view of which is illustrated on Fig. 5. It is made in dark blue flannel, trimmed with broad white braid. Net of oil silk, bound on the edges with red braid, and having a band of embroidery down the middle. The pattern of the bathing suit is in two sizes, medium and large. Price, thirty cents each.

FIG. 2. – A bathing cloak, for use before entering and upon leaving the water. It is in circle shape, with a hood, and is made of

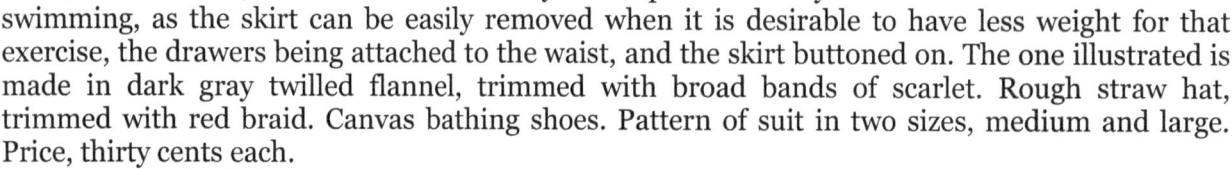

unbleached Turkish toweling, trimmed with *point Russe* embroidery in black and yellow silks, on red flannel. Broad-brimmed hat, of coarse leghorn braid. Pattern of cloak, thirty cents.

FIG. 3. – A favorite style of bathing suit, comprising a full blouse waist, a short skirt, and full drawers. Many ladies prefer this style for swimming, as the skirt can be easily removed when it is desirable to have less weight for that exercise, the drawers being attached to the waist, and the skirt buttoned on. The one illustrated is made in dark gray twilled flannel, trimmed with broad bands of scarlet. Rough straw hat, trimmed with red braid. Canvas bathing shoes. Pattern of suit in two sizes, medium and large. Price, thirty cents each.

FIG. 4. – The "Victor" suit, made in dark blue flannel, trimmed with black braid. This design can either be used for a bathing suit or a street costume. Pattern in sizes for from four to eight years. Price, thirty cents each.

FIG. 5. – The front view of the "Brighton" bathing suit, the back of which is shown on Fig. 1. See description of that figure for prices and sizes. [ ↙ ↘ ]

FIG. 6. – The "Undine" bathing costume, for a miss of ten years. It is made of heavy all-wool suitings, mixed gray, and is trimmed with cross-stitch embroidery of red and white worsted on blue bands. Red and white, striped stockings. Bathing hat of coarse straw, red and blue. Pattern of suit in sizes for from ten to fourteen years. Price twenty-five cents each. ...

Brighton Bathing Suit. – A most convenient, comfortable, and becoming style of bathing suit, cut with a yoke, front and back, to which the lower parts are attached in broad box-plaits, and side gores under the arms, and fitted by a belt worn on the outside. It can be appropriately made up in serge, moreen, or twilled flannel, as these materials do not cling to the figure when wet, and trimmed with braid, or bands of all-wool delaine, either forming the entire garniture, or in combination with rows of alpaca braid of a contrasting color. The one

illustrated is in dark blue flannel, ornamented with rows of white galloon of different widths.

This design is illustrated on the full-page engraving. Pattern in two sizes, medium and large. Price, thirty cents each. ...

The "Undine" bathing suit is very pretty in gray or navy-blue flannel, trimmed with black or red wool, embroidered in white, or a plain or figured woolen braid may be used. The blouse is yoked only at the back, and is cut in one with the front, with a square neck that will be found both pretty and convenient. ...

Undine Bathing Suit. – A sensible and becoming bathing suit for children, consisting of a half-long, sacque-shaped blouse, and full drawers. The blouse has the neck cut in Pompadour shape in front, and a yoke at the back to which the lower part is attached in gathers, and the whole is rendered tight-fitting by a belt. The lower edges of the drawers are gathered into bands and finished with ruffles. The design is appropriate for heavy serge, twilled flannel, moreen, or any material that does not cling to the figure when wet, and can be suitably trimmed with alpaca braid or bands of a contrasting shade of the material. This design is illustrated in the full page engraving. Pattern in sizes for from ten to fourteen years. Price, twenty-five cents each.

*Demorest's Monthly Magazine*, August 1879

Fig. 5. – Bathing shoe of canvass, with sole of cord; rosette and sandals of red braid; either plain écru or colored stockings are worn with this shoe when bathing. ...

Fig. 7. – Bathing costume in pale blue flannel, consisting of drawers. with trimming of embroidery of several different shades of wall-flowers. Blouse with pleated plastron in front, fastened by a band and buckle; long sleeves, both the upper and lower part of which, as well as the edges of the blouse, being embroidered in the same manner as the drawers.

*Godey's Lady's Book*, September 1879

[Biarritz] For ladies and gentlemen array themselves in bathing costume, in which they march down to the water from the establishment – the ladies in general wearing over all a cloak or shawl, which they drop ere they reach the edge, and it is taken charge of by a friend or a bathing man. The ladies' habit, of which the fanciful patterns (possibly imagined and engraved in far-away Paris) exhibited in dressmakers' shop windows afford but a faint and incorrect idea (as, for example, in representing ladies appearing in lace frills, and trig, tight, little laced boots), usually consists of a short tunic with equally short sleeves, not reaching to the elbows, and knee-breeches reaching barely to the knees, the tunic girt at the waste by a girdle, to which is attached in the majority of cases, *á la* John Gilpin, two empty yellow gourds as floats. Then very often a straw hat is stuck upon the head, and tied by a ribbon over the crown and broad brim and under the chin, giving the appearance of a frightful "ugly;" while on the feet are generally worn a pair of local shoes made of canvas, with thick hemp soles, which, decorated with devices in worsted, are very commonly worn by the residents, and even for walking about the beach by many of the visitors, and are sold for two or three francs per pair. The bathing dresses vary in pattern and shape, and are of all colours. White is seldom worn. Bright colours – red, scarlet, green, light blue, yellow, amber – are often seen; in short, the aim with many is apparently at something stunning, suitable for the adornment of a pretty mermaid. To add to the effect, smart young ladies will also have their dresses embroidered, and otherwise made attractive and bewitching, in the way only a graceful girl knows how; and really it must be confessed that this bloomer costume is exceedingly becoming, at all events to the younger ladies. Stout old ladies cut a figure in it sometimes remarkable.

The gentlemen, on the other hand, look like harlequins, for their costume in general consists of a somewhat tight-fitting dress either of cotton or woollen, and most commonly in stripes of two colours, and of all colours and shades, though white and blue stripes are the most common. Their dresses costs from 6f. to 2of. (a very good woollen one in red-and-black stripes cost me 13f.). Some of the old gentleman wear a straw hat loose on their heads, so that occasionally it is seen floating away from the wearer by reason of an accidental wave or submersion. I suppose the object of the straw hat is to obtain protection against the beams of the sun, but it suggests the uncomfortable idea that the wearer never plunges his or her head under water, the doing of which would, I doubt not, afford equal protection against the sun's heat, and is in any view always necessary to prevent a flow of blood to the brain in bathing.

In these varied and brightly-coloured costumes, the bathers cut gay figures. But the picture is composed and completed when they enter into action. At the edge of the water, the gentlemen bathers, sometimes portly and rotund, having threaded in bare feet their way down through the ladies sitting on the stairs, and through the crowd of spectators on the sand, wait with patience in their brilliant, tight, and unusual attire, the observed of all observers, the arrival of their lady friends, if they any have, and on their arrival, taking their hand, accompany them into the water; or the ladies take the hand of a bathing man engaged to attend them, and march in under their charge, and presently they are in the clear salt water, alive with bathers in every colour and in every form of movement practised by those who go down to the sea to bathe. Some rush from the shore wildly and inhumanly into the water, and, wickedly regardless of frightening the small fishes, dive head foremost with a splash, and strike out. Others stalk in majestically, and either quietly push far out, or paddle about pretending or attempting to swim in shallow water. Then other gentlemen are giving encouragement to their little boys or girls, or to their wives, or possibly their lovers, or improbably their sisters, either dipping them, or helping them to swim, or teaching them to float, or joining in other usual maritime gyrations. Others catch hold of the rope stretched out if the water be low, and dance about in a mad and profitless way, or if the tide be high, the swimmers catch at it as they pass and take a rest; and sometimes, if at a proper height, an adventurous one will sit upon the rope, like a sparrow on a telegraph wire, when (perhaps beholding admiringly from the treacherous seat some fat lady floating on her back on the surface, her bathing integuments undulating in the water like the tentacular folds of a jelly fish) of a sudden somebody else, perhaps waggishly, perhaps innocently, clutches at the slack rope, and with unexpected shock upsets the unwary, abstracted philosopher, who with a whirl capsizes heels in the air, and head making discoveries though eyegate, nosegate, and mouthgate in the brine below. Or two recently arrived English young ladies will walk in, hand in hand, scorning the aid of a bathing man, and perform together, with all the regularity of clockwork, an endless series of curtsey ducks in the water without stirring from the safely selected spot. Other ladies, to vary the programme, are carried out by a bathing man and dipped horizontally in the wave, so that head and feet obtain ablution simultaneously; or a stout matron will take hold of a bathing man, who swims out with her on his back apparently, so that she enjoys the luxury of being buoyed up and drawn through the water, and can say, "I'm afloat," But these sham swimmers are notably the exceptions. The great matter of observation is that the vast majority of the ladies, young and old, swim about as easily as the gentlemen, though they are in doing so generally accompanied by a man swimming behind or beside them in case of accident; and, indeed, one important occupation of those employed as bathing men is to teach the young idea how to swim, an accomplishment which, after a few lessons, they are usually able to master, and young girls are constantly seen swimming about among the others, like minnows among the tritons. Some ladies, after long practice, are very adventurous; two of them will go out together in a boat a considerable distance, when, throwing off their cloaks, they will dive head foremost from the side of the boat and swim ashore, the boat following. One little girl was most clever. She would go out to what looks like the vestige of an old pier, and, jumping high, perform a somersault, and, diving under the water, "come up smiling," swim about, and do it again and again. I have, however, seen many older diving belles jumping from the same pier. In fact, bathing in all its forms is here carried by the ladies to an enviable perfection altogether unknown at home; and while it not merely affords a most invigorating exercise, it becomes a most valuable branch of education, tending to lessen the risk of casualties at sea. It were well that at home the good example could be followed.

*The Literary World*, September 5, 1879

[ ← ] Bazar Glove-Fitting Patterns, 1879

**1339.**—Lady's and Miss's Bathing Suit. 10 sizes. 32 to 40 ins. and 6 to 14 yrs. 7 yds. 25 cts. each.

**503.**—Lady's and Children's Bathing Suit 5¼ yds. 25 cts. each.

Deb Salisbury

The "bathing dress" to which we wish to draw attention, and which, after testing it ourselves, we have no hesitation in recommending, might with equal correctness be termed a life-jacket, or life-vest. It may be described as an inflated bodice, fitting closely round the waist and round the neck, and may be either worn over an ordinary knickerbocker bathing suit, or be made a complete bathing dress in itself, with sleeves, and knickerbockers or drawers, attached, but the body alone being inflated. It must not, however, be supposed that it is an india-rubber dress; it is composed of nothing but ordinary fine linen, which – although doubtless few of our readers will be aware of the fact – becomes air-tight when wet. It has merely to be saturated with water before being put on, and is then inflated through a small tube within easy reach of the mouth. Its buoyancy is so great that the wearer can float buoyantly in any position, and can lie on his back without moving hand or foot, as comfortably as if he were lying on a bed.

If, after being some time in the water, a portion of the air should have escaped, it can be re-inflated by the wearer whilst floating, without difficulty or inconvenience. When dried, after use, it can be folded up in as small a compass as an ordinary shirt.

The inventor of the Safety Bathing Dress is Captain G. PEACOCK, formerly a master in the Royal Navy, and inventor of the celebrated paint for ships known as "PEACOCK and BUCHAN'S Paint," and author of several other inventions.

Captain PEACOCK states that he designed this dress as far back as the year 1828, and has had one in use himself ever since that period. He has, however, only recently been induced to make it public, which he has now done, and placed its manufacture in the hands of Messrs. PINDER and TUCKWELL, clothiers and outfitters, at Exeter, having registered it under the title of the "Nautilus Safety Bathing Dress." Its cost is, for a man's dress 15s., and for a female's from that sum upwards.

*The Life-Boat*, November 1, 1879

## 1880

*The bathing dresses* are made of flannel or serge, but the flannel will be found to be the warmest and softest; they may be of any color that is preferred, but dark blue and white are the most usual; white has the disadvantage of soiling soon with the dirty seaweed, but looks very pretty when new. If the dress is of white, colored worsted braids may be employed an a trimming; if of colored material, white braid in most worn. Abroad it is customary to wear short sleeves, in America the long sleeve is preferred. An oilcloth cap to protect the hair from the water, and a large, strong, coarse straw hat to protect the face from the sun, and long thick stockings or canvas shoes to protect the feet from the stones, are all necessary adjuncts.

*Peterson's Magazine*, July 1880

She [Lady Dolly] rang, and sent one of her maids for one of her bathing costumes, which were many and of all hues.

Vere looked at the brilliant object when it arrived, puzzled and troubled by it. She could not understand it. It appeared to be cut off at the shoulders and the knees.

"It is like what the circus-riders wear," she said, with a deep breath.

"Well, it is, now you name it," said Lady Dolly amused. "You shall have one to-morrow."

Vere's face crimsoned.

"But what covers one's legs and arms?"

Moths, a novel by "Ouida." 1880

Deb Salisbury

Bathing Dresses. – A bathing dress for the summer is almost as much a *sine qua non* as a morning dress, for few ladies like to subject themselves to the chances of such as can be hired from the proprietors of bathing-houses; while for those who spend the summer near salt water the cost of the material would be absorbed in a very few days. There is no doubt that the less cumbersome the clothing the more beneficial the bath, and ladies who are fortunate in having private bathing places will find a flannel dress, made with a loose blouse waist and short closed drawers, very nearly perfection; but for the ordinary bather, who has to take her chances with many others, there is no better design than the one which serves also as a gymnastic suit, and consists of a sailor blouse, skirt and trousers. The skirt is plain in front, and there is no more fullness in either blouse or skirt than is necessary to its good appearance. The amount of material required for this entire suit is little less than nine yards. Twilled flannel, dark blue or Russian gray, is the most serviceable material for bathing dresses, as it does not chill or hold the water. White, black, or red braids are the usual trimmings, put on broad and in clusters, or simply as bindings, according to taste.

Home and Health and Home Economics, 1880

# 1881

Addie. – 1. A fine, dark-blue reps would be much lighter than serge for your bathing dress, flannel is also used sometimes, but does not answer so well, except for children. 2. Blue trimmed with white mohair braid is the prettiest combination of colours. 3. Trousers fastened at the side, and put into a shaped band at the waist, the edge reaching nearly to the ankle. A very plain tunic reaching to the knees, and fastened round the waist with a band; short sleeves. Madame Goubaud will send you the pattern complete for 1s.

*Myra's Threepenny Journal*, April 1, 1882

BATHING SLIPPER. – Slipper of white elastic cloth, lined with linen, and soled with manilla straw, covered inside with white elastic cloth. The toe is braided with very narrow red worsted braid, sewn on with knotted stitches of black silk. Round the slipper is a border of loops of red braid, meeting in front in a rosette of braid, and a white seashell.

*Arthur's Home Magazine*, May 1881

FIGURE NO. 12. – The bathing-dress here illustrated is a simple garment, appropriate for flannel, Fashion No. 2235 supplying the design. The waist and drawers are in one piece, while the skirt, which is separate, is attached to a belt, which in turn fastens to the waist. The more simple the trimming the more suitable a bathing-dress appears, and the best finish for any design is one of white braid and bone buttons here employed. ... *Quantity of Material (45 inches wide) for* **30** inches, 4 yards; **32** inches, 4 1/8 yards; **34** inches, 4 1/4 yards; **36** inches, 4 3/8 yards; **38** inches, 4 1/2 yards; **40** inches, 4 3/4 yards; **42** inches, 5 yards; **44** inches, 5 1/4 yards; **46** inches, 5 1/2 yards.

*The Domestic Monthly*, June 1881

FIGURE NO. 20. – This suit, which is intended for a young girl, shows the waist and trousers cut together, the skirt consisting of plain breadths gathered at the top, and fastened to the belt. A sailor collar is added to the neck, and a bright braid is employed for a trimming. ... *Quantity of Material* (45 *inches wide*) *for* **27** inches, 3 1/4 yards; **28** inches, 3 3/8 yards; **29** inches, 3 1/2 yards; **30** inches, 3 5/8 yards; **31** inches, 3 3/4 yards; **32** inches, 3 7/8 yards.

*The Domestic Monthly*, June 1881

FIG. 20.
No. 2254.–Misses' Bathing Suit.
Price. 20 cents.

FIG. 26.
No. 2252.–Boys' Bathing Suit.
Price, 20 cents.

FIGURE NO. 26. – This simple bathing dress, for a boy from four to ten yeas of age, is copied from Fashion No. 2252. The body and trousers are cut in one piece, and a belt holds the fullness of the waist to the figure, the garment fastening at the front. A sailor collar is placed at the neck, and a trimming of braid finishes the suit, which is of flannel. ... *Quantity of Material* (45 *inches wide*) *for* **21** inches, 1 3/8 yards; **22** inches, 1 3/8 yards; **23** inches, 1 1/2 yards; **24** inches, 1 1/2 yards; **25** inches, 1 5/8 yards; **26** inches, 1 5/8 yards; **27** inches, 1 3/4 yards.

*The Domestic Monthly*, June 1881

*No. 45. The Hubbard Bathing Costume.* – The latest fancy for a bathing-dress to be made of fine serge, any colour preferred. The drawers are gathered in at knee with a thick cord, which ties at the sides, then the blouse is gathered on shoulders and across back, forming quite a yoke, with the neck finished by a roll collar and plissé. Sleeves are gathered with a cord, forming a frill to match the drawers, then a girdle encircles the waist. Flat pattern, 9d.; untrimmed, 1s. 9d.; trimmed, 3s. [ → ]

*Household Words*, July 16, 1881

COMBINATION SWIMMING OR BATHING COSTUMES.

Upon the Continent very young children require to be clothed for sea bathing, and the combination garment was so admirably suited to the purpose that it was instantly adopted for children of all ages. For some time past it has been gaining favour among ladies, particularly with those who swim or who are learning to swim,

and certainly the absence of anything like petticoats or of girth about the waist, the perfect security of the dress, and its freedom and comfort to the wearer, render it of irresistible attraction to the swimmer. When the machines are not able to be pushed into the sea, and also for use upon the beach, a wrap is very desirable with these costumes; the circular cloak is the usual shape chosen. The dress may be made of any cotton material, and a band of ingrain linen, stitched on as a border, gives it a gay and picturesque effect; frills are added midway on each leg to simulate a skirt. No. 372, lady's combination bathing dress, full size, pattern 1s.; No. 373, young lady's combination bathing dress, pattern 1s.; No. 373a, child's combination bathing dress, pattern 9d.

*The Bazaar, The Exchange and Mart*, July 11 1881

Deb Salisbury

BATHING COSTUMES.

Bathing gowns, like riding habits, are open to certain changes, and receive them as all other branches of dress do season by season, indeed costumes for the sea, river, and London swimming baths (of which, alas! there are so few for women's use, and nearly all of those but grudgingly allowed at such inconvenient hours as to be almost prohibitive), have a trace of prevailing fashions in their construction. When crewel work smothered walking and house dresses it appeared in designs of shells and weeds, or water plants and reeds, on bathing suits. Now it is unknown, and gauging, which is the mainstay of present dressmaking art, is the principal feature for aquatic raiment. Similarly when edges of overskirts were fringed, scalloped, or battlemented, the hems of bathing tunics were finished in like manner, but now all are straight, and fringe or fancy trimmings are discarded in favour of flat braids. But even braid is applied with a view to suggesting this year's novelty of "shading," for it is used in rows of different widths, running from wide to narrow and then beginning at the wide again, instead of having a wide band in the middle and those each side of it corresponding in gradually decreased size. If only three sizes are used they are still monotonously run on as large, lesser, less, without any greater break between the smallest and largest than there is between the other rows. One year we had a whim for three bars of inch wide braid; the next we broke out in the Greek key pattern, done in Russia braid; the following there was a craze for one very wide braid flanked either side by a narrow one, or two medium widths placed alternately. This summer braid is mostly in shaded widths as described above, but there are a great many gowns trimmed with numerous rows of extremely narrow braid, which is generally spaced equally, but sometimes is grouped.

River swimming and town tanks permit greater variety of clothing than sea does, because salt water is so destructive to most colours, and, moreover, materials that are light and clinging may be chosen for the two first, although the far greater publicity of a beach renders them unsuitable for the seaside. A very pretty costume for fresh water was of grey homespun, trimmed with a Turkey red twill band, on which was laid rows of white Russia; the neck, short knickerbockers, and puffed sleeves were finished off by tatting, done in scarlet wool. I do not see why homespun should not do for the sea, if the body were full by means of gauging, and the trousers a good width, banded in at the knee, so that when wet they would cling in folds instead of smoothly. The idea of braid on a contrasting band was being carried out on another costume, and extremely handsome it looked, but I have never yet found a blue or a black braid that would stand sea water well. The gown was fine blue serge, and the neck was a yoke of honeycombing sewn with cardinal; the drawers were loose at the leg and a band round them and the tunic, was of cardinal twilled flannel with narrow navy and black braid alternately; short puffed sleeves with a braided band to match the rest. The best swimmers wear high combination garments with a band round the waist, but a short tunic is no perceptible impediment, and decidedly prettier than skirtless combinations, for those who are not so at home in the waves that they are always immersed. Combinations can be made with gauging, and I would suggest as a new departure that there should be no waistbelt – gauging at the waist, front and back, alone drawing the dress to the figure. Gauging is eminently suited to swimming robes because it allows of roominess where there should be freedom, and yet the gauged parts give nattiness and form. The idea of beltless combinations occurred to me because I have just made a bathing costume as a beltless gauged tunic, and it is as comfortable as it is new looking. It is of Egerton Burnett's cheap (1s. 2 1/2 d.) all wool navy serge – he has two at that price, but one feels stiffer than the other – and I recommend the looser; 6 1/2 yds. is ample for tunic and drawers. The tunic is cut high at the sides of the neck, and is square back and front, but only short, or it would pull over the shoulders, and it is closely gauged for a few inches, as wide as the base of the square is. The square is about as large as that of *Bazaar* pattern No. 13. The fullness caused by the gauging gives the necessary play-room for chest and shoulder blades, but is again confined by some inches of gauging at the waist on the fronts and back. Sloping under the arms well, and giving one bosom pleat, makes the tunic fit as tightly as is advisable, and then the band of the drawers (which button at the sides) is buttoned to the inside of the back gauging, and again at the under arm seam, while the front band is buttoned to the inside of the waist gauging of each front. The advantage of not sewing the back band to the bodice is that it is so much easier to wring out, dry, and fold the two parts separately. By this means, too, the dual portions of the dress become one, and there is no more drag on the waist than with combinations. A wide hem with buttons and buttonholes fastens the tunic throughout its length, the gauging being on each side of it; and let no one imagine it is the same thing to sew up the skirt part and button from the waist only, for then it is a perfect maze to get in or out of, whereas with completely parting hems the suit is the easiest possible to don and doff. Gauging must have tapes or a brace of material under it on which to sew the gauged lines, for no thread will bear the strain unsupported. Gauging is ornamental in itself, but it can be made still more so by feather stitching the lines with wool or coarse crochet cotton. Like day dresses, sleeves to bathing suits are puffed and set high on the shoulder. If the armhole is large and the sleeve not set too high, there is much less draw on the arm socket than with the old long shoulder seam, but in this, as in other things, one must hit the happy medium – "it is no mean happiness to be seated in the mean." A white flannel gown destined for the banks of Father Thames was tastefully worked in German cross-stitch with fast-coloured crewel wools, and cross-stitching in white Berlin ornamented some of the serges and buntings for sea wear. Scarlet bunting is too glaringly conspicuous to be nice for the purpose of bathing, yet it is used. It makes the wearers look like boiled shrimps. Blue bunting is a good material, and can be trimmed with overlapping rows of parti-coloured buntings laid on and stitched down by machine. A rather peculiar dress of blue bunting had the shoulders gauged round and round, as zephyr dresses are done, and white star braid was along the runnings; the drawers were full and drawn in as knickerbockers to the knee by many rows of running, leaving a frill at the edge, and had braid like the neck; full sleeves nearly to the elbow, banded in with gauging like the drawers. Square yokes of gauging are seen also, but they are the least commendable form, as they are ugly if shallow, and if deep they gird across the back – circular runnings have not the same effect, nor need they be carried so long on the shoulder. Another variety of gauging is to have it across each shoulder, but to leave the centre of back and front plain.

In materials, serge stands first, as it probably always will, for it possesses all the virtues called for; bunting comes next, and then a few new introductions, such as homespun, men's shirting flannel, and some natural woollens, by which I mean kinds of serges and flannels made from mixtures of brown and white sheep wool without dyeing. In this, of course, there is nothing to be injured by salt, and it is quickly growing popular for wear in the sea and by the sea. Its sandy colour makes it good for beach frocks for girls and suits for boys. True, nothing beats navy serge for the same purposes, but this light brown stuff looks cooler than dark blue.

Despite all the preaching of the faculty as to the dangers of bathing without first wetting the head, there is increased disregard of their sermonettes now that curly polls are so abundant. But the old bladder-like oilskin cap cannot be tolerated in its pristine frightful mess, and a fisher cap, Tam O'Shanter, soft toque, Palmer, Gipsy or other cap of the same as the dress, or a contrast to it, is worn over the oilskin to hide it. By far the most consistent head dress is a square kerchief tied on as a handkerchief cap is arranged. One of Turkey red twill is quite pretty with a navy dress; white ones should have plenty of showy embroidery on the borders.

*The Bazaar, The Exchange and Mart*, July 20, 1881

No. 66. *The Bathing-Shoe*. – Shows a pretty bathing-shoe, which is ornamented with chain-stitch embroidery, then laced up the leg with red braid. The pattern may be had for 3d.

No. 67. *The Bathing-Glove* is made of Turkish towelling, and has a piece of elastic across the inside of wrist to secure it when worn.

No. 68. *The Sarah Bernhardt Bathing-Cap*. – Shows the now fashionable bathing-cap, called the Sarah Bernhardt, made of crême oil-cloth, box pleated from side to side across front, while the back has double draw-strings run in so that it may be made to fit any size head. Rows of fancy red or blue braid trim it, finished by bows. ...

Deb Salisbury

### Bathing-Dresses.

The bathing-costume receives as much attention now as one's toilette; indeed, so fanciful are some made, that they seem too pretty for the sea. However, it is just as well to make a shapeable one as the unsightly sacques so often seen, so a few hints will be welcome.

In the first place, the material used must be stout or elastic, so as not to cling in an unsightly manner to the figure when wet, and must readily permit the water to drain through, while the style chosen depends upon the wearer's fancy, not forgetting that perfect freedom to the use and movement of the limbs is most essential.

The shape that receives most favour is decidedly the combination dress; that is, body and drawers cut in one, with the neck made quite high at back, open in a small V shape in front, finished by a sailor collar, while the sleeves can be short, demi, or long, as the wearer may fancy.

Another style is the Hubbard combination garment, gathered at neck like the Hubbard dress, then a belt worn round waist; or a pretty design, as shown in No. 12, p. 234, which consists of pants and blouse, gathered on each shoulder, forming a stylish costume. For those not liking the combined garment, a skirt is fixed to belt, or they can have the ordinary drawers with deep blouse; but I decide most certainly in favour of the combined garments, which are easier, more comfortable, and far prettier-looking; besides, there is no fear of the waves washing the skirt up, as in the ordinary blouse and drawers, thus showing two or three inches of flesh between drawers band and blouse waist, as is often the case. The material most used for bathing-dresses is a stout soft twill flannel, or a fine soft serge, although many use a strong, coarse linen; or, for those well able to afford it, fine camel's hair makes up beautifully. Navy-blue flannel, I think, makes up best, and should be trimmed rows of very narrow white or red braid; still, white, dark red, black, and pale-blue serges are now employed for bathing-dresses, which are made very pretty by the addition of cross bands of another colour, ornamented feather stitch in wool to correspond; then the sailor collar, cuffs, and belt are ornamented. I was shown a charming bathing-dress, made as a combined garment, of fine white twill flannel with sailor collar, cuffs, and outside of drawers beautifully embroidered with sprays of seaweed, which looked just the thing; in fact, I think, a fancy stitch worked in coloured wools far supersedes braid for effect, white flannel embroidered in black, red, or navy blue, or blue flannel embroidered in white, make charming costumes, and the embroidery is generally of arabesque designs. The bath-cloak must not be forgotten, for many ladies bathe off the sand without a machine; therefore, a cloak is very handy to throw over them while running to their dressing-place; and the Hubbard style takes the lead here, as in all other garments. Fine flannel, any colour desired, should be used, and the cloak is of a sacque form, gathered round neck, with loose sleeves, while a hood is added for putting over the head; then it is ornamented with embroidery. Many of our readers have experienced the annoyance of the sun's glaring rays on the face while bathing, therefore a bathing-hat comes into great demand. The shape used has a wide brim, with moderate crown; in fact, it is the shape known as the gipsy hat, which abodes the eyes and face so well, and the brim and crown are ornamented embroidery, with a plissé of serge round crown, then tape or braid passed over crown and sides to tie under hair behind; and when ornamented with bright colours they are pleasingly picturesque and unique.

The question as to whether or not the sea-water is beneficial to the hair is still a mooted one; besides, it is not convenient to get the hair wet, which at once removes the curled forehead fringe now so fashionable; therefore ladies wear a waterproof cap, which should be made of oilskin, or very light indiarubber cloth, made after the style of a French nurse's cap, sufficiently large to entirely cover the hair, so that the head may first be dipped in without fear of disarranging or wetting the hair.

Some time since bathing-caps were merely made as a net with an elastic or tape run in, but since the elaborate bathing-costumes have been used, we find the caps more fanciful, and often they are finished by a plissé, finished in front by a rosette; but 'the Sarah Bernhardt cap, price 2s. 6d., or post free, 2s. 8d., is very pretty and becoming.

Bathing-slippers are very necessary, especially on stony beaches, and are made with soles of twisted straw, with embroidered serge or crash tops, then laced over foot and up leg. Our illustrations will serve as a guide for making all necessary items for bathers. Next to the costume, we require a bag or basket for carrying it when wet, for when dry it can be strapped up; but then, after bathing, what is to be done with it? The best plan is to make a bag of oilskin or thin indiarubber cloth, which cover with serge, cashmere, or crash, and make the mouth of it with deep frill and double-draw strings. It may be embroidered or braided to match dress. Many ladies prefer a basket which can be had of wicker for about 1s., and lined oilskin to prevent the wet dress dripping, for, although it may be well squeezed after being taken from the water, flannel will hold water more than any other material, and if it drips through the basket spoils one's dress; whereas, if the basket is lined oilskin, the dress can be carried with safety. After use it should be shaken out ready for next dip, as should the cap and slippers.

*Household Words*, August 13, 1881

A FRIEND of mine, who has returned from accompanying Ins wife to a French watering-place, has revealed to me secrets which are calculated to destroy the illusions appertaining to the nymphs that disport in French waves. He went with his wife to buy a bathing dress in Paris. There he discovered that beneath the tight-fitting jersey which is now the fashionable dress for the water, stays are worn, and many other appliances to aid in fashioning a beauteous figure.

I REMEMBER going with a lady to bathe at one of these French watering-places. We both emerged from our respective machines. Near me I saw a beauteous vision. Her hair was flowing round her shoulders, her eyes glistened, her cheeks were bright with colour, and her dress lent beauty to a beautiful figure. Soon a wave came. I missed my friend. Close by me was a haggard female; her form was angular and scraggy; her nose was blue and her checks hollow; a wisp of hair, not larger than a rat's tail, was hanging from her head. Where was the glorious vision that had stood by me? A voice came from the chattering teeth of the hag. It was the vision; but, O, how changed!

*Truth*, August 25, 1881

Open air bathing necessitates a shroud for the unrobing and robing process, some ladies even having a maid at the water's edge ready with a cloak to throw on. Circular cloaks are good, and dressing gowns or ulsters the worst; in fact, the latter are useless. First in comfort are the cloaks of very primitive cut, resembling, as they do, the blanket cloak of a savage, being only a large square with a slit in the centre for the head to go through. They are easily entered, are perfectly secure, and have plenty of space for easy movement of the arms underneath during the toilet. They might be made of Egerton Burnett's waterproof serge or fine cloth, and serve the double purpose of cloak and rolled gown case.

*The Bazaar, The Exchange and Mart*, August 15, 1881

I WENT to Brighton in October, when the season was at its height. ...

A great deal of bathing goes on in Brighton, though less than at other places where the fashionable season comes earlier in the year.

English bathing is something altogether different from French or American; it is the very triumph of discomfort and inconvenience, the most unpleasant pleasure that can ever have been devised.

At every English seaside place there are two sets of rough wooden boxes on wheels, – bathing-machines they are called, – one set for ladies and children, and the other for gentlemen.

These machines seem to be studiously so contrived as to be as unendurable as possible. You approach them in a spirit of martyrdom, and pay from a sixpence to a shilling – it is a shilling at Brighton – for the use of the machine, including a bathing-dress. Each little box has a small shelf, a peg or two, and a useless bit of looking-glass about as large as the palm of your hand. The floor is gritty with sand. The door of entrance at the landward end seldom closes, and that at the seaward end never, so that the wind blows straight through.

These machines are usually drawn into the water by horses, though sometimes they are let down from a steep beach by a capstan.

"Hold hard !" cries out the driver, as he is about to start the thing off; and, indeed, you need to "hold hard," for unless you clung desperately to the seat, you would be thrown to the floor, as the machine has no springs, and jolts horribly, giving you a sensation like a donkey's trot. You must sit on your bathing-dress, or that is pretty sure to get shaken into the sea.

Deb Salisbury

When your box has been drawn well into the water, horse and driver take leave of you, and go in search of some other unfortunate; but first the same voice that has bidden you to hold hard cries out "Remember Jack!" which means that you are to give him a penny or two. You are always giving a penny or two in England. Your pockets ought to be lined with copper, like a steam-boiler, to get on here at all.

When Jack has departed, you put on your bathing-clothes. If they are the ordinary hired ones, they are sure to be very ugly. A sort of long blue flannel sacque, with no trousers, is the commonest style, though occasionally there is a queer union of waist and trousers, somewhat more comfortable than the other, but scarcely more sightly.

Having thus made a guy of yourself, you descend some steps into the water. In England, men and women never bathe in company. Ladies are under the charge of a sort of amphibious animal, called a bathing-woman, who spends her whole time in the sea.

You find here none of the graceful picturesqueness of French bathing. It is the rarest thing in the world for an Englishwoman to be able to swim; and there is nothing very charming in the sight of a line of figures clad in blue flannel night-gowns, and with oil-skin caps on their heads, clinging frantically to ropes, and bobbing and courtesying to a row of wooden boxes. The hours for this enchanting performance are from seven or eight in the morning till about noon.

Sometimes it happens that a bathing-machine is forgotten by the lad who should come on horseback to fetch it back. In vain the lady puts her towel out of a hole designed for that purpose at the landward end, which is the proper signal to say that she is in readiness.

"Jack" is bent on something else, and does not heed her flag of distress. She finds the rising tide caressing her feet, and gradually flooding her box, and soaking her apparel. She waits to be remembered, not patiently, but with her fears rising like the tide. However, Jack usually turns out better than the lover in the ballad, who rides away, and never comes again. Before it is quite too late, he tears down the shingle, and again Venus rises from the sea, safe, though salt. Frights of this sort happen not altogether infrequently; but I have never heard of any serious accident in connection with Jack's forgetfulness.

All English people hate this system of bathing. They all grumble at it, but no one tries to change it.

It is the same thing everywhere, even in the Channel Islands, which belong to Great Britain. The only variety is that the larger and more fashionable the watering-place, the greater the misery, and the less you get of space or convenience.

Random Rambles, 1881

# 1882

The bathing costumes are, as usual, composed of the pantaloons, blouse, and waistband, like last year. Red is the predominate color this season at the sea-side.

*The London and Paris Ladies' Magazine of Fashion*, July 1882

Our attention and our wishes are undoubtedly tending seawards, and Dame Fashion, concurring with our mood, has given us in Nos. 280, 281, and 282, charming models for our bathing costumes; the first, the Biarritz, is in thin dark-blue flannel serge, trimmed with coloured embroidery in a lighter shade of blue; the shape is exceedingly comfortable, giving full play to the limbs in swimming. The Dieppe bathing costume is a trifle more dressy, made in white or light-blue serge, embroidered in colours. The gauged yoke is both becoming and modest. The Trouville is the third of our illustrations, and is made of blue serge, with trimming of washing silk, and bouffant waistcoat of the same. ...

No. 280. – THE BIARRITZ BATHING DRESS.

Bathing dress of blue serge, made with a deep gathered flounce and yoke trimmed with coloured embroidery. Trousers to match. Quantity of material required, 8 yards. [ ↖ ]

No. 281. – THE DIEPPE BATHING DRESS.
Costume of white flannel ornamented with bouillonnés and coloured embroidery. Bow and sash of washing silk. Quantity of material required, 8 yards.
[ → ]

No. 282. – THE TROUVILLE BATHING DRESS.
Bathing dress of serge with bouffant waistcoat of washing silk, and flounces of silk to match. Quantity of material required, serge, 8 yards.
[ ← ]
*Myra's Threepenny Journal*, July 1, 1882

Sea Nymph. – Bathing dresses are made of flannel or serge; flannel is the lightest, but serge is generally preferred as it clings less to the figure. You will find a good model in this number. ...
No. 350. Bathing costume of blue flannel ornamented with white braid, the scallops worked with cream wool. Rosettes of braid. Tunic gauged at the neck and sleeves, and trousers gauged near the edge. Quantity of material required, 6 yards. [ → ]
*Myra's Threepenny Journal*, August 1, 1882

A new model for a bathing suit has the blouse and drawers made in one piece, with a short skirt to button on at the waist. Another style has a shirred yoke set in, like the Mother Hubbard dresses and cloaks for children. The shirred yoke is also seen in a bathing-cloak intended to be worn when leaving the water. Bathing-cloaks are made of serge, waterproof of Turkish toweling.
*Arthur's Home Magazine*, August 1882

FIG. XX. – BATHING-DRESS, OF BLUE FLANNEL, trimmed with dark-red flannel, pinked and cut out, so as to show the blue flannel underneath.
[ ← ]
FIG. XXI. – BATHING-DRESS, OF WHITE FLANNEL, trimmed with a cross-stitch embroidery in red.
*Peterson's Magazine*, August 1882

Bathing-dresses are equally rich; they are made of cashmere, serge, flannel, and even washing-silk; and are embroidered and braided in the richest colours and patterns. The Amelia sandal shoe is worn for bathing, also a little strapped stay, to keep the waist and bust in place.
The Ladies Treasury for 1882, 1882

No. 38. Doll in Bathing Dress. Costume of dark red serge, trimmed with white lace. Waistband of blue ribbon worked in point russe with red silk and tied at the back. Bows of similar ribbon on the shoulders. Bathing cap and sponge bag of oilskin, bound with blue braid. [ → ]
<u>Children's Fancy Work</u>, 1882

And when Miss Brown saw Miss Risley and Miss Brook making their stout ticking swimming-suits uncommonly coquettish, all the detective in her rose;
<u>Hester Stanley at St. Marks</u>, a novel, 1882

# 1883

FIG. V – BATHING-SUIT, FOR A CHILD. It is made of blue flannel, has a red sash around the waist, and is trimmed with red braid. ...

FIG. XVII. – BATHING-DRESS, OF MAROON-COLORED FLANNEL. It is gathered back and front, and the tops of the sleeves, as well as the trousers, are laid in plaits, and fastened across with ornamented straps.

FIG. XVIII. – BATHING-DRESS, OF DARK-BLUE SERGE. The bottom, the collar, and the sleeves are cut in tabs and bound with white.

*Peterson's Magazine*, July 1883

A most important and necessary garment – one which must be included in our workroom preparations – is a good bathing dress. The pattern given is one which requires no great skill in cutting out; but it will be found both comfortable and becoming, and can be easily taken off. It should be made of thick flannel or serge, and trimmed with scarlet or white Hercules braid. The tunic is like a very loose jacket, and buttons all down the front; three rows of white braid are laid on all round the edge and on each side of the front. There is a sloped seam down the back and at each side, but no side-pieces; nor is there need for darts in front; the fewer seams made, the neater and more comfortable will be the tunic. It is cut in a point at the neck, where it is finished by a sailor collar, like that shown in the engraving; this is edged with braid, and ornamented at each corner with an anchor worked in

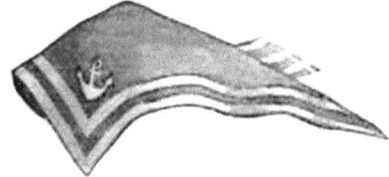

crewel of the same colour as the braid. The waistband is fastened to the back seam; it is edged with braid, and is pointed at one end. The drawers are loose and open round the knee, and have three rows of braid to match the tunic. They should fasten at the sides, being put into two bands, as I explained in making children's knickerbockers, and have a button on one band and button-hole on the other. The length of the sleeves of the tunic may be according to the taste of the wearer; but be sure and make them wide enough, so that they may be easily slipped off. A modification of this dress would suit a little girl; or you might make something still more simple, by copying a combination garment, fastening it round the waist with a band, and adding a sailor collar and short sleeves, trimmed with braid. The great thing to be remembered in making a bathing-dress is, to have it loose enough; it is so distressing to have to struggle out of wet clinging draperies, especially for children, who are very likely to be injured, instead of benefitted, by standing shivering in the draught after their morning dip.

Many ladies object to wet their hair with sea water. I am not sure that it is injurious. It leaves an unpleasant stickiness, and the hair does not curl or crimp well after the bath; but this difficulty maybe obviated by rinsing it in soft water previous to drying it.

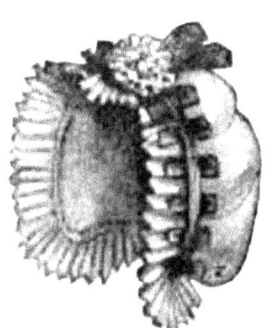

The cap illustrated is composed of oil-silk or shepherd's plaid waterproofing, and has a pleating round the edge, with band and bows of braid to match the trimming of the dress. This is of course for a grown person. I should not recommend the use of a cap for children, because I think it so much better to wet the head first; and with them there is less trouble in drying the hair, especially now it is fashionable for little ones to wear it so short.

The necessity for wearing shoes when bathing depends upon the place selected for spending the summer holiday. At Swanage, that delightfully quiet and picturesque spot, with its quaint stone-built houses and gently-sloping hills, and its extensive bay, where the children may gambol in the waves with perfect safety; at Yarmouth, and at most of the watering-places on the Kentish coast, the beach is sandy and soft; but on a shingly beach it is more comfortable to have the protection of shoes, which may be of canvas or straw, with india-rubber soles.

White serge is an excellent material for the costumes of very little girls at the seaside. They may be made to look most effective by adding a bright-coloured sash of wide silk ribbon with hand-painted ends, and collar and cuffs of silk, which should be separate from the dress, for the convenience of washing.

For little boys, nothing can be better than the Jersey suits, now so much worn. They are not, perhaps, quite so durable as those made from serge; but they may be bought at a very reasonable rate, and it is desirable to save the trouble of making, if the expense is not much increased thereby. The best way of making a little boy's serge suit is to have drawers fastening at the side and loose round the knee, and loose shirt, put into a band at the waist and falling loosely over, like a Garibaldi, with sailor collar fastened at the throat with black ribbons. I prefer a sailor straw hat to the woollen caps worn with the Jersey costumes. They are lighter, cooler, and more protection to the face. With one of these, a suit of serge, india-rubber-soled shoes, spade and pail, a little boy may be said to be fairly equipped and ready for any emergency.
Letts's Illustrated Household Magazine, 1883


Another successful venture was the making of pretty bathing-dresses. One of our party had spent some weeks of the summer at a French watering-place, and had bought there an elegant costume, which served for a pattern. It was made of thick Bolton sheeting, and knickerbockers and tunic were both elaborately trimmed with bands and frills of Turkey red twill, and at the waist a cord and tassels of red worsted. The red twill will stand salt water without losing or changing colour, and looks bright and pretty enough to quite eclipse our ordinary clumsy serge dress. Bathing shoes, to complete the costume, we made of coarse canvas; the soles were crocheted of thick twine or cord, and on the toe was roughly embroidered an anchor or some such nautical device in worsted of the colour of the dress.

To several of these bathing costumes was added a loose dressing-gown – of which French ladies know the comfort so well – to slip on directly the bath is over. The shape is either like a long sleeveless cloak, or else simply a large edition of an ordinary dressing-gown. The material is bath-towelling, bound with coloured twill to match the bathing-dress.
The Master's Service, 1883


Deb Salisbury

# 1884

No. 4 – Is a new pattern for a bathing-costume, to be made of navy-blue flannel, and trimmed with white worsted braid. The waist and skirt are all in one; the fullness of the body, both back and front, being gathered at the neck, and plaited at the waist; front and back of the skirt are kilted, and the side-fullness of the skirt is put into box-plaits; extra width is put into the skirt for the fullness over the hips. Elbow sleeves, with plaited ruffle, and pants full to below the knee, and terminating in a ruffle. An elastic is run into the casing for the pants. A belt of the material is arranged for the waist, but many girls prefer the white worsted girthing-belt, with straps to buckle. ...

No. 6 – Is another seaside-costume for a boy of eight years. It is also made of marine-blue serge or flannel, and trimmed with a band of white, stitched on by the machine. This costume will serve either for a bathing-suit, or for morning wear on the beach: for the latter, substitute long sleeves and long stockings and boots, and, of course, finer material. The knee-pants and blouse, with belt or sash, make a stylish everyday-suit for a boy of this age.

*Peterson's Magazine*, July 1884

IT is always better to take your own bathing-gown with you. It is a little expense at starting, but "the first expense is the last." It is much healthier and safer to have your own gown, instead of depending on what the bathing-woman may be able to lend you, and pleasanter too, for if you borrow, you go through a different experience of wretchedness every day, getting one day something long enough to trip you up, and one day something short enough for a child of seven. Perhaps, at last, on horror's head horrors accumulate, and you are given a gown with the string run out. If you have your own dress yon can be sure of getting what you like, and are able to look to the buttons being on, from time to time – a very needful precaution, as threads soon wax weak in the sea. Thin serge is the best material for bathing-gowns, and they can be nicely trimmed with braid, and made to look pretty. Navy-blue serge, with a large sailor-collar braided in white, looks very well. Some of the new-fashioned gowns are made of plaid, and have a plain piece let in like a waistcoat They are often made high to the throat in this case, and down to the wrists also, but we do not advise this, as it is much healthier to have the arms free. A gown ought to be rinsed out in cold water directly after it has been worn, as this keeps it from rotting. It is better to take it home for this purpose, if possible, and also to make sure that the bathing-woman does not lend it to anybody else. If you make a point of carrying it home, it is as well to provide yourself with an oilskin bag, large enough to take it comfortably, and this will save your walking-dress from also taking a sea-bath which would not be so beneficial to its health as to your own.

*Household Words*, July 5, 1884

LADIES with sufficient courage to admit that they are old enough to remember the first introduction of a bathing-suit, when a tunic and trousers superseded the serge gown of our grandmothers, will recall the severity of public criticism upon the new costume. The objections were more to the idea than to the article itself, for the change had much in its favour, and it has been a case of the survival of the fittest. The advanced bathing-costume of this year has come in quietly, crept in unnoticed, being a combination garment – vest and trousers in one, but rather too pronounced in form to suit English tastes. The addition of a short skirt, gathered to a band

and fastened round the waist, does away with all objections to a combination bathing-suit. The eccentricities of embroidery in crewels on serge for bathing dresses has quite disappeared, sunflowers and yellow daisies being looked upon as vulgar. The heavier makes of navy-blue serge, with white braid, or red, large sailor collar, and simulated cuffs, make an unexceptionable costume.

*Household Words*, July 26, 1884

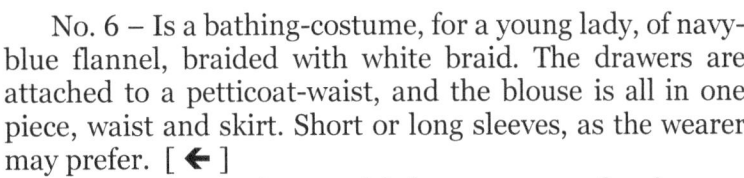

The latest fashion at French watering places is to be photographed in your bathing dress. If the fashion comes over here, it will give a spurt to the business of the itinerant seaside photographer. It is to be hoped, however, before this comes about that the hideous bathing dress of Margate and elsewhere will be a thing of the past.

*The Photographic News*, August 15, 1884

No. 6 – Is a bathing-costume, for a young lady, of navy-blue flannel, braided with white braid. The drawers are attached to a petticoat-waist, and the blouse is all in one piece, waist and skirt. Short or long sleeves, as the wearer may prefer. [ ← ]

No. 7 – Is another model for a costume for the sea-bath, made as the above, only the trimming is simply of three rows of braid. [ → ]

*Peterson's Magazine*, August 1884

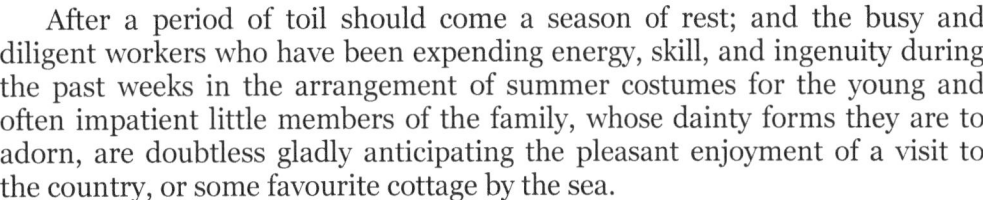

After a period of toil should come a season of rest; and the busy and diligent workers who have been expending energy, skill, and ingenuity during the past weeks in the arrangement of summer costumes for the young and often impatient little members of the family, whose dainty forms they are to adorn, are doubtless gladly anticipating the pleasant enjoyment of a visit to the country, or some favourite cottage by the sea.

Time was when such periods of relaxation were to the majority of people few and far between, but, in the present day, rich and poor alike recognise the necessity for a change of scene and perfect rest from mental anxiety and bodily fatigue; and an annual trip to the sea is considered indispensable for the preservation of the health and active vigour which is needed to sustain the struggle and race for life. Every facility is given to the public, in these days of enterprising effort, for carrying out so laudable a purpose; cheap trains carry them far away, and so numerous and varied are the resting places scattered around our coasts that none need feel it an impossibility to find a suitable retreat.

One of the principal attractions of the visit to the seaside is of course the *sea-bathing*. Mothers of large little-families usually select a watering-place where the sands are extensive and afford a safe playground for the children, who spend their mornings digging mimic trenches and building castles of the sand, but oh, mothers, let this be *before,* not *after* the bath. When they have had their dip in the sea, gentle exercise is more healthful than standing or sitting about in draughty corners.

In order that children may enjoy their bath, it is desirable they should have a proper dress to wear. This should be made of wool, because the body is not so apt to be chilled by wet serge or flannel as by wet cotton or linen. Bathing dresses are made sometimes of silk or striped cotton material, but they cling most ungracefully, and are not so useful as a serge costume. The ordinary serge for bathing dresses is not expensive, it is true it loses its colour, but daily immersion in the sea will spoil the best material in course of time.

The only difficulty then is the making, but none will object to this addition to the summer needlework, when they realise the increased comfort the extra trouble ensures.

The absence of clothing adds very much to the dread which a child has of trusting itself to the watery element. We can sympathise with the feelings of fear which children experience when a door is suddenly opened and they see a vast expanse of water, and presently behold a strange old woman attired in a hideous head-gear with a miniature hood of a bathing machine lowered over her weather-beaten face, who, coming close to them, in a hoarse voice tells them to let her help them down the steps into the warm sea. It is far better that they should be first taken in by their mother, for the shock of the cold water is a sufficient strain on the nervous system of a child, without the addition of fright. Of course, some children are physically unable to bathe in the open sea, and a child should never be compelled to go into the water if on emerging it shivers and looks blue or livid. Another difficulty is how to dry the skin thoroughly, for on this depends the child's comfort and happiness for the remainder of the day.

It has been truly said that sea-water does not give cold, and this has led to the supposition that partial removal of the moisture is all that is necessary; but it must be remembered that the salt property of the water causes an irritability of the skin which is most objectionable, and which promotes a corresponding irritability of temper, and calls forth exhibitions of fretfulness which demand frequent reproof and repression. The best method to avoid such a painful result is to prepare for each child a *peignoir* or loose gown of bath towelling, which can be slipped on in a moment, when the wet bathing dress is discarded. In many of the Continental bathing establishments these *peignoirs* are supplied by the proprietors, but it is not yet the custom in England. The proper material for making such a useful "Companion of the Bath" may be bought by the yard; it is similar to that of which ladies' dresses were made a season or two ago.

While on the subject of bathing, it may be remarked that it is better, if possible, to allow children to bathe from the beach; and in some instances, where the sands are extensive, small tents are very useful, which can be erected and taken down with very little trouble. They are not expensive; indeed, if a family includes many young people, the cost of such a tent would be saved in one season, and the owners would be spared the worry of waiting for bathing machines, and be free from the danger of catching any infectious complaint, too often the unhappy result of the summer holiday.

The easiest and simplest form of bathing dress for quite a young child, is an adaptation of the combination garment. The accompanying sketch may, perhaps, be sufficient to indicate the method of making and trimming this comfortable and useful covering for a little bather.

It would look very pretty made in white or striped flannel, or in white serge, trimmed with scarlet bands, and the frills round the legs and arms scalloped and worked round with scarlet wool, with a small leaf or ornament in each scallop. The square sailors' collar, in each corner of which is worked an anchor in scarlet, is tied in front with scarlet ribbon, the opening down the front being fastened with scarlet bone buttons, the buttonholes worked with scarlet silk. This little dress has the advantage of being easily put on and taken off, and is, therefore, preferable to a more dressy and elaborate costume for children of tender years.

The second illustration is more appropriate for young ladies of more mature age. It is composed of dark navy serge, and consists of a blouse or tunic and knickerbockers. The tunic is made in three pieces, the back being cut in one, the shoulders fitting loosely, the side-seams very much sloped, the fulness being confined at the waist with a band. It is trimmed with bands of white serge, stitched on at each side with scarlet ingrain silk or cotton; the turn-over round collar is of the same material, with an anchor embroidered in each corner. A band of white serge is placed down the front, and round the edge and sleeves of the tunic; the knickerbockers, which are let into two bands and fasten with a button on each side, are trimmed at the edge to correspond. It is a good plan to wear some covering for the head, either a broad-brimmed Japanese hat, or a pretty hood of oiled silk or waterproofed material, nicely trimmed and becomingly made. Some ladies prefer to wet their hair with the sea water, and let it afterwards dry in the sun. Whether this is or is not beneficial is a subject that has been much discussed, and is a matter that must be left to individual judgment. Children do not, as a rule, wear hats or hoods,

and it is presumable that the fashion has been adopted of late years by ladies, more to avoid the trouble of undressing and re-arranging the *coiffure,* than from fear of incurring injury from the hot rays of the sun on the salt water.

<u>Letts's Household Magazine</u>, 1884

# 1885

There is considerable variety in bathing suits this year, and there is seemingly a greater regard for modesty and taste than ever before. The suits are made as formerly in two pieces, trousers and waist combined, and a short skirt which should extend just a little below the knees. The trousers are made fuller than they used to be, and are now invariably finished at the knee in Knickerbocker fashion, never being allowed to hang loosely. A broad elastic band is used in confining them at the knees. Some women prefer their bathing suits made with the skirt and waist combined, instead of the waist and trousers being in one piece; but this is not nearly as healthful or comfortable a way in which to have one made as that first described. The materials most used in making up bathing suits are flannel, camel's hair, and cashmere. The latter material is only used, however, when a particularly fancy suit is desired, and then two colors are generally employed. Flannel is by all odds much the best material to bathe in. It should not be too heavy, but it should be of the best quality, which does not hold the water like the poorer goods, and is much more comfortable and durable. Olive green, dark red, and seal brown flannel are all much used now, but the dark blue still remains most in favor. It is becoming to the majority of complexions and does not fade as quickly as some of the other colors mentioned. Bathing suits in plain shades are enlivened by rows of either white or black braid, or have dashes of bright red or yellow about them that look very attractive. Stockings that match the suit in color, and turbans that are cleverly made of the trimming are worn. Gloves and corsets are now considered superfluous and affected, and are never worn by sensible women. A costume recently made for a dainty Newport belle is composed of cream-white flannel of the finest quality, trimmed with very narrow tinsel braid that glitters in the sunlight like diamonds, and which does not tarnish. There is a yoke waist adorned with innumerable rows of the braid, which is also placed in a Greek design around the skirt. The cream-colored stockings have yellow flowers embroidered up their sides, and the turban made of the same material as the dress, has a band of tinsel braid bordering it. The effect of the costume is very pretty. A few women have utilized the new woollen plaids for bathing. But they are not at all attractive after they have once been in the water.

*Brooklyn Magazine*, August 1885

Bathing suits grow more and more fanciful, and those of European build are equal to the most abbreviated costumes of a burlesque company. Low neck and no sleeves, with the shortest of knickerbockers, and a dainty skirt that reminds one of the baby's flannel petticoat, with a pair of stockings matching or harmonizing in color with the dress, is supposed to constitute the apparel required by Miss Aphrodite. ...

2405  Lady's Bathing Costume. The pattern of this garment is cut in three sizes, 34, 36, and 38 inches bust measure. 8 1/2 yards material, 24 inches wide, and 58 buttons for the medium size. Price 30 cents, any size.

*The Cottage Hearth*, August 1885

FRENCH women improvise novelties in bathing costumes just as they would any other kind of dress, and with as much facility. The fashionable watering-places in France have been rife with fresh modes for those who delight in a matutinal plunge, or rather, dabble. French women disport themselves in the water, and rarely go in for the energetic bathing which English women affect. The latter, in fact, do not consider the toilette an important point at all, and keep faithful, as a rule, to blue serge trimmed with red, in the form of knickerbockers, and a banded paletot. But I have a novelty to describe which my countrywomen are patronising largely, viz., bathing suits made of navy blue knitted yarns, bordered with red crochet. They have great merit. They adhere to the figure, but not unduly, are pretty to look at, and healthy, and they are made in the same shapes as the blue serges. The only choice about them is in the ornamentation, which varies in the width of the collar and the length of the sleeve, half the depth being often of a contrasting colour. There are caps to go with them for those who wear them, but bathing is more healthy without.

*Cassell's Family Magazine*, October 1885

## 1886

Fig. XV. – Bathing-Dress For a Little Girl. It is made of white flannel, and trimmed with three rows of blue braid.

Fig. XVI. – Bathing-Dress For a Little Girl. It is made of crimson serge, and is finished with white machine-stitching. ...

Fig. XVIII. – Woman's Bathing-Dress, of Navy-Blue Serge, trimmed with scarlet braid and bone buttons. The blouse has a yoke and sailor-collar.

*Peterson's Magazine*, July 1886

The bathing costumes have a little that is new to commend them this year. Moreover they are more becoming. Some are made loose, like a Breton jacket, in serge, trimmed with white and red braid, the ornamentation carried out on the knickerbockers. Others have sailor collars worn over distinct waistcoats in stripes. But there is an inclination to use striped flannel, and provided the colours bear the water, it is a move in the right direction. Another idea is knitted suits made like those Italian fishermen wear, with woollen frills at the neck and sleeves; but they fit the figure too closely. Some of the vests fasten on the shoulder, so are not liable to open unduly at the back or neck. Nearly all this year's bathing dresses have the trousers and tunic in one, the drapery attached to a waistband – the less ornamentation the better; imagine tufts of wool made up as rosettes placed down the front of the tunic! One introduction to be avoided is a waterproof dress for bathing. Why should people venture into the water with clothes intended to protect them from that element? Netted bags to place the wet dresses in are, however, a very good idea, as the water oozes through them.

*Cassell's Family Magazine*, Autumn 1886

Knitting and crocheting effects have been introduced into bathing suits late this season. Probably the idea will be carried further, so that fancy edgings, rosettes, and the like, in silk and wool, will be used with woolen dresses.

*Arthur's Home Magazine*, November 1886

## 1887

Messrs. Yeatts & Troth, whose cosy store on Chestnut street, out by Broad, is the source of supply for a large proportion of the best dressed gentlemen in town, have been handling a few tasty novelties of their own get up. ... Bathing suits, which are all important to existence here, they have gotten up in stockinette of solid colors that makes a really beautiful costume for the purpose.

*The Clothier and Furnisher*, July 1887

NEW YORK FASHIONS.
BATHING DRESSES.

Navy blue and white twilled flannels, striped flannels, serges, and jersey webbing are the popular materials for bathing suits. The favorite plan for making these suits has the waist and drawers in one piece, with a separate skirt that is attached by buttons in the belt. This design is susceptible of much variation, as it may be made with a plain blouse-waist or with a yoke, with long sleeves, elbow sleeves, or the short cap sleeves, and the drawers may be straight and short, or else full and long, and gathered about the ankles in Turkish fashion. The blouse with sailor collar is a pretty waist for stout figures, while those who are slight look better with a yoke and pleated waist. The drawers and waist are attached to the same belt, while the skirt has a false belt or lining for button-holes to meet buttons that are set around the belt of the waist and drawers. Swimmers prefer short sleeves that leave the arms free; sometimes the arms are protected by flesh-colored Balbriggan covers, which may be made of stocking legs; for general bathing the long sleeves are used with a slight fulness gathered to a band at the wrist. Plain drawers reach just below the knees, and the limbs are covered below by long stockings, which are now provided with cork soles or with rubber slippers to protect the feet when walking in the sand on the beach. Blue flannel suits have white or red flannel stitched on as trimming. All flannels should be well shrunken before the garments are made. A white flannel sailor collar and a V plastron or shirt front are pretty on a on a blue flannel blouse; the skirt then has two white bands an inch wide stitched around it, and just above its edge is another band that is cut in points at the top, with a blue braid button set in each point; the drawers have similar bands; there are other blue suits trimmed in the

same way with red flannel, and white suits with either red or blue trimming. Striped flannel skirts for plain blue waists and drawers are also liked, and may be of the striped flannel, or else white or red flannel may be sewed in lengthwise bands down a blue skirt to form stripes; as, for instance, nine or ten white bands, each two inches wide, are stitched lengthwise on the skirt from the belt nearly to the hem, and each stripe is shaped in a point at the lower end. Four pointed stripes are then stitched on the lower part of each leg of the drawers, and there are similar stripes on the sleeves. Some of the sailor blouses have four box pleats in front and back, others have but two pleats, and still others have stripes of white or red flannel stitched on. Mohair braid, black, white, or red, is used in rows on sailor collars, across the shirt plastron, and on the sleeves; the skirt and drawers also have braided borders. The woven jersey suits come plain, or striped in blue, garnet, or black, with long stockings to match, attached to rubber slippers, and a pretty cap with two points finished with tassels; the skirt is amply full, and buttons on at the waist line. Some of the jersey suits have fitted waists, while others are as loose as blouses; the latter have the sailor collar now so popular, while the plain waists have high standing collars and short sleeves. Caps of oiled silk or of gossamer rubber are merely a large puff with rubber band,

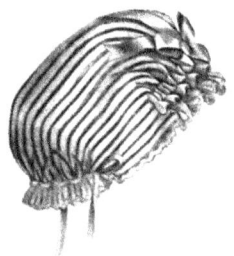

to cover the hair well; hats of the same materials are gathered in the crown, and have brim enough to protect the face. ...

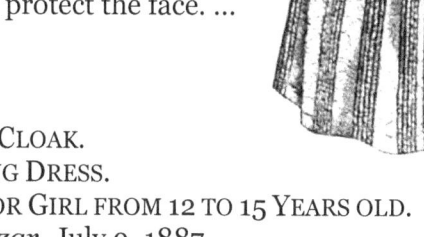

BATHING CAP.
GIRL'S BATHING CLOAK.
LADY'S SWIMMING DRESS.
BATHING SUIT FOR GIRL FROM 12 TO 15 YEARS OLD.
   *Harper's Bazar*, July 9, 1887

FIG. XI – BATHING-SUIT, OF NAVY-BLUE FLANNEL. The pants are fastened to a petticoat-body of the flannel, which is trimmed at the neck with three rows of braid, to show where the blouse opens. The entire suit is trimmed with white cotton braid, put on in the pattern shown in the illustration.

[ ← ]

*Peterson's Magazine*, August 1887

In bathing-gear there is a novelty, viz., the combination dresses in elastic cloth, or stockingette. They are very good indeed for children, and for swimming; but they require additional tunics for sea-bathing.

*Cassell's Family Magazine*, October 1887

### Bathing.

A very large proportion of the visitors to Coney Island find the source of their greatest pleasure in the surf-bathing. There is little to choose in the matter of location, as from one extremity of the island to the other, the beach is equally smooth and safe, and the magnificent surf of the same character. The uniform price for the use of a bathing-house and dress is 25 cents, but at a few places toward the west end, 15 or 20 cents only is charged, but 25 cents is the maximum price at the best places. At the Manhattan Beach Bathing Pavilion, Brighton Beach Bathing Pavilion, and at the Iron Pier will be found the most luxurious bathing facilities. The bathing dress should be made of a woolen fabric, as it retains the heat of the body, and therefore prevents a too rapid evaporation. Maroon and blue are the proper colors, as they resist the corrosive and bleaching effects of the salt-water. A broad-brimmed straw hat may be worn, but all cover (such as oil skin caps, so commonly worn to prevent the hair from being wet) preventing a free perspiration .on the scalp, are injurious. Do not bathe just after a meal, or when over-fatigued, chilly or over-heated, or (unless with the sanction of your physician) when suffering from any acute disease, or laboring under any organic affection.

The proper time to bathe is, when in a healthful condition, when comfortably warm, two to four hours after meals, at any time between 7 a. m. and 9 p. m., from the beginning of June to the end of September. The best time is during high water. Fifteen minutes should be the average duration of a bath. One bath a day is enough for most people, although robust people may occasionally enter twice a day unharmed, and extraordinary people as often as they please. Children should never be forced to bathe. All the good effects which are expected from the bathing are nullified by the fright and nervous shock. The proper way is to get them gradually accustomed to the sea; to let them have their bathing clothes on, and play on the beach, when they will go to the edge of the water, and by-and-by find their own way in. Do not undress and dash into the water after a long walk or run, or when much heated. Do not enter the water when the stomach is entirely empty nor when you are fatigued by hard mental or physcial [sic] labor. The most common cause of cramps in the legs or arms is due to ignorance of or neglect of these simple precautions. Do not go into the water sooner than two or three hours after a hearty meal, as it interferes with digestion and nullifies any good to be obtained by the excercise [sic]. For beginners especially do not stay in the water too long. Ten minutes, or at most, twenty, will be enough for one not accustomed to the water.

The Tourists Companion and Guide to Coney Island, 1887

## 1888

No. 9 – Is a simple bathing-costume for a of four to six years, made of navy-blue flannel edged with white braid. [ ➜ ]
*Peterson's Magazine*, July 1888

People sometimes experience a great disappointment, and occasionally suffer in totally unexpected ways from a short sojourn at the sea-side. The sea and sea-bathing are great restoratives, but they require to be taken and used judiciously.

But the inexperienced and unaccustomed should begin at the right season, in July, when the water is warm, and the desire is likely to be strongest. They should, at first, have the aid of a trainer, or, at least, fearless swimmer, with whom the first plunge may be made with a feeling of absolute safety. The little "dippings" to which so many women and girls confine themselves are absolutely dangerous – not to life, but to health – because the surface of the body ought to be completely under water, and ought to be active, moving with the element, and be able to partake of its buoyancy. Little children ought not be forced into the water. If they are permitted to play in the sand and see other children enjoy bathing, they will gradually lose fear, and acquire a love for it. But there is a risk in doing this if the body is not in a perfectly healthy condition. Playing or bathing upon chilly and damp days sometimes precipitates attacks of rheumatism, even in children, and the old should never bathe in the sea without precautions, on account of the liability to cramp.

On the other hand, a course of sea-bathing is, not infrequently, the finest possible medicine, and to the accustomed, and healthy, active individual, it is a pleasure, and means of restoration, for the absence of which nothing would compensate. A young woman living in a little town in the interior of New York had become "run down" without knowing precisely what was the matter with her. A physician advised the sea-side and salt-water bathing for a month. She went, but felt so much worse, that at the end of a week she returned home sure that *that* was not the cure for her. The doctor sent her back, and told her to remain and follow his instructions, whatever happened. At the end of four weeks she was covered with a terrible rash from head to foot, but she remained two weeks longer, until it had disappeared, and went home a bright, happy, because well, woman. Such a course of treatment would make over many women who now suffer simply from stagnation of body and mind.

The bathing-dress proper consists of two pieces – drawers, set into a hip band or yoke, and a blouse tunic, belted in with canvas belt and leather buckle. Six to eight yards of material will make it, according to width, and ten yards or a "piece" of braid will trim it.

We have of late modeled our dresses upon the European costumes for bathing, and in many ways greatly improved them. But the European bath-houses are usually set upon wheels, which run across the sandy shore into the sea, and, descending by three steps, the bather leaps in, without being obliged to walk over the gritty space between the ocean and the dressing-place, as we do at all our sea-side watering places in this country, thus exposing arms and face to the sun, and the person, in bathing costume, to the hundreds of eyes that are usually watching from the shore. This makes a cloak, or wrap necessary, and none have been found so suitable as the "Terry" cloak, a gathered or plaited circular garment mad of soft cream or wine-colored Angora flannel, which needs no lining – and may be finished neatly enough for a promenade on the beach if desired.

Deb Salisbury

The two best materials for bathing dresses are twilled flannel and English serge. Unless one can afford to go to a first-class place and pay a high price, it will be economy to buy good material, a pattern, and make the dress for one's self. In this way you secure a choice in colors and fabrics such as cannot be found in the cheap, ready-made suits. It is true the cost of material alone will amount to almost as much as the price of a cheap bathing-costume, ready-made, so if time as well as money is an object, and sea-bathing an incident which does not often enter your life, it may be just as well to content yourself with the baggy and stereotyped dark-blue or iron-gray suit you can find at any furnishing store.

There is a consideration, however, which should have weight with young women – it is this, that it is a bathing-dress and that its fashion does not materially change. Once acquired, neatly cut, and neatly made out of well-chosen material, it will be available, if properly taken care of, as long as a bathing-dress will be needed. Then if she is expert at fancy work she can embroider it with a monogram in red or white in front or upon the collar, and in various ways render it distinctive, and quite different from common bathing-suits.

Undoubtedly the most refined costumes for bathing are those made in cream-colored serge flannel, and finished simply with rows of stitching in pure silk, cream color or gold, or cream and gold. This adds nothing to the cost of the owner can do her own stitching, and even if one gets it done by the yard it will cost little more, silk included, than braid. What is true in regard to the finish of cream color is true of other colors; three or five rows of chain stitch, or saddlers' stitching, in ivory white upon peach-blow flannel, or Gobelin blue, is far more elegant than the rows of time-out-of-mind braid which are common in every shop.

The canvas boot is better for obvious reasons than the canvas shoe as part of a bathing-costume. It is more protective, gives better support, but should be discarded before going into the water. It is better for both feet and ankles to be uncovered, and have freedom, but if there is a repugnance to going into the water with the feet uncovered, soles, with the canvas tips, tied on with tapes should be used.

*Our Country Home*, July 1888

A DESPATCH from Asbury Park is headed "The Bathing Suit Must Go." Now, this is shocking. There is so very little of it that it ought to be allowed to remain. It is better than nothing. If the bathing suit goes, newspaper men and other modest persons will also go. – *Norristown Herald*.

*Puck*, September 5, 1888

## BATHING SUITS.

At ultra-fashionable seaside resorts some exceedingly fancy bathing toilettes are seen daily on the beach, such as the fish scale costume, tights with tunic, the bodice, from waist-line up, covered with luminous scales, and other gay looking dresses trimmed with real metal braid; however, such garments are exceptions, for the generally useful bathing suit is of soft serge or flannel, in combinations of red and blue, blue, copper color or red, and black or white, such hues being really the only ones which will endure the frequent exposure to salt water and hot sunshine.

The bodice with yoke and full waist is still |popular, so is the regular blouse; but young ladies with shapely figures now wear fitted corsages, trimmed after fancied models. One new suit in navy flannel serge, has drawers and tunic cut out in tabs at lower edge, and bound with gold braid, plain waist, with collar, belt, vest and sleeves finished to match. The waist is closed in front with buttons and buttonholes, and the collar points, below vest, are tied together with ribbons.

A garnet suit, which also has a tight waist, is adorned with black braid, put on in odd pattern, while a light blue flannel dress for a little girl has trimmings of white flannel, spotted all over with a dark blue polka dot. Two suits for small boys are pretty and simple; one has short pants and waist garnished in odd design with white braid; the other suit, of striped red and blue flannel, has belt, collar and bands on short sleeves of dark blue flannel.

*Ladies' Home Journal*, September 1888

# 1889

SOME of the leading retailers are showing an assortment of men's bathing suits, which partake of the dominant gaudiness of the season. With some of the suits stockings and shoes are included. The stockings in fast colors and of a shade to comport well with the pattern and color of the suit.

THERE is a certain Baltimore swell who, being an excellent swimmer, proposes to spend the greater part of the coming season upon the seashore. He will take with him a repertoire of bathing suits and all the paraphernalia of lavement in the shape of bath trousers, gowns and the various ablutionary appurtenances, which the man of luxury utilizes in the privacy of his town house. A valet will accompany him and each day a portable bathing house will be set up on the beach, adjacent to the place where he proposes to enter the surf.

*The Clothier and Furnisher,* June 1889

No. 9 – Is a simple model for a bathing-suit, of dark-blue flannel or serge, trimmed with a band of white worsted braid. Long sleeves may be added to suit the taste of the wearer. The trousers may be longer and put on a band. [ ← ]
*Peterson's Magazine,* July 1889

No. 9 – Is a novelty in the way of a bathing-suit. It is made of marine blue serge and trimmed with white worsted braid. Long sleeves may be added. [ → ]
*Peterson's Magazine,* August 1889

A charming material for seaside wear, indeed the very best fabric of its kind, is English serge, which comes only in white and navy blues. It is especially useful for bathing dresses as it is not injured by sea water. It is not harsh as its name might indicate as the American and Irish serges are, but it is soft to the touch.

*Good Housekeeping,* August 3, 1889

*A Metropolitan Beauty Doctor – The New York World*

A shrewd little business woman who keeps a beauty parlor... Of all the remarkable things done by this very remarkable woman that of dressing a lady's arm exceeds everything else. Some otherwise beautiful arms are marred by a light growth of hair, to which sleeveless bathing suits and lace-sleeved walking dresses have so largely conduced. One season of bare arms on the beach is all the lesson a society woman needs; after that she takes her ocean dip in long sleeves, silk mitts and a broad-brimmed hat. But the mischief accomplished, it is necessary to pluck the arms before the fair creature can appear in evening dress. In this operation the madame is an expert. She goes over the arm with a pair of tweezers on the day of the opera, ball, or carpet party, and drawing out the darker hair from shoulder to wrist, resorts to some delicate paste to conceal the down that remains. Of course, this treatment has to be repeated for each subsequent occasion, and those ladies who go in society a great deal find the low-neck and short-sleeve bodice a most expensive fashion. These visits are kept profoundly secret and are made by appointment.

*Current Literature,* November 1889

And here we come to another branch of summer dress, viz., bathing and swimming costumes. We put the two together, for we hope in time that all our girls will have learnt this useful accomplishment, and for which there are now facilities in nearly every large town. So far as bathing is concerned, the arrangements made for it at French watering-places are far more conducive to health – not to speak of comfort – than those in vogue on our own coast. Hot linen, and especially a hot bathing sheet, in which to envelop the whole body at once, and a hot foot-bath, are both regarded as essential requisites in France. The first undoubtedly prevents chill through a too rapid and extensive evaporation, and aids in producing a proper reaction; and the latter will prevent the headache from which the majority of people suffer on coming from their morning's dip in the 'sad sea waves.' The 'usual thing' supplied at an English watering-place is a shabby old bathing-dress of brown, blue, or pale sand-colour, and two very small and sometimes ragged towels, stiff enough from recent wettings to stand on end if desired.

But though we may not yet be as advanced in these matters of comfort as the French, we are not quite without the power to help ourselves. There are few people who cannot manage to provide themselves with some elderly cotton sheets, when they pay their annual visit to the sea; and when the large-sized, rough Turkish towels can be obtained for one shilling everywhere, no one need go unprovided with them. They can even be purchased for sixpence, if of a smaller size. On emerging from the sea, the wet bathing-dress should be taken off as quickly as possible; and to exclude the external air and retain the animal heat, the body should be wholly enveloped in the bathing-sheet, and under its shelter the flesh should be well rubbed with the rough towel. After the drying, no time should be lost in putting on the clothes, and then proceeding to take that brisk walking exercise which will establish the full and permanent reaction of the circulation for the day. A hot-water tin, such as is generally used for the feet, will keep both the sheet and towel hot while the bather is in the sea, and the water it contains will also provide a hot foot-bath, if it be possible to procure a basin in which to put it.

Having finished the purely sanitary suggestions which, by long personal experience, have been found by ourselves the most beneficial, we will resume our chat upon the bathing-dress. There is a diversity of opinion existing about the material of which bathing-dresses should be made. For sea water and for swimming, many people prefer linen or cotton, in the form of ticking, or a stout holland or linen cloth. Others, again, prefer serge, flannel, or bunting for both fresh and sea-water bathing, as well as for wearing when swimming in the covered bath or the open sea.

We must confess that we think flannel, serge, or bunting the best and most becoming for any and every such purpose, and now that a bathing-dress can be procured for *4s. 6d.* ready-made – as we saw them sold ourselves at a south-coast watering-place – there is no excuse to be made for any girl who bathes without a suitable and thoroughly comfortable garment. The drawback to these bought garments is that they rarely fit the purchaser, and nothing can be more unbecoming than to bathe in a dress which is too low in the neck or too short in the legs, and by its tight proportions is only too admirably fitted to show off any personal drawback, either of extreme fatness or emaciation.

Deb Salisbury

There are two shapes in which bathing costumes can be made: the 'smock,' and the ' union' or 'combination' dress, to which latter a short skirt can be added, if only needed for bathing in the sea when no swimming is in question. The first named is the proper garment for the middle-aged and the stout. It is made in the shape of a smock or a long 'Norfolk jacket,' and is buttoned down the whole length of the front, confined by a band round the waist, and is supplied with half-long sleeves. The drawers worn under it are moderately full, and fasten with a button at the waist on each hip. These latter may be either long or short, to suit the wearer's requirements.

The combination bathing-dress is too well known to need much description. As we have said before, it needs a short skirt in addition for bathing in the sea, and also when used by stout or inelegantly thin people. This skirt has very little fulness, is put on over the dress, and is fastened round the waist with a band and button. Very excellent paper patterns for these can be purchased at any of the numberless paper-pattern shops, and the 'smock' bathing-dress can be obtained by asking for it under the name of the 'Norfolk jacket,' or any jacket of a straight shape, either with or without a yoke on the shoulders.

Navy blue flannel or serge is usually trimmed with rows of very narrow white or scarlet braid, or else a row of moderately wide, and two rows of narrow on each side. Some young ladies have three graduated rows of braid, the first wide, the second medium, and the last narrow. White, dark red, pale blue, and black serges and flannels are also employed, and these are sometimes ornamented with wide bands, cut on the bias, and of a contrasting colour, such as blue or red on white; blue, black, or white on dark red; red, white, or black on pale blue; and white or pale blue, on black serge. The edges of the bands are ornamented with ' featherstitch,' 'long-stitch,' or 'coral-stitch,' in wool, and the 'sailor's collar,' bands of the sleeves and waist-belt are trimmed to correspond. We recently saw a charming bathing-dress of dark blue serge embroidered with sprays of red coral, worked in coarse worsted. Nor must we forget that the 'Hubbard ' style of making gatherings at the neck and below the waist has found its way into the fashions of our bathing-dresses.

No one must be offended if we lay great stress on the acquirement of a becoming garment in which to bathe at the sea, for old and young alike. One only needs to stand for a few moments on the shore at any large bathing-place to see the bathers, and hear the remarks upon them, to understand thoroughly the necessity for paying more attention to this really important matter.

Bathing-slippers should not be forgotten, nor their immediate purchase neglected, particularly if the shore be a frequented one, for then there will certainly be an ample store of broken glass, besides the usual sharp flints, oyster shells, and pebbles, to cut or bruise your feet. At many seaside places they may be procured, being made of plaited straw or of felt. In either case they need some embellishment, which may be given by the small expenditure of a piece of scarlet braid, and the turning of it into rosettes or bows, and sandals which cross over the foot and ankle, and are tied above it in a bow and short ends. These bathing-shoes and slippers may also be made by clever amateur hands out of felt or blanketing, or of very coarse flannel, embroidered in coarse crewel-work, and bound neatly with worsted braid. They may be soled also with a pair of cork soles, to be found everywhere, which should first be covered on both sides with flannel. Another method of making a bathing-slipper is to take a pair of old boots or shoes, cut them down to the required shape, and to cover the fronts – the only part left – with flannel to match the bathing-dress, trimming with worsted braid, and attaching sandals of the same to them, to keep up the heel.

The only article now left to be mentioned is the bathing-cap or hat, which, in France and America, is usually one of the prettiest portions of the costume; for you should know that in both these countries it is thought indispensable to shelter the head from the sun and wind. In the above-named places they are made of straw, or of *piqué,* like those white washing hats so much used for children's wear. In our own land, however, we have adopted a much more foolish practice – that of covering the head with a waterproof cap, closely fitting to it. No harm is considered to result from wetting the head with sea water, so far as we can hear from any reliable authorities on the subject.

The Girl's Own Outdoor Book, 1889

HINTS ON SEA BATHING.

By "Life's" Doctor.

1. Invalids, particularly in the northern states should not indulge in surf-bathing between the first of November and the first of March.

2. The best time for the bath, if you have no bathing-suit, is between 9 P.M. and 4 A.M.

3. Bathing before breakfast is not recommended, unless you have been out all night with the boys.

4. Never neglect to protect the head while in the water. A silk hat should not be used for this purpose as it attracts the sun's rays.

5. In case you are seized with cramp while in the water, rub the affected part vigorously for ten or fifteen minutes with chloroform liniment. Many valuable lives might be saved every year if this advice were more generally followed.

6. Children should never be permitted to bathe except in the company of their parents. They are apt to become nuisances and may require spanking at any moment.

7. Should you become sea-sick from the motion of the waves, repair to the nearest drug-store and give the soda-water clerk the usual wink.

8. Do not become frightened if you swallow a little salt-water. It is not poisonous even to bathers from the Blue Grass region.

9. Ladies should not wear corsets when bathing, unless they happen to be corpulent and there are men about.

10. Fast-color bathing suits are recommended for ladies who expect to wear *décolleté* gowns in the evening.

11. Practical jokers who think that the greatest enjoyment of the bath consists in ducking someone else, should not hold their victim's head under water more than five minutes at a time.

12. In case you are seized by a shark, present him with a copy of Life. When he begins to laugh, he will open his mouth and you can make your escape.

*Life*, August 1, 1889

# 1890

Lilla has been buying a bathing-suit. She is off to Normandy, and has chosen a compromise between the smartness of the "toilette pour les bains de mer" that hails from Paris, and the unmitigated hideosity of the bathing-gown *vulgaris Anglicanus*. Hers is very pretty, consisting of knickerbockers and tunic of dark blue serge, with a tan leather belt, short sleeves, and a sailor collar. I fancy she wears a corset while bathing, but so do many others who object to their figures spreading away, as they would otherwise do, perhaps beyond the power of the owners to collect them again into their previous limited compass. But what would Lady Harberton say?

Black silk bathing-dresses are the newest and most fashionable articles in that line at Newport, where the American belles perform their dilettante bathing. The bodices are gathered in at the waist, and are worn over tightly-fitting corsets – so I see by an American paper that Laurel has sent me.

*Truth*, July 24, 1890

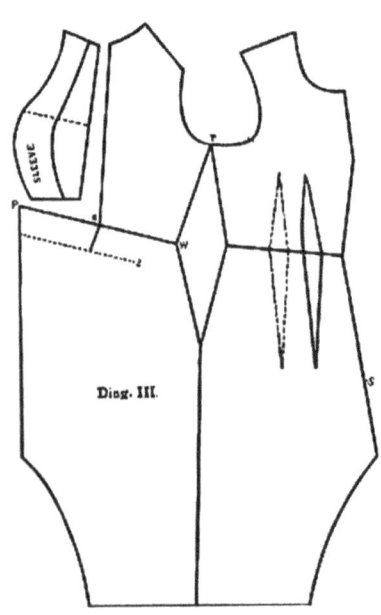

Diag. III.

IN offering a pattern for a bathing-dress [◄], I feel called upon to consider all young lady bathers as swimmers, present or prospective, and I am therefore giving a style of dress in which this class of bathers is more particularly considered. I give a close-fitting combination garment, sufficiently long from neck to knee for comfort and style, and loose enough in the body length to make exercise in it agreeable and pleasant. Non-swimmers always wear a short scanty skirt over this, fastening it at the waist with a broad belt. Swimmers sometimes dispense with the skirt, but that is simply a matter of individual fancy, as the skirt does not interfere with the pastime to any appreciable degree, if it is not made too full, and it has a distinct advantage where the combination alone, heavy with the water, might be felt to define the figure too closely. This is, however, altogether a matter for personal decision. If the combination is worn without a skirt, it should be made close-fitting to the sides and waist by means of darts and hip-scams. There is not a word of extenuation to be offered for the shapeless bag of flannel – tied in sharp at the waist and bulging out both above and below it, filling with air and water at every movement, and rendering its wearer ridiculous and uncomfortable – which some bothers affect, with the idea that it is more delicate than a close-fitting garment. To all such bathers, and any who are at all self-conscious or sensitive on the score of appearances, I give one brief scrap of advice – wear skirts. With the skirt the baggy style of dress is all right, and a girl floating on the water in one can feel that she looks like a flower, even if her unskirted sister does look like a mermaid.

Woman's World, 1890

### HER ECCENTRICITIES.

JUDGING from the description given in private letters received from American women who have been visiting French watering-places, the most startling bathing-costumes seen at Narragansett Pier or Long Branch this season are commonplace when compared with the creations of French women. The most remarkable were of plain black cashmere – very thin, too – with a white scarf around the waist. It is hardly necessary to say that few of these costumes were seen. In another costume no corsets were worn, their place being taken by fine, flesh-colored silken tulle tights. The suits had white flannel Russian blouses embroidered in metallic thread, with sleeves to the wrists. The trousers ceased at the knee, where they were confined by embroidered bands. Leggins of white buckskin were worn or not, according to fancy.

*The Illustrated American*, September 20, 1890

## 1891

One reads a great deal in the papers of the startling bathing-dresses worn by fair Americans at the sea-side. There are no signs of them at Narragansett. A bathing-suit can never be very becoming, but the fair bathers at the Pier make them as attractive as it is possible to do, and are never guilty of the offences against good taste and propriety committed by some of their English sisters at such French watering-places as Dieppe, Trouville, and Dinan. There is a great deal of lolling about on the sand by bathers of both sexes in bathing-costumes, but at what resort is this not the case?

One of the prettiest bathing-costumes on the beach – pretty because of its simplicity – is worn by Miss La France, of Buffalo, a very pretty brunette of beautiful figure. She wears a blue flannel sailor-suit with large white collar, and blue stockings to match. Her pretty head is adorned with a blue polka-dot handkerchief, and a long white sash encircles her slim waist. Miss La France is a famous long-distance swimmer, and daily can be seen in company with Miss Jennie McSweeney, another charming young lady and daring swimmer, swimming far out at sea. These two are by no means the sole representatives of their sex who are famous at the Pier for their natatorial achievements; but, on the contrary, there are several others who give the men sharp competition. ...

Deb Salisbury

[Answer to a letter to the Editor] Lady Bug. – Make your bathing-suit of dark blue alpaca. Very recently it has been discovered that this light wiry stuff sheds the water admirably, is not clinging or heavy as water-soaked flannel, and yet will make up into most charming suits. Make full trousers of the alpaca, to button at the knee; then over your shoulders draw a seamless jersey to match the alpaca's color; cut the jersey open at the throat, and turn back a sailor collar of alpaca. Over the jersey and trousers slip an alpaca bodice cut out round at the back and front, sleeveless, and gathered full into the band of the short alpaca skirt. Wear long stockings and an oil silk cap. If you should choose blue alpaca and jersey, trim lavishly with narrowest pipings of red silk.

*The Illustrated American*, August 15, 1891

## 1892

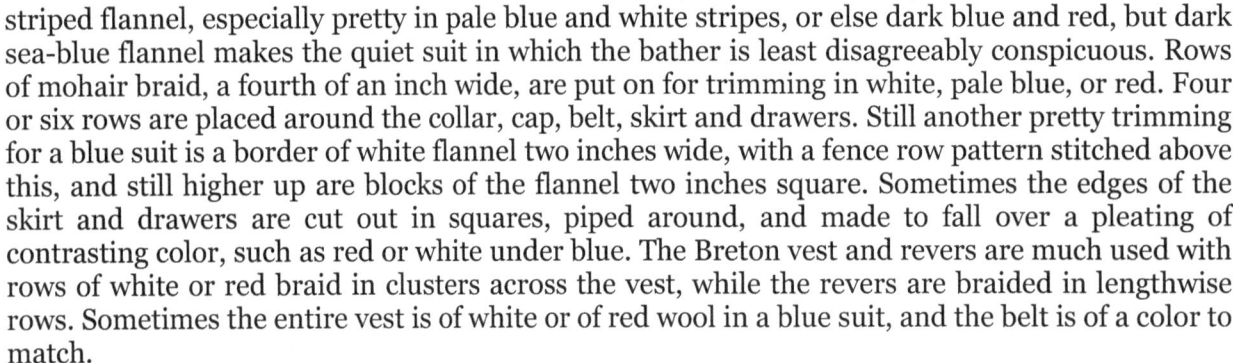

No. 139 pictures a bathing suit, modeled after the Russian blouse pattern; it is a blue flannel, trimmed with white mohair braid, and cross-stitched in white on the bodice and sleeves, and also on the stockings.

| | | |
|---|---|---|
| 8 yards flannel, | @ 63c, | $5.04 |
| 6 yards mohair braid, | @ 20c, | 1.20 |
| | | ------ |
| | | $6.24 |

*The Illustrated American*, June 25, 1892

### BATHING SUITS

Navy blue flannels or serges that do not hold much water are the favorite materials for bathing suits. White flannels and serges are also used, and there are combination suits that have a skirt, vest, and revers-collar of striped flannel, especially pretty in pale blue and white stripes, or else dark blue and red, but dark sea-blue flannel makes the quiet suit in which the bather is least disagreeably conspicuous. Rows of mohair braid, a fourth of an inch wide, are put on for trimming in white, pale blue, or red. Four or six rows are placed around the collar, cap, belt, skirt and drawers. Still another pretty trimming for a blue suit is a border of white flannel two inches wide, with a fence row pattern stitched above this, and still higher up are blocks of the flannel two inches square. Sometimes the edges of the skirt and drawers are cut out in squares, piped around, and made to fall over a pleating of contrasting color, such as red or white under blue. The Breton vest and revers are much used with rows of white or red braid in clusters across the vest, while the revers are braided in lengthwise rows. Sometimes the entire vest is of white or of red wool in a blue suit, and the belt is of a color to match.

The favorite bathing suit consists of a long garment with the waist and drawers in one, joined together by a belt on which the skirt is buttoned. The neck is cut high, with a sailor collar, but the preference is for short sleeves that leave the arms free for swimming. There is, however, the choice of several kinds of sleeves given with most suits, viz., the mere cap in the armhole, the short sleeve, the half-long, which reaches to the elbow, and the long coat sleeve extending low on the hand to protect it from the sun. The cap sleeves are narrow at the top and lapped there, but are wider underneath, and turned downward, so that no matter how the arm is lifted the armpits are well covered.

The waist with a yoke and box-pleats extending to a belt is one of the best designs, with ample fulness for concealing the figure. The yoke is cut very deep and square across to the arm and may be confined to the front of the garment, while the back has three wide box-pleats from the neck to the belt, and is covered at the top by the large square-cornered sailor collar. The drawers are sewed to the lower edge of the belt of the waist; they are buttoned down the front, and are made large and quite straight at the knee, and plainly hemmed, instead of being gathered to a band as they formerly were. The skirt is about two yards wide, and falls just below the cap of the knee, and the drawers extend two or three inches below the skirt. There should be an inside belt lining to the skirt (like that in children's kilt skirts) supplied with button-holes for the buttons on the belt of the waist. The outside of the belt does not show the buttons, and may be made of a contrasting color of flannel, or else trimmed with rows of braid; and this is so pretty, and to effectively holds the skirt, that it is not necessary to wear the canvas belt sometimes considered indispensable.

Besides the suit described, bathers who are well-dressed, wear long stockings, either black or matching in color the suit. Striped or fancy hose are never in the best taste. Ordinary bathers wear no shoes, but for those whose feet are tender or who desire to be shod, regular bathing shoes made of duck and similar materials are always to be purchased in cities near the sea. The oilskin cap, which is easily procured, is the proper head covering for ladies who do not wish their hair to get wet. Besides this, one requires some sort of hat or cap that will shade the eyes and face. A pretty straw hat tied under the chin but with no trimming does this effectually and is not injured by the water. Ladies sometimes show very pretty muslin bonnets shirred on reeds for the front and with short capes and full crowns that are very pretty. These require to be rinsed out and ironed after each wearing to be really presentable. A large full circular cloak of cloth or flannel should also be provided to complete a bathing outfit. This necessarily need not be exactly like the bathing suit in color, although if they correspond, it is in better taste. This is worn on the beach when the bather is not really in the water and aside from all questions of modesty is a desirable protection from undue exposure and chill.

Little girls wear bathing suits very similar to those of the ladies in material and make. Some machine embroidery, or else rows of bright braid, trim them. For boys and very small girls, are one-piece suits with waist and trousers together, made of stockinet in narrow stripes, or else of flannel.

Home Dressmaking, 1892

THE ETHICS OF THE BATHING DRESS.

The return of the season when the bathing dress becomes a standard costume in certain portions of the country suggests a consideration of the nature and essence of modesty in attire. During the next two months many thousands of women will appear upon the beaches along the North Atlantic coast clad in garments which, as the New York *Sun* remarks, "reveal the figure not less generously than its proportions are exposed by the tights worn upon the stage. Nay, the exposure of the bathing costume is even franker ... The stage figure may be made up by art. The figure of the feminine bather clad in the conventional bathing costume of the day is as nature made it. As it is, it frankly appears as the wearer walks along the beach and plunges in the surf."

The annual reign of this abbreviated garb of the seaside has been made the ground of an assertion that its wearers are deficient in womanly modesty. This sweeping charge is commonly made by those who have little or no first hand acquaintance with the subject, and like most sweeping charges it will not bear the light of dispassionate investigation. On the contrary, it is undoubtedly true that the regulation bathing dress is worn by thousands of women who would not tolerate anything that approached the improper or indelicate. That maidenly modesty and matronly virtue need not shrink from donning it is shown by the fact that they do not shrink.

The basis of modesty is the convention of civilized society; convention in matters of dress is justified by the appropriateness of the costume. In these two principles lies the whole philosophy of the bathing dress. To quote again from the *Sun's* essay, "when a manner of dress becomes conventional it cannot be immodest, whether it be the costume of the South Sea Islanders or of New York. When it is usual and prescribed it ceases to attract attention. Hence women who would shrink with horror from exposing their legs in a ball room think nothing of wearing low necked dresses there, while at the sea beach they will show their legs and hide their busts."

It is proverbially impossible to indict a nation. The question of a proper and suitable costume for bathing has been settled by the women of America, and their authority is amply sufficient to overrule any allegation of supposed immodesty. The pattern they have adopted is the one best fitted to the use for which it is designed. It is the one upon whose lines the women of the future may be dressed at all times. The most sensible suggestions for the reform of the ordinary feminine dress advocate models more or less similar to it. Last summer at Chautauqua one of the most interesting and important topics of discussion was the apparel of working women. It was generally agreed that as woman is more and more competing with man for her share of the world's work, her need of a more suitable costume is becoming urgent; and the model

recommended for adoption was designed after the style of the bathing dress.
*Munsey's Magazine*, July 1892

## COSTUMES FOR THE BRINY.

There are few costumes that call for more discrimination than those used by the feminine surf-bather. There are two deplorable extremes, and the medium is not always easy to strike. A bathing suit made conspicuous in any way – by its color, its trimming, or, most especially, by its cut – is an abomination. Scarcely less so is the suit made with so rigid a regard for respectability that it seems a hideous menace to all those surrounding. Women who go into the surf for the love of it, and they are the only ones who should brave the exertion, should dress themselves so as to best enjoy the advantages and insure their own comfort. It is one of the few occasions when appearance becomes a secondary consideration. The old model that combines the plaited bodice and trousers and in which the short skirt conceals the latter, cannot be improved upon. There are several details to be observed in order to avoid ungraceful effects. The skirt should always cover the knee, and the loose trousers meeting black or dark-blue stockings, should garter above the knee. Separate blouses or bodices that fasten over the skirt are by no means so secure as are those made in one with the trousers. A wide belt of canvas buckled over the skirt-band gives a neat and comfortable finish. A costume so made out of dark-blue or black – dark-blue is preferable as the brine soon causes black to rust – serge or flannel could not offend the most fastidious. The woman who fastens her bulgy surf-trousers low over her ankles, wears a skirt as long, and a shapeless gathered waist high up about her throat, who covers her feet with heavy canvas rubber-soled shoes, may be true to the connections she so hideously professes, but she presents a ludicrous sight and could not if she wanted to enjoy a swim or a dive so arrayed. But there are those who pine for novelty even in their bathing suits and for them may be noted the Russian blouse, belted and hanging over the skirt, which is short enough to display a ruffled finish to the trousers. Shoulder-straps several inches in width, starting from the belt behind and buttoning in front, as noticeable in the suspender-bodices, are innovations. There can be no objections to slightly sloping the neck of a bathing-dress, supplementing it with a pointed sailor collar, or simply tying the rolled collar with a scarf, nautical fashion; but a pronounced square-cut or rounded neck to a bathing-dress is inappropriate, to put it mildly. The bathing-hat is obsolete quite. The belle of to-day is too acute to crown her fair head with so unsightly an appendage, so she substitutes a silken kerchief of bright hue, as best suits her complexion. This she knots coquettishly about her head, and to further protect her tresses from the sea's rough usage, she coils them in an oiled silk cap that the kerchief of becoming hue quite hides. Galetea is a cloth that is much liked this season for bathing costumes, and Jersey cloth is likewise found to suit the purpose admirably. Galetea, it should be said, is a narrow-striped material, combining quiet shadings; the Jersey cloth is quite plain, as most of us know. In justice, it should be added, that the sailor collars that have so long supplemented the bathing-suit à la mode, have come to be termed "shoppy," as so many of the "ready-made" suits own them, and they are to be noted more generally on children's suits.
*Table Talk*, August 1892

## THE BATHING COSTUME

IF you are well and strong you are going to add to your strength by going in to find out whether the waves are really sad, or whether they won't tell you a story of their merriment, and of their acquaintance with fascinating mermaids and jolly mermen.

Of course, you want a pretty dress for this occasion. People of refinement choose for their bathing costumes those which, while they are most comfortable and permit the greatest freedom of the body, are yet absolutely modest. We read, and occasionally see very elaborate suits of white and pink, and those that are trimmed until they seem belter suited for a Roman chariot race than a sea bath. However, very dark blue or black coarse serge, or flannel, makes the most comfortable suit, and perfect modesty is achieved when this suit is in two pieces; that is, the trousers which reach just below the knees, and the bodice, which comes up well about the throat, and has elbow sleeves, are in combination, making one, while over this is worn the short skirt which fastens to buttons about the waist, the mode of attachment being hidden under a canvas belt. Long black woolen stockings are in order, and if you are going to bathe much, and wish to keep them from wearing out, it will be wise to get them a size larger, and to insert in their feet the soles sold in the stores for knitted slippers. It is best to wear a rubber cap, and so protect one's hair from the salt water, because this is certain, in time, to injure it, though one often sees articles recommending the salt bath for the hair.

By the by, that woman will feel the best who takes her plunge after having a very light breakfast; she will come out feeling desperately hungry, and then she should eat something, after which she should rest, and, if possible, sleep awhile. If you are inclined to be chilly as you come out of the water, have a long cloak of red Turkish toweling, with a pointed hood attached to it; throw this about yourself, drawing the hood over your head. I advise red for this, because it will not so readily fade when the salt water has to dry upon it. Then, too, it makes a pretty spot on the beach. It is scarcely necessary to say to a well-bred girl that I do not advise her lingering on the beach in her bathing dress, though she sometimes does this from thoughtlessness. What she should do is to go right from the bath house to the water, and when she has plunged and dived and floated and swum until she believes that nature intended her to live in the water, and when somebody else is telling her that it is time for her to come in, she must go right from the embrace of the big billows to her dressing room.

*The Ladies' Home Journal*, August 1892

**Bathing Suits and Trunks.** Bathing "trunks" are usually made of knitted cotton or worsted, and shaped to cover the loins and trunk of the body. Bathing "suits" are of various shapes and made of many materials. Surah silk of thick quality is used extensively. It is claimed that it does not retain as much water as flannel, and that it does not cling so closely to the figure. The medium quality bathing suits are manufactured of flannel and of a coarse wiry cheviot. The more modest suits are made with the waist and drawers in one, cut in continuous pieces or attached to the same belt; a seperate [sic] skirt reaching to the knees is then buttoned on to this belt. The drawers fall below the knees and are quite wide with rubber in the hem to draw them into shape. Jersey suits are also manufactured and these do not shrink. The waist and skirt are all in one piece in this variety, and the skirt is made full. The drawers are close fitting like equestrian tights and have stockings woven with them – but how and where they are fastened no man has ever found out. ...

**Moreen**. [Formerly *moireen,* from moire]. A fabric of mohair or wool filling and cotton warp; formerly made in imitation of moire silk, for purposes of upholstery. It was sometimes plain, but more commonly "watered" with embossed patterns by passing the cloth over a hot brass cylinder, on which was engraved various flowers and other fancy figures. At present it is manufactured to some extent and used for petticoats, bathing dresses, etc., and the heavier qualities for curtains.

A Complete Dictionary of Dry Goods, 1892

# 1893

Storm serge is an admirable material for bathing-suits, as being so prepared to repel moisture, it clings less to the body than ordinary serge when in the water. Cardinal red is a favorite color this season.

*Frank Leslie's Illustrated Weekly,* July 6, 1893

She almost fainted when she saw
    She showed a bit of stocking;
But later, in her bathing-dress
    Which barely reached her knees,
She walked the beach in carelessness,
    Complacent as you please.
      *Life,* August 10, 1893

BATHING SUITS.

If there is any thing specially noticeable in eastern illustrations of women's bathing costumes this summer, it is the shortness of the skirts and the lowness of the necks. Now, no one questions the disagreeable feeling caused by heavy and voluminous clothing in the water. Especially is this the case if one is learning to swim. But I very seriously question the propriety, to say nothing of the modesty, of women going into the water with low-necked costumes and little protection in the way of clothing for the lower limbs. Some people appear to be very much shocked if they go into a gymnasium and find woman clothed in a divided skirt and blouse. But such people seem to be quite willing to go into the water at our Lake resorts where there is a very mixed assembly of men, good, bad and indifferent, mostly indifferent and some decidedly bad, with little clothes on. They have small protection for the limbs, and less – when the water has once soaked their clothing – for the upper part of the body. I am sure bathing is a delightful and healthful luxury, but confess to an old-fashioned prejudice against seeing women so exposed in our public bathing resorts. Small need then to cut the neck lower and shorten the skirts. By the way, there is nothing better for bathing suits than lined Turkish toweling; and have the neck high, the sleeves at least to the elbows, and the drawers fastened below the knee, while the skirt reaches to that distance also. Next to Turkish is our own home made linsey.

*The Deseret Weekly*, August 12, 1893

"There are many English people here, and we are told that they come early in the season and stay late. The season at Trouville begins about the middle of June and closes soon after October 1st. French people of fashion would not be seen here before the opening or after the close, as they would consider their characters ruined by doing anything so much out of the common course of things. A considerable number of visitors are those who travel with the *billet-circulaire,* or circular ticket, which enables the traveller to visit several cities and points on the coast within a certain specified time. As the holder of a circular ticket wants to see as many places as possible, he can only afford a day or two to each point where he stops off from the railway train. The circular ticket is by no means unknown in America; neither is the circular tourist and his ways, as every hotel-keeper can testify.

"The scene in general reminds me of much that we saw at Frascati's, which may be taken as a miniature edition of Trouville. But Frascati cannot compare with Trouville in its beach, which is of the softest sand that the bather could wish for to walk upon with his bare feet. There is no need of bathing-shoes here, but fashion prescribes them. The style of bathing-shoe worn at Trouville is a linen gaiter with the front cut away and lacing around the ankle. Every traveller is supposed to carry them in his baggage, but any one who comes here without them may find an abundance in the shops or at the bathing-houses.

"Bathing may take place at any hour, but the proper time for it is at high tide, provided it does not interfere with dinner or some other entertainment of a practical character. Then everybody goes to the beach, either to bathe or gaze at the bathers, or upon other people who don't go into the water. The non-bathers are far more numerous than those who dip into the sea, and of those who venture upon bathing there is only a small proportion who can swim. And now a word as to the bathing-dresses which are the fashion here.

"Trousers and jacket, the latter gathered in at the waist, compose the feminine costume of Trouville, together with an oilskin cap to keep the hair dry, and Amelias (as the linen slippers, or gaiters, are called) for protection to the feet. (Mary says I must say 'basque' instead of jacket, and then it will be better understood by feminine readers. Well, then, here goes for basque.)

"Some of the bathing-dresses are elaborately ornamented, while others are plain enough to satisfy a Quaker of the time of Roger Williams. Occasionally you see an American woman with a dress of the style in vogue at Newport or Bar Harbor, and we are told that a few of the French visitors have copied it. But the fashion is not likely to change, as the company that owns the bathing-houses has a large stock on hand of the old pattern, and you can readily understand that the views of the managers will be conservative.

"Everything is done by rule here, and if you want to do as you please your only course will be to please to do as the regulations require. The 'bureau' looks after everything, and when you want a bath you must begin at the bureau by buying the needed tickets. I say tickets, because there are several things for which you must pay, and each payment requires a ticket. There is the simple bath, the bath with a cabin, and the *bain de luxe;* then there is the costume (the *peignoir),* towels.

head-dress, slippers, the *baigneur* (whose occupations were described at Havre), the master or mistress of the baths, together with a variety of extras and supplementary things. Doctor Bronson says he is reminded of the hotel somewhere along the Missouri River which required the traveller to pay three dollars a day, with meals and lodging extra. The bathing-cabins are on wheels, so that they can be moved to suit the tide; and though you pay by ticket for the cabin, the driver of the horse that moves your cabin expects a gratuity for the service. If the horse had been educated up to the ability to demand a gratuity, you may be sure he would have exacted it before we left him.

"The part of the beach allotted to bathers is divided into three parts by means of cables that run far out into the water. The middle section is for families, and on either side of it are the sections for women or men exclusively. Out in front of each section is a boat securely anchored, and each boat has steps which hang over the stern a foot or more into the water. The swimmers go out to these boats, which are in charge of skilful *baigneurs,* and they may have instruction in the art of swimming if they desire it, though necessarily the lessons will be short.

"We have had our share of fun, sitting on the beach and watching the bathers. There are fewer swimmers among them than you will see in the bathing assemblages at an American sea-side resort, and many of those who are able to swim do so very awkwardly. They flounder around like porpoises – no, not like porpoises, because those denizens of the deep are graceful and know how to take care of themselves, and such is not the case with the people we are considering.

"Yesterday two women who wanted to display their abilities in bathing created a scene by losing control of themselves, screaming loudly, swallowing a quantity of salt-water, and running quite a risk of being strangled. The *baigneurs* seized them and brought them up to the shore as soon as possible. One of the women fainted, and the other became hysterical and kept on screaming after she had been stretched on the sand. Both were liberally drenched with water from buckets, which stopped the shrieks of the hysterical one and brought the other to her senses. Then they were hurried off to their cabins, where the attendants bathed their feet in hot water and helped them assume their ordinary apparel. As Byron says, 'Both were young, and one was beautiful.' Fortunately they were light in weight, or they would have been somewhat difficult for the *baigneurs* to manage.

"There is a delightful stretch of beach for walking, and for children and dogs to play upon when the tide is out. When the beach happens to be uncovered on a warm afternoon all the visiting population of Trouville seems to be gathered there. The older ones saunter about, young people and middle-aged ones play at croquet, children romp and have a thoroughly 'good time,' and the dogs accompany them in their rompings, unless they happen to belong to adult and dignified persons, whom they are obliged to follow demurely. Some of the young people are in their bathing-dresses, and wander about in the pools armed with nets and baskets for the purpose of catching shrimps. 'We don't get many shrimps,' said an English girl to Mary yesterday, 'but there's a great deal of fun in trying to catch them.'

The Boy Travellers in Central Europe, 1893

Deb Salisbury

# 1894

[ad for] Continental Knitting Mills, ...
MEN'S AND BOYS'
BATHING SUITS
In Worsted, Wool, Flannel and Cotton
[ ← ]
*The Clothier and Furnisher*, February 1894

The bicycle suits and swimming suits are best in washables or blue flannel, and are in the drills and ducks with stripings and in solid colors.
*The Clothier and Furnisher*, May 1894

An attractive bathing costume made of navy-blue flannel is represented at figure No. 3 SS, the style being a vast improvement upon the unshapely garments formerly in vogue. The waist and trousers are made together. A casing adjusted underneath at the waist-line holds an elastic band that regulates the fulness to the body, and an elastic inserted in a casing made a little above the lower edge of each leg draws the fulness and forms a frill below. The neck is cut out in moderately low, round outline, and to the upper edge is joined a circular Bertha that falls naturally in waves and is decorated with two rows of narrow white worsted braid above one row of wide braid. Similarly trimmed double caps fall over the arms in lieu of sleeves. A short, full skirt bordered with one row of very wide below three rows of narrower braid falls from a belt that is covered with wide braid, and in the seam joining the skirt and belt is included a fluted peplum trimmed with two rows of narrow braid. The pattern of this costume is No. 6838,

**9284**
Ladies' and Misses'
Bathing and
Dusting Cap:
2 sizes.
Either size,
5d. or 10 cents.

which costs 1s. 3d. or 30 cents. If a less fanciful effect were desired, the neck could be finished high with a standing collar, long sleeves could be added, and the trousers could be allowed to hang loosely at the knee. Several modifications of this style may easily be effected, the various modes of shaping being indicated in the pattern. With the suit are worn black cashmere hose, and a cap formed of a blue silk handkerchief jauntily arranged to fit the head. A cap of this kind is to be preferred to the regulation cap of oiled silk, which, although eminently practical, is far from becoming.

At figure No. 4 SS a bathing costume for a miss is pictured made up in cream-white French flannel showing blue dots. It corresponds in style with the ladies' costume shown at figure No. 3 SS. The skirt is trimmed at the bottom with blue braid applied in points, and the Bertha is similarly decorated and is cut away below the braid. The sleeves are short, and over each falls a cap that is ornamented and cut out to correspond with the Bertha. The sleeves are edged with braid, and a blue webbing belt encircles the waist. Black

**3285**    **3285**
Ladies' Bathing Corset
(Copyright): 10 sizes.
Bust measures,
28 to 46 inches.
Any size, 10d. or 20 cents.

**3033 3033**
Pattern for a Cap
(Available for Tam
O'Shanter or
Sailor Style):
7 sizes.
Hat sizes, 6 to 6¾;
or Head measures,
19¼ to 21½ inches.
Any size, 5d. or 10 cents.

stockings are worn, and about the head is tied a white silk handkerchief. The pattern used in making the suit is No. 6894, price 1s. or 25 cents.
*The Delineator*, June 1894

Deb Salisbury

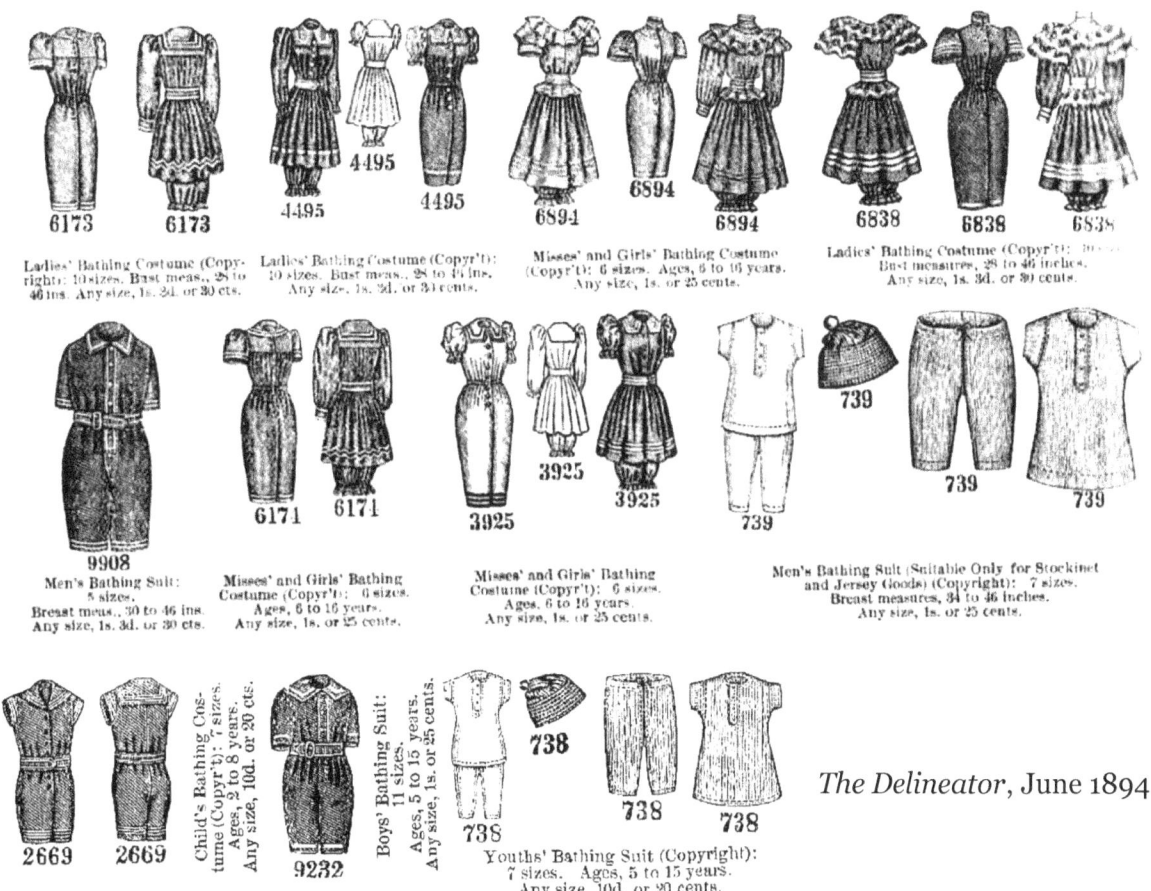

Ladies' Bathing Costume (Copyright): 10 sizes. Bust meas., 28 to 46 ins. Any size, 1s. 3d. or 30 cts.

Ladies' Bathing Costume (Copyr't): 10 sizes. Bust meas., 28 to 46 ins. Any size, 1s. 3d. or 30 cts.

Misses' and Girls' Bathing Costume (Copyr't): 6 sizes. Ages, 6 to 16 years. Any size, 1s. or 25 cents.

Ladies' Bathing Costume (Copyr't): 10 sizes. Bust measures, 28 to 46 inches. Any size, 1s. 3d. or 30 cents.

Men's Bathing Suit: 5 sizes. Breast meas., 30 to 46 ins. Any size, 1s. 3d. or 30 cts.

Misses' and Girls' Bathing Costume (Copyr't): 6 sizes. Ages, 6 to 16 years. Any size, 1s. or 25 cents.

Misses' and Girls' Bathing Costume (Copyr't): 6 sizes. Ages, 6 to 16 years. Any size, 1s. or 25 cents.

Men's Bathing Suit (Suitable Only for Stockinet and Jersey Goods) (Copyright): 7 sizes. Breast measures, 34 to 46 inches. Any size, 1s. or 25 cents.

Child's Bathing Costume (Copyr't): 7 sizes. Ages, 2 to 8 years. Any size, 10d. or 20 cts.

Boys' Bathing Suit: 11 sizes. Ages, 5 to 15 years. Any size, 1s. or 25 cents.

Youths' Bathing Suit (Copyright): 7 sizes. Ages, 5 to 15 years. Any size, 10d. or 20 cents.

*The Delineator*, June 1894

## BATHING SUITS.

This year's bathing suits are by this time well drenched with salt water, and having in a measure lost their freshness, may safely be commented on by the most savage critics. The first thing to be said about them is that they differ very much at the different resorts. At Newport they are never conspicuous, as the "smart set" there bathe, if at all, at an early hour of the morning, and are rarely exposed to the observation of any but their maids and the bathing master. Their costumes, therefore, are of the plainest, and often two or three years old. On the opposite side of the bay, at Narragansett Pier, the bathing hour is the most important period of the day, and all the fun and jollity goes on after bathing, when the band plays on the Casino piazza. The bathing costumes here are always *chic* and picturesque, but they no longer have the reputation they once had for being unduly abbreviated and too *fin de siècle*. The prettiest women at the Pier this summer have worn black serge or black mohair, quite plain, or with white, red, or blue trimmings of hercules braid. The Turkish trousers, which were formerly quite universal, have been superseded this year by tights, which, of course, are not bulky and do not tend to magnify the size of the waist; but the trouble with them is in the shrinkage, and the fact that they are obliged to be absolutely peeled off when the wearer reaches her bath-house. Over the tights is worn a skirt of the length that the bather pleases. Some ladies have it only to the knee, others wear it a few inches longer. A blouse waist buttoning on to the band of the skirt, so that the waves may not detach them and leave the wearer minus one or the other, is the most usual make, with large balloon sleeves reaching just below the shoulder, and as many capes, furbelows, and epaulettes as may be supposed to suit the taste of Neptune's kingdom. A bright-colored turban tied over the oil-skin cap, similar to those worn by the Southern negress, completes the costume, which is as modest and comfortable as a bathing dress can be made. At Long Branch, Asbury Park, and indeed all along the Jersey shore, in common with the several places on Long Island, fashion runs riot on the beaches. All the colors of the rainbow may be seen there, and one of the favorite combinations is orange and black, in stripes, with arms naked from the shoulders, and skirts that, as the

Frenchman said, "are hardly begun before they come to an end." A party of four women astonished the boarders at a hotel on Long Island by appearing in the surf on the Fourth of July in red skirts with bands of white edged with blue running around the skirt: shirts of blue cambric with white dots, and sailor collars of red. Turbans made out of American flags completed this highly patriotic costume. White duck has been largely employed this summer for bathing gowns; and although it absorbs the water and becomes very heavy, yet it does not cling to the figure, and is more becoming than a woollen material. A pretty suit of it has been worn at New London by a lady who is celebrated for her fearless swimming and diving. It is made in the prevailing fashion, with a blouse waist, and skirt coming half way between knee and ankle. Several bands of light blue serge encircle the skirt, and the bust is held up and the blouse kept in place by a broad belt or peasant's waist of blue which fastens in front and is finished by a rosette. A sailor collar of blue and large sleeves of the same, without capes or frills, make this one of the prettiest salt water costumes of the season.

At one or two places the Bloomer suit has been worn, but, we are happy to say, not where modest women most do congregate. The Bloomer is not unlike a man's pajamas, being without a skirt, and with a pair of Turkish trousers tied over, or perhaps buttoned – we will give it the benefit of the doubt – to a loose shirt of wool or cotton material. These are no doubt very comfortable for swimming, and are worn a great deal on the coast of France: but there, as in England, huge machines or bathing houses on wheels take the bathers down to the edge of the water, and they are engulfed by the waves before they can be seen. There is no running up and down the beach, or talking with friends and acquaintances between the bath-house and the waves, as is so common here. Many ladies sacrifice so much to their appearance on the beaches that they bathe in corsets. They might as well sleep in them, as far as health is concerned, as nothing is so important as unobstructed circulation and a free action of the heart when swimming, diving, and indulging in the violent exercise of buffeting with the salt sea waves.

*Godey's Magazine*, August 1894

FIG. 226. BATHING COSTUMES. – The figure at upper left corner shows bathing costume of dark blue alpaca, with square yoke belt, and band about the skirt of white flannel with blue polka dots. The hat is a blue Tam-o'Shanter. The lower figure on the left shows black serge costume trimmed with white. The upper figure on the right shows a perfectly plain black serge with pointed yoke and bodice. The lower figure on the right shows gown of striped tennis cloth trimmed with red braid. The hat, a fashion rarely seen now, is of rough straw trimmed with red. [ ← ]

*Godey's Magazine*, August 1894

*Bathing Dress.*

The favourite marine-blue serge is unrivalled for these costumes, and when relieved with white or red looks quite charming. Yokes and collars of white have lines of narrow red braid following the outline, and white braid in different widths is used to adorn a costume of dark blue.

A pretty gown of blue serge was made with a blouse jacket smocked at the neck with rows of red stitching and a tiny heading standing up, lined with red Turkey twill; a deep piece of serge cut on the bias was gathered into the arm-hole and the outer edge encased an elastic, forming thus a large puff-sleeve at the top of the arm. A wide scarf belt of red crossed the back of the jacket, and was sewn at each under-arm seam, fastening in the front, the jacket forming a deep basque beneath. Wide serge "bloomers" reaching half-way below the knee, with a one-inch band and frill embroidered with red, completed this becoming costume.

Health and hygiene insist upon the wisdom of immersing the head, and argue with truth of violated precepts and consequent giddiness and headache. On the other hand fashion, and in some instances vanity, assert that the hair should be prettily coiled in a high Greek twist and the head and face held up out of the water, otherwise sunburn is as imminent as dank locks.

*Cassell's Magazine*, Summer 1894

THE ART OF SOCIAL BATHING.

THE spontaneous, unpremeditated bathe is best of all, when sunbeams light the water, and the rocks are dry and hot. Yet it has drawbacks inseparable from its character. In all forms of civilised bathing there are three periods, each of which offers room for failure, – that of undressing, of bathing, and of dressing. In the spontaneous bathe, the first is usually too rapid for criticism, the second too exhilarating for description, and the third too depressing for recollection, from lack of towels. Moreover, even on the most unfrequented shore it is seldom sacred from interruption. Hence the predicaments of bathers, which mainly occur to those who indulge in this delightful but inartistic form. Besides, it is limited to male bathers, and if the development of sea-bathing as a social institution is to make the progress it deserves, this solitary and selfish enjoyment of its pleasures, so dear to the English male mind, must be discouraged by the offer of something equally delightful to the swimmer, and more attractive to both sexes.

Bathing, in the present month, means as a rule sea-bathing, and as generally practised, it follows the custom of fifty years ago, without change, and, it must be added, without much enjoyment either. The art of bathing in society, as a delightful marine amusement for all ages and sexes, was never contemplated when sea-bathing first became an English institution. It was looked upon as a wholesome but somewhat unpleasant duty, by most men, and nearly all women, to be got over as quickly as possible before making a toilet and appearing in general company. The bathing-machine was for the moment the Englishman's, or Englishwoman's, "castle," with a private piece of sea attached to it, limited so far as rights of ownership could be exercised, to a width corresponding to that of the "machine," and in point of time to the utmost which could be had for sixpence. "Trespassing" was indignantly resented, and it was, and in many places is still, very "bad form" even to look at your neighbours, a feeling which in cases where ladies and gentlemen were bathing in juxtaposition was hardly to be wondered at. For the costume of the former was as hideous as it was uncomfortable. A tunic, of the roughest and coarsest dark-blue serge, tied round the waist with a string, a pair of sacks, reaching half-way between the knees and ankles, and a cap of oilskin, suited for the head-gear of a fish-wife landing herrings, being supplied, with the two sandy towels, as part of the outfit included in the hire of the "machine." The name given to this marine contrivance argues a Scotch or French origin, though it possesses neither the comfort which is suggested by the first, nor the elegance inferred from the second. Its merits, if any, were those of comfort, for it kept out wind and rain, and though its damp, sandy, cold, gritty floor was disagreeable, and the wooden steps on its "sea-face " were the cause of sad disaster to tender feet and shins in ascending before the impulse of a breaker, it enabled clothes to be kept dry, and its cracked looking-glass gave some aid in completing a rough toilet. On the other hand, its moving powers were seldom such as to enable the bathers to take a header in deep water; and the order by which a proprietor endeavoured to comply with the demand for its removal into deeper water, – " Gent, says he wants to have a 'header,' take him out into the *drain*," – is believed to be based on the actual practice of a well-known Sussex seaside town.

If bathing is to take a place among social institutions, the question of costume takes perhaps the first place. There is nothing so indelicate as clothes, when they are "off," as the author of "Troy Town" justly observes, and nothing so charming when they are on, and are suitable and becoming; and as this is mainly, though not entirely, a ladies' question, the adoption of a pretty sea-dress is all-important. Form and material have already been settled, so far as authority can do so, in the pages of the volume of the "Badminton Library " devoted to " Swimming;" and the pretty picture of ladies bathing in costume, which there appears, should reconcile the most exacting to its use. "The best material," we read, "is Turkey twill," and the cut of the dress is quite charming. "The costume should be tight-fitting, and made with knickerbockers and a short skirt;

if for speed-swimming, the absence of skirt is preferable. The dress should be trimmed with the club colours, and made neatly but not elaborately. Waterproof-caps are worn by many ladies; while for men the University costume is best." By this is meant, not a cap and gown, but a close-fitting cotton garment, made in one piece, and reaching from the shoulders to above the knee. These can be bought of almost any colour, and to judge by the variety worn where social bathing is in vogue, there is no lack of care displayed by the other sex in the selection of a becoming costume. It is said that even the Radley boys, who, like the Etonians, much resented the idea of any costume at all when bathing in the Thames, were induced to wear it by the judicious provision of suits adorned with the colours of their "houses" and elevens, and Boon became as eager to obtain them as they had before been contumacious in refusal. With a "neat and appropriate" costume provided for both sexes, the difficulty of joint enjoyment of the greatest pleasure of the sea-side disappears. The rest is a matter of detail which can easily be arranged; for that exuberance of marine attire by which Continental and American lady bathers sometimes defeat their object, is likely to be sternly discouraged by the practical good sense of English women when engaged in an amusement which they seem to enjoy even more than men. The following extract from an American magazine of fashion is, however, perhaps worth quoting by way of warning: – "The unbecoming appearance of many lady-bathers has led us to ask the particulars of the toilet of one whom we have remarked as looking equally well dressed, when in the water and on shore. She first dons a thin woollen under-garment, and over this she wears a corset with most of the 'bones' removed. She then puts on a pair of black stockings, and the bathing-dress, which should have an upper skirt reaching almost to the tops of the bathing-shoes, which should be of white canvas. The bathing-dress should be dark, blue or black, as it makes the figure look better than a light one. The details should be left to taste, but a few white embroidered anchors or a little white or red fringe will give lightness. She plaits her hair underneath a close-fitting bathing-cap, but in order to avoid the unbecoming appearance which this lends to the head, she fixes a false plait, pinned on below the hair, to fall below the bathing-cap behind, and a few little curls, arranged in a *négligé* fashion, are sewn inside the bathing-cap to fall over the forehead." The effect of this over-thoughtful attention to detail, and especially of the long dark skirt, when soaked with sea-water, must have tended to produce the vision of that–

"Wet shroud wrapped round lady gay,"

which so appalled the seer of Ravensheuch in prophetic mood; for it is a fact that long clinging costumes have a far more "undressed" appearance in the water than the shorter dress now generally adopted by lady swimmers. The other means and appliances for the art of bathing properly understood, are suitable dressing-rooms and a moveable spring-board. The old bathing-machines, drawn up above high-water mark, are available in most sea-side towns. But tents, pitched on the shingle, so as to avoid a sandy floor, are more convenient, and easily removeable at the end of the season. At "Sea View," in the Eastern corner of the Isle of Wight, these pairs of "family tents" are pitched in a long row just beneath the trees which overhang the beach, and make a very pretty background to the bright line of the bay. A moveable spring-board is easily made by fixing the board on to a pair of wheels, which can be run out into the water as far as is wished, and withdrawn before the flowing tide. Diving from the board is a source of endless amusement, and makes a change from the monotony of swimming in deep water. Ladies, now that a weekly visit to the swimming-bath in summer has become a recognised part of the routine of girls' schools, are often equally good, or better, swimmers than men, and are at least as enthusiastic in the pursuit of their pet amusement. One well-known hostess has for some years made fresh-water swimming one of the features of her country-house hospitality, and usually holds a "water-competition " as the closing entertainment for her guests' amusement. Such water-parties, held daily between breakfast and luncheon, would be the greatest possible attraction which could be arranged by those whose country-houses lie near the sea, and make the morning hours between breakfast and luncheon a time of active enjoyment instead of a period of rather bored lounging, or not too successful efforts to kill time in groups, or in the anti-social occupations of reading and correspondence.

*The Spectator*, August 11, 1894

# 1895

To meet the requirements of a public bath, the average American bather is clothed from his neck to his knees. The American suit for the male bather consists generally of a Jersey shirt with flannel trousers, or else of a flannel suit in one piece, belted at the waist. If this is so with the male American bather, it is still more so with the American woman. The proper suit for her consists of a garment similar in cut to the one-garment suit of the man, over which is worn a skirt which should reach at least to the knees. Stockings are, of course, as indispensable to the woman bather in America as they are in ordinary life.

In considering the European types of bathers, we find that they narrow down to two classes, English and French. All continental nations, of course, bathe, but the bathers of these two nations are found in so much greater numbers that any comparison is naturally limited to them. The other continental nations imitate closely the French in their bathing customs. The French bathing-suit is more like the American than the English, because the French permit "mixed bathing," that is, the bathing of men and women together. The skirt on the Frenchwoman's suit, however, exists more in courtesy than in fact, not averaging more than six inches in length from the belt, while the trouser leg, if the male observer is permitted to speak of such articles of apparel, usually reaches to within a few inches of the ankle, while stockings are not worn at all. Sandals, however, commonly complete the costume. The material of the suit is generally dark in color and heavy in texture; that abomination of abominations, the white suit, being rarely seen.

The Frenchman's suit is made in one piece of some thin material, striped in gayest shades of red and blue; it is made without the slightest pretension to fit, and hangs like a gaudy meal bag from the shoulders. As far as colors go, the Frenchman is the butterfly of the two, but neither sex look in the water like anything but guys. This is a surprise and shock to those Americans who have heard so much of the beautiful but risqué bathing costumes of the French watering resorts.

*The Cosmopolitan*, June 1895

There is a great impression prevailing in Europe that our bathing dresses and customs are grossly bold and suggestive. This mistaken idea grows undoubtedly from the class of illustration and incident which goes abroad, just as, similarly, French bathing has been grossly libeled by French writers and artists. It is a much vexed question anyway, this idea of modesty. Like the definition of beauty, it is impossible, almost, to draw the line in bathing or in the ball-room. The individual case must be decided on its own merits. After all is said, the question of modesty simply resolves itself into a question of custom. The authorities may attempt to regulate the suits, as they do at Asbury Park, but it is futile. It is far better to rest on the existence of a healthy public sentiment, which, after all, settles all questions. I remember seeing a young woman wear the ordinary knickerbocker costume of our resorts at an inland bathing-place in South Jersey, where the old-fashioned ankle trousers with long skirts were still in vogue. The feeling of horror at such daring spread to all there, for it was a breach of custom, and the costume, which would have been modest and pretty elsewhere, looked most shocking in the midst of its uglier companions. Consequently, while American society now accepts the short skirt, knickerbockers, and long, black stockings as the proper suit for a woman bather, yet it is a costume that in the city, or even on the sea-shore board-walk, would be simply scandalous.

There has grown up at the various resorts the use of lighter shaded flannels, silks, and serges as suitings for bathing dresses. In most instances they should be avoided by the right-minded American woman, for most of them become more or less transparent on being wet, and cling as if dipped in glue. Black, dark blue, and deep maroon are the only proper colors for the salt-water bath.

When the American woman becomes daring in her dress or conduct, she follows the great American tendency and goes to the last extremes. I never saw at any European sea-shore resorts costumes that were as suggestive or indecent as the thin, white suits which a dozen women bathers wear every summer at Atlantic City. Nor do we see abroad such looseness of behavior as is tolerated occasionally at our larger resorts. To the credit of the vast majority of bathers it must be conceded that such dressing or conduct is conspicuous more from its rarity, and exists simply from the great underlying principle that the authorities cannot interfere with one's personal tastes

or ideas of propriety.
*The Cosmopolitan*, July 1895

THE Englishman shows nothing more typical of himself than the manner in which he bathes; the habits, the views, and the very life-history of that nation are expressed at the sea-shore. The simplest consideration of the question shows this fact. The English look upon ocean bathing as immodest; therefore, they go to the whole length that is possible, and bathe in a manner that is an indescribable shock to their visitors. The English are blunt and direct in thought and speech; their bathing customs are expressive of these two great national characteristics. As they believe ocean bathing to be immodest, they have decided, like the French, that it should be done in private, and, being a more logical people, they have carried this idea to a more rational conclusion. The first essential, of course, in private ocean bathing is that there should be no commingling of the sexes; the French, in permitting this, stand in a very illogical position; in consequence, in England, men and women bathe separately. As a simple, unqualified assertion, this statement sounds extremely well; but the English, being only human, have not carried out their ideas as consistently as they might have done. The bathing-grounds of the two sexes at the various resorts are, as a rule, only a few hundred feet distant from each other; consequently, each set of bathers is in plain sight of the other, while the beach at each point is often crowded with men and women watching the bathing. As a practical result, therefore, as far as any seclusion or privacy is concerned, the bathers might just as well use the same grounds.

It is just here that the great inconsistency of English bathing comes in, for the most critical cannot complain that they have not carried out their ideas of privacy in their bathing-suits to its fullest degree. The English bathing costumes, if such a dignified term may be applied to them, are most extraordinary. The suits for the women are made in one piece, skirts not considered necessary; in short, they are simply the old-fashioned bathing-suits worn in America by men. As women, as a rule, wear their clothes much tighter than men, and as the materials are generally much flimsier than those used in French and American suits, the effect upon the looker-on, who is a stranger to English bathing, is often startling. In addition, these suits are cut, as a rule, quite low in the neck, frequently being as low as a décolleté ball-gown, necessitating considerable care on the part of the wearers to keep them from being washed away by the waves; while the trouser leg is cut short, frequently not reaching to the knee, occasionally edged with white lace, while, of course, no stockings are worn. As these suits are not supposed to be seen by the male spectator, they express fully the English sense of propriety; to the American who does not possess such a logical mind, their existence at first sight is wholly incomprehensible; they correspond far nearer to the conceptions which Americans have of the French bathing-resorts than do those of Ostend or Trouville.

But if the English woman's suit is a shock to the modesty of an American traveler, no words will express his surprise on seeing the remarkable garb of the bathing Englishman. This costume is nothing but the familiar swimming-tights worn by American boys when they slip away for a quiet swim to some unfrequented spot on lake or river. An American boy in an English suit would hide in the bushes on the approach of a passer-by. Personally, I shall never forget my feelings when I ventured to step out of my bathing-machine into the water at Brighton, in full view of fully five thousand people, many of them not twenty-five feet away. Involuntarily I could not rid myself of the expectation of seeing the great crowd rise up, inexpressibly shocked, and call for a "Bobby" to drag me back to my senses and to my bathing-machine; but human nature is intensely imitative, and a few minutes in the water restored my confidence, and I swam wholly forgetful of my unadorned appearance. There is one advantage of this style of bathing; it is the delightful reaction of the salt water on the bare flesh; it is interfered with, or lost entirely, when the limbs are enveloped in clinging flannel.

In consequence of this method of bathing, when the untraveled Englishman hears that in America and France men and women bathe together, he is unspeakably shocked, for he cannot imagine for a moment that there is any other style of bathing dress than that of his own country. As a result of this separate bathing, the English bath is stupid and unpleasant. That pleasant, proper camaraderie, which is possible at French and American resorts, is wholly lacking. The women have not the confidence and comfort inspired by the presence of male bathers, while the men lose that attraction which comes in helping women in any athletic sport. Probably it is as a result of this separate method of bathing that there are no great crowds seen in the water at English resorts, such as are found in America. The English, unlike the French, as a nation, are fond of salt-water bathing, looking upon it as a very healthful sport; but unwittingly they miss the essence of its great attraction.

The English use the bathing-machine in a similar manner to the French; the bathing-masters follow the ebb and rise of the tide religiously; as a result it is no uncommon matter to find that one's machine has been shifted many feet from its original position, and the bather is then compelled to spend many weary minutes hunting for his own particular van. As the little houses are as alike as peas in a pod, he is likely to ruffle the tempers of the occupants of the other vans, if not his own, by breaking in upon their privacy in an apparently unpardonable manner. This hunt for one's bathing-machine constitutes one of the daily joys of English bathing. Each little house is generally girdled with the patent-medicine sign of some enterprising Briton, and the bather is advised to try all sorts of doubtful compounds for his various ailments. There was a society founded in London to discourage advertisements in public places, by pledging its members to refuse to buy anything advertised in a railway station or other conspicuous spot. Apparently, to judge by the frequency of signs everywhere, this society is not in a very flourishing condition.

Each English woman, when she appears upon the beach, must bring her walking-stick with her; she could never take her morning constitutional without it. It is no uncommon sight to see a party of English people out for a walk, each woman with a stick, each man without one. They make the walking-stick a great aid, testing rocks in the midst of streams with them, probing suspiciously soft spots in the sand; a bath is never complete that does not include the use of this stick to and from the bathing-machine.

The sea-bath in England, as in America, costs a fixed price, which includes everything except the services of the bathing-master. The details of the bath are less intricate than in France: the peignoir is unknown, and hot water is never placed in the bathing-machine. The machines themselves are all of one style, not varying in size or comfort. If a bather requires the aid of the bathing-master, no set price is fixed for his services, the amount of remuneration being left to the judgment of the bather. The bathing-vans are very small, poorly lighted and ventilated, and they seem doubly inconvenient from the habit of the bathing-master, who rolls them into the surf while their occupants are undressing. The bathing-master is not so important in England as on the continent, but he is far more in evidence than he is in America. He keeps a close supervision of the women and children bathers, but, as the English woman is as a rule more athletic and more daring than her continental sister, his work is less arduous.

*The Cosmopolitan*, August 1895

There have been instances of actual heroism among the ladies who go in bathing at Narragansett Pier, at Seabright and at Long Branch. Look at the illustrations in your Sunday newspapers and judge for yourself if I am not right. Of course when I say heroism I do not mean the melodramatic emotion of hysterical drama; but there are heroines of the beach who defy the cold, calculating criticism of the inartistic male by making their bathing dresses as nearly ideal as conditions and the prudery of the age will permit – without police interference. I am sorry that the word police slipped into this article at all. The police should not be judges of seaside society. Who ever heard of a policeman with a true eye for artistic ensemble? Who ever heard of a policeman with an intuitive appreciation of the ideal? What do they know of the boundary line between the proprieties of a ball dress and a bathing costume? I contend that the interference of a village policeman with the privileges of idealism that the summer girl can advance at the seashore vulgarizes the whole scheme of the modern *toilette de mer*.

Probably the most "fetching" (I don't like the word, but it is in this sense most conservative) bathing costumes ever seen in America were those worn by the young women who appeared in. the "Gaiety Girl" at Daly's Theatre. At the time it was suggested that they were only fit for stage wear. The property bathing machine and the painted water were their security of grace, The audiences who witnessed the performance of the Gaiety Girls at Daly's Theatre last winter were impressed with the taste and natty style of the bathing costumes worn there, but of course never

applied them to practical value for future use.

Yet these costumes were designed after the most approved style of the dresses worn by the élite of Paris at Trouville. They were made in Paris. I confess that, with very slight modification, I have seen the identical costumes at Narragansett Pier and at Long Branch.

The portrait of Florence Lloyd in her stage bathing costume is a fair example of the dresses worn by many ladies on the seashore at these resorts. To be sure the skirt worn by the actress is a trifle short, but in France a long cloak is worn while the lady crosses the sands from her bathing tent to the water, which she hands to her maid just before she makes her first plunge.

The costumes worn by the Gaiety dancers were made of silk, instead of flannel.

Cissy Fitzgerald's bathing dress was an exact pattern of a similar costume worn by a very fashionable and titled Frenchwoman at Trouville. The colors were white and blue, and the bonnet was made of oil-silk.

I talked with Miss Fitzgerald about the practical advantages of the costume she wore, and she assured me that it was not in the least exaggerated for stage effect. Even the high-heeled slippers are worn on the beach at Trouville. The cloak modifies the apparent audacity of the costume, and as the wearer hurriedly wraps it about her immediately she leaves the water, the inartistic mob need not be shocked by what is, after all, merely a graceful picture.

To speak seriously of this question of propriety in ladies' bathing dresses, the fault lies more conspicuously with the manner in which the wearer conducts herself than in the costume she wears. We are so accustomed to abuse the motives of the swimmer girl on the score of feminine vanity that we very often misjudge the decorum of her costume on such grounds.

The temptation to be admired leads to indiscreet posing and lounging on the sands during bathing hours that is worse than savage, because it is suggestive.

*Frank Leslie's Popular Monthly*, August 1895

## 1896

IF you are interested in the growth of things ugly to things beautiful, and are a bit of an evolutionist in a way, we would suggest, as a field for your observations, that you travel on any perfect summer day to one of our fashionable watering-places, and cast a comprehensive eye at the costumes of those who sport upon the shore. And as you sit there on the beach, recall, if you can, that so-considered modest apparel of the most hideous gray flannel which used to be proclaimed the correct thing when our mothers were girls. Allow the retrospective mind to catch a glimpse once more of those graciously artistic full trousers reaching to the very ankles and finished with a frill which was as awfully simple as it was simply awful. Remember, too, the bag-fitting blouse to which was attached an exceedingly scanty skirt, the sleeves which came to the wrist and were tied there like the neck of a meal-sack, and the big straw hat which completely hid the identity of the wearer. It is (or was) indeed a charming

picture, a thing of shreds and patches; a something which savored as strongly of the rag-bag as of the tailor's art, a bathing-suit that was in fact made up of any old scraps that could be gathered at random in a blind search of the house closets. Such was the frightfully constructed rig (it hardly deserves to be called a dress) which the ethics of fashion demanded in those days. Let us hope that, in this respect at least, history does not repeat itself, and that our eyes shall never be again inflicted by painful spectacles like unto these. The march towards things beautiful in late years has indeed been undergone at a sharp pace, but there has nevertheless been side-issue retreats; we can only pray against the time when it will be considered as *a la mode* to dress one's self again in old-fashion clothes as it has been to furnish one's room with old-fashion furniture.

It is with a refreshing feeling of contrast that we see to-day, in place of these antediluvian nondescripts, the more pleasing costumes of those who are bathers in the deep. Some of them seem verily too marvellous creations to be subjected to so destructive an element as the salt water. They possess all the appearance and quality of material that the smartest street gown requires. Black satin, mohair, and rich wash silks figure so conspicuously amid these scenes where the surf of the sea rolls incessant that one marvels at the wealth of a tailor's resource and his ability to introduce the beautiful even under the most inauspicious circumstances. Of course we are all well aware, and say so on the sly, that some of his designs were never intended to be submerged in the water, but were only planned to grace its fair owner as she poses on the sand under the shade of a becoming parasol. But there are not many such. On the other hand it is the more practical girl clothed in the more sensible dress who predominates. She it is who combines the beautiful in effect and the adaptability in material. She is not a "show" bather; her dress is not a nom-de-plume, it is in nature as well as in name a bathing-suit.

Of these inexpensive ready-made bathing-suits, the serges and flannels, there is one model which seems to have a wide-spread popularity. This is composed of a short skirt and high gathered bodice, all in one, with full under trousers in a separate piece. The sleeves of these suits are usually in short puffs and the neck of the bodice is commonly finished with a broad sailor collar. The more inexpensive the suit the more it runs to white braid, zig-zag and plain, and the bigger its collar.

Of the more expensive suits those made out of heavy gros-grain silks are exceedingly stylish, any of these materials admitting of much elaboration in the way of trimming. Many of the waists are almost as elaborate as those made for an evening gown. There are large puffs for sleeves, which are lined with crinoline, and the epaulettes over them are also lined and stiffened.

Although crinoline takes water very quickly, when it dries it regains its rigidity, so that madame on donning her suit the second time has the satisfaction of knowing it looks quite as fresh as when new.

As a rule, the puff sleeve ends before it reached the elbow, and mitts are being revived to protect the white arms of the fair bather, so that they may be presentable by gaslight. For neck trimming, large sailor collars, heavy with braid or embroidery, are seen on many of the new silk suits. Others have revers, and it must be remembered that these are well lined with a material which will keep them in place.

Skirts are a trifle longer than those worn last season, and much fuller. When white is combined with black a band in used as trimming around the bottom.

For the feet nothing is more suitable than the generally acceptable little sandals of black or colored satin with cork soles. These are strapped daintily around the ankle with narrow satin ribbons crossed over the instep. With a shapely foot the effect is all that could be wished.

Of the designs for bathing-suits that are at once serviceable, inexpensive, and artistically effective, perhaps there is none more popular nor more simple than that which is presented first in this current number of the magazine. It is made of any color serge, black, blue, or red, and trimmed with whatever colored braid that will contrast with the body of the suit. The skirt is made separable, while the waist and trousers are of one piece. Usually half-puff sleeves are worn, although, when desired, long ones are added. The great advantage of a costume of this style is derived from the fact that the collar can be turned down from the neck, thus permitting of a high and low service. A serge of this stamp is much preferable to flannel because the wiry nature of its material sheds the water much more quickly than does the flannel. Of the different colors black and a dark navy-blue are generally considered to be in the best taste, because the harmony of colors is more pleasing, and the bright trimmings will lighten the body up as much as is necessary.

The second illustration is a suit made of black or navy-blue brilliantine, the difference from serge being of course that it presents a more dressy appearance combined with the additional merit of being somewhat lighter in weight. In many cases a small sailor collar and skirt bands of another tint is added to this dress, and if the bodice is in the shape of a blouse the sailor collar will often open low over a highly ornamented shield front. Again, it is sometimes constructed with a deep yoke back and front, three box-plaits running from yoke to belt. Naturally, minor variations of this sort are well nigh innumerable, even the least of which, may, in some cases, either entirely make or wholly mar the general effect. One cannot be too careful as a rule in the looking out for the small points. In order that well-fitting stockings may be assured with all suits it is advisable to always purchase them a size smaller than is ordinarily worn, so that they will not stretch too much.

Concerning Design 3, scarce nothing can be said by way of explanation, except that it is by far the more pleasing to the eye when made of mohair. Of this material it is likely that most of the stylish costumes will be made in the future.

Mohair after all makes, perhaps, the most sensible bathing-suit of any material used. It is light in weight and when soaked does not cling to the body as do the serges and flannels.

*The National Magazine*, August 1896

I will give you the programme of the day as it is lived by guests at one of the large hotels – hotels where it costs a pound a day to live with any degree of comfort.

As your bedroom will, in all probability, face the sea, the first rays of light from the sun as it lifts out of old Atlantic will call you out of dreamland. If wide awake, and keen, very keen, on 'surf-bathing,' you will tumble into dressing-gown and slippers, and make your way down to the beach for a 'buff bath,' a tumble and toss in the dear old ocean, unencumbered with the orthodox bathing-costume all must wear at the regular bathing hours. On a clear, crisp, sunshiny morning, this 'bare-breasted' battle with the breakers is a glorious tonic, and sends you home with an appetite for breakfast that spells bankruptcy for 'mine host' if discretion does not hold it in check.

After breakfast, stretched out on a wicker chair or lounge in a breezy corner of the wide verandah, you lazily read the morning papers brought by special train from Philadelphia and New York; meanwhile a splendid orchestra of forty pieces is playing music of a kind which mingles naturally with the lazy mood of place and hour.

About 11 A.M. the after-breakfast idlers disappear, but only to reappear a few minutes later in long lines of 'bath-robed' and dressing-gowned figures, trailing down to the seashore for a surf-bath. It is an attenuated crowd, for as much of the usual garb as Mrs. Grundy, mamma, or modesty will sanction is left behind in the hotel, so that the small frame bath-house – which takes the place of the English bathing-machine – may not be uncomfortably crowded. These small frame bath-houses stand in long lines, 100 deep, at right angles with the beach, and are in charge of an attendant who not only keeps the place clean and dry, but looks after your bathing-suit, drying it after the bath, and in a measure freeing it from the sand which during that bath works its way into every seam. These bathing-suits, by the way, are built on one pattern, originally designed, I believe, by a hater of mankind. They emphasise [sic] every weak point. The thin look thinner, the stout more aggressively rotund. One leg of the breeches is always shorter than the other; and the buttonholes are invariably too large to exercise the slightest control over the undersized buttons. A doleful and dreary blue in colour, the white braid, supposed to add a fashionable frivolity, only aggravates the picture; while the straw hat which bathers in the 'postmeridian' period of life wear as protection against the sun, and which is tied with white tapes under the chin, will demoralise the most self-satisfied bather on his first walk down to the surf. For that walk must be taken through a crowd of people – people who are on pleasure bent, who have a quick eye and keen sense of the ridiculous, and who are not afraid criticism will disturb the bather.

But having run this gauntlet, and reached the kindly shelter of the sea, all memory of caustic criticism is swallowed up in a joy that is mental and moral, as well as physical. And the first breaker not only tumbles you shoreward, but sweeps you out of the careworn present, back to the days when 'you and the world were young together.'

*Cornhill Magazine*, November 1896

## 1897

Strict observance of the following rules, being necessary for the safety and comfort of the bathers, will be insisted upon by the Superintendent and his assistants: –

1. All persons must wear bathing suits or trunks. Only bathing suits of cotton, mohair, Danish cloth, or other material without nap, are allowed, and the colors (preferably blue, gray, black or white) such as will not run.

The 191st Annual Report of the Town Officers of Brookline, Massachusetts, 1897

No. 200. LADIES' BATHING COSTUME.

(Front view on page 38, back view given below.)

This costume combines all the practical features of excellency to be desired in a suit of this kind. It is simple of construction. The blouse and drawers are in one. The skirt is arranged over the body part and the whole completed with a belt. The sailor collar is short in the back and ends in long revers in front, which continue down the edges of the plain vest to the waist line. The skirt is as plain as possible, which is very necessary, as a full skirt is a great disadvantage when water-soaked. As shown in these illustrations is made of serge and trimmed with plain braid. May be made of brilliantine or Shaker flannel. Requires 5 1/2 yds. 44 in. wide for medium size.

*American Home Magazine*, July 1897

## 1898

**BATHING SUITS**

**MEN'S**

Pure worsted, in black, navy and maroon, decorated with woven stripes of silk in Roman colors around knees, shoulder and bottom of jersey.

**$7.50 a suit**

**Caps to match, $1 each**

Other fancy Worsted Suits with colored silk stripes, $4 and $5.50.

Pure worsted suits with colored trimmings, $3 and $5.

**Boys'**

Cotton Suits, striped all over, navy with white or red stripes; fast colors, 75c.

All worsted suits, plain black or blue, $1.75.

*Printers' Ink*, June 22, 1898

I have asked Mme. Sykes Josephine about the bathing corset for your friends of the houseboat. She tells me that the correct corset is made of flannel (price a guinea), and comes to the waist. It has shoulder-straps, and crosses over in fastening. I hope this is the information required. It must be a pretty bathing dress that she writes about – white serge with facings of washing silk.

*Truth*, August 18, 1898

Here I am in Paris, you see, only for a few days. It is much too hot to shop, and yet I do it all day. I have been out buying a bathing costume, in which to delight the wanderers by the seashore at Trouville. It is made of white, and it is cut without any fulness in the tunic save on the hem, which is decorated with one of those shaped flounces bordered with a round scollop. It has a large collar, open at the neck, made of white embroidery, and underneath this ties a sailor knot of red and blue and white plaid, and a cap and shoes of red and blue and white plaid have I purchased to complete this. I have also bought a black bathing gown with a large guipure collar, and knickerbockers of the new shape, turning up like the Cromwellian cuff. I felt convinced I should look particularly beautiful in this black gown. I saw a woman last year at Trouville showing her complexion off to special advantage under such influence.
*Country Life Illustrated*, August 18, 1898

One word in conclusion about dress. Certainly in swimming I am an advocate for 'rational' dress and no skirt, and I think simple knickerbockers and a high body with short sleeves is a much more decent garment than the usual skirted costume with low neck and no sleeves. The lower limbs of the bather are only seen as she enters and quits the water, and the *dry* skirt alone conceals them, not the wet skirt, which, as she leaves the water, clings tightly round her. So as the skirt only fulfils its purpose when the bather walks or dives into the water, and it seriously impedes her swimming powers, I do not think it worth her while in a general way to wear one. If, however, social custom, the opinion or practice of companions in the water, or the fact of bathing with both sexes, renders it advisable to wear a skirt, the swimmer should have one which buttons down the front, like an ulster, and so arranged that it can unbutton and be fastened back to the waistband, and thus leave the legs quite free if the wearer wishes to take a long swim. Cotton twill is an excellent material for a bathing dress; it carries much less weight of water than serge, and also stands wringing out better, and dries immeasurably faster. But in dress ladies will always please themselves, and if shop costumes are any guide to the public taste, it would seem that most of us prefer to carry several pounds weight of woollen braid and limp frills and flounces, which, in reality, are very unsuitable for the lady who 'means business' in the water.
*The Badminton Magazine of Sports and Pastimes*, August 1898

**A Swimming Jacket** may be procured to fasten around the waist under the arms. It is made of cork or some similar material, and the support which it affords gives a timid child confidence in the water and makes bathing a delight instead of a terror. ...
**Bathing Suits.** Alpaca is the most satisfactory material for these suits. They may be trimmed with bands of white duck and a white duck collar added if desired. Those for girls look well made with a full waist and short puff sleeves. For little boys they are made in one piece, with a belt around the waist, sailor collar, short sleeves and reaching to the knee.
*The Ladies' Home Journal*, September 1898

At the present day it is not regarded as incompatible with modesty to exhibit the lower part of the thigh when in swimming costume, but it is immodest to exhibit the upper part of the thigh. In swimming competitions a minimum of clothing must be combined with the demands of modesty. The regulations of the Swimming Clubs affiliated to the Amateur Swimming Association require that the male swimmer's costume shall extend not less than eight inches from the bifurcation downward, and that the female swimmer's costume shall extend to within not more than three inches from the knee. (A prolonged discussion, we are told, arose as to whether the costume should come to one, two, or three inches from the knee, and the proposal of the youngest lady swimmer present, that the costume ought to be very scanty, met with little approval.) The modesty of women is thus seen to be greater than that of men by, roughly speaking, about two inches. The same difference may be seen in the sleeves: the male sleeve must extend for two inches, the female sleeve four inches, down the arm. (Daily papers, September 26, 1898.)
Studies in the Psychology of Sex, 1900

# 1899

THE bathing dress deserves consideration. It is preferably brown; a good, clean bronzy brown, to supersede the blue for which we have almost a superstitious reverence. First, of course, Parisian women declared for brown, and the prime reason for their choice is that it is the most becoming shade for a bathing dress, and then it is one of the few tones that remain firm and fast after hundreds of dippings in salt water.

Those who experiment with green, or red, or purple, all of them good becoming tones, will quickly grow sadder and wiser at their own expense, for the sea water will wring the color out of such pretty water togs, and not infrequently the bather herself will be stained by the running dye until her own pretty neck and arms much resemble a badly decorated Easter egg. So let us be content with brown, and according to one's complexion select the suit. Cream, twine, and wood brown are the gradations to choose from, and, of course, if you simply cannot wear brown, then try gray, or a deep golden cream color. The lovely bathing suits made of oyster shell or mother-of-pearl gray offset with white or black trimmings are quite surprising. Middle aged women will do well to remember that stoutish figures are seen to best advantage in dark brown and dark gray, and only slender young folks should indulge in white, pale gray, and yellow brown for wave riding costumes.

Now for the material wherewith sweet Thetis shall be clothed. Flannel is still regarded as the standard goods for the bathing dress, yet the majority of women have transferred their allegiance from flannel to alpaca and brilliantine. Flannel is decidedly heavy when saturated and dries with provoking deliberation, while brilliantine, or good mohair, or the best alpaca, seem no weight at all in the water; in fact their fiber rejects the fluid, and they all dry speedily. There is no extra expense involved in this last mentioned goods. Again, it is impossible to make a graceful wool bathing dress without allowing a great thickening of goods in the blouse and at the skirt belt, and on a woman who has a comfortable covering of flesh on her bones the fulled flannel produces an extra bungling girth that is not an enhancement to her looks. Mohair

**BROWN BRILLIANTINE**

knows none of these failings, it does not shrink and pull, and no one can deny its durability. Mohair braid and wool braid continue in great demand for ornamentation and it is quite impossible to ignore the fact that flannel is very much employed in bands and belts and collars on the mohair skirts and blouses.

Consider the making of a bathing suit very largely with regard to the figure. If you can and will only wear flannel, then take a bit of advice and make your knickerbockers of mohair. Cut them pear shape – that is to set into a snug, flat yoke at the hips and widening a bit at the knee. Nothing will so relieve the undue weight of a water-logged wool bathing dress as the light, springy knickers. No inventress has yet risen to show us an improvement on the combination of blouse and trousers in one and the short skirt buttoning on to this union garment at the waist. However, there is a marked alteration in many of the skirts; those of flannel, particularly, are shaped to close in without a pleat or gather, at the hips.

A purely conventional bathing dress of this season is of brown mohair. About the foot of its up-to-date skirt runs a widish band of fine deep cream serge, with a narrower fold an inch above that (this fold, by the way, is set on to give the skirt necessary solidity and weight at the bottom). A sailor blouse of brown mohair forms the upper half of the costume and over its shoulders falls a really huge square sailor collar of cream serge. The collar in front has points that converge and taper nearly to the waist line and where its ends come together a scarf of cream wash silk is softly knotted in a sailor's twist. The vest is of mohair, barred with bands of cream wool braid no wider than bébé ribbon, and the long sleeves have cuffs of cream serge.

An ornamental idea, for a slim young girl, is very adequately set forth in the accompanying picture. Here is a yellow brown alpaca suit that is full of body and skirt and buttoned up behind. Madam Paris says the most graceful and novel swimming costumes are so fastened – the yoke and belt, sleeve bands and skirt border, are made of clear blue flannel pierced with a leaf pattern through which shows the pale brown mohair. Elaborate as this looks, it is the labor of one who does the simplest sewing, for at any art needle workshop a pattern can be inexpensively stamped on bands of sapphire or navy blue wool. These are then basted on the dress in the proper places and the line of the stamping followed on the sewing machine threaded with cream sewing silk. After the pattern has thus been secured, the inside of the design is clipped out, and the brown shows up prettily through the blue. By means of a mingled braid of dark and creamy threads the edges of the ornamental bands are finished off, and then, on to the fashionable box pleat decorating the skirt's front and for the back fastening of the blouse, big, round, dark blue crystal buttons are sewed. These are pierced buttons without metal eyes.

Important details of the bathing dress are the gay silk bandannas and polka dotted squares used for tying over the ugly oiled silk bath cap and the ribbed wool hose that ought in color to match the wearer's dress. Now and then on the beaches are seen women in dark blue hose smartly polka dotted, or a woman in brown hose with thread-like stripes running the length of the stockings, but it is well to linger on the side of stern conventionality in the bathing costume, for no fashionable and ladylike person appears on the beach in anything suggesting conspicuous sensationalism.

*Good Housekeeping*, July 1899

And now a single suggestion as to children's bathing-suits for the season of 99. Materials of present preference are flannel, serge, or Turkish toweling, the favorite style of making alike for boys and girls the "one piece suit," – shirt and drawers together. A skirt just reaching the knees is added to the little girl's costume. The bathing-stocking is much improved, being re-enforced in the foot in a sort of moccasin fashion, rendering it a better shape and more durable.

*Table Talk*, July 1899

By the way, there is a princess bathing dress that has much to recommend it. All devotees of the surf have experienced the disagreeable uncertainties of the bathing-dress skirt made to belt around the waist. The bodice and trousers made in one piece are, of course, a great security, but when the flannel or serge skirt becomes water-soaked it is extremely heavy, sags below the belt, and if buttons and loops are supplied, as extra precautions, the skirt band gaps between these in most untidy fashion; most, if not all, women have been subjected to these annoyances which go far toward marring the pleasures of the surf-dip. The advantage of the princess suit will be promptly appreciated. Skirt and bodice are made in one after the usual princess cut. The bodice is lined, curved and darted just enough to follow the lines of the figure without compressing it in any way. If properly curved into the waist no belt is required. The Knickerbockers button on to an inside belt. A model made in blue-black brilliantine and trimmed with wide bands of mohair braid, is voted to be the most stylish, as well as the most refined bathing costume noted at Cape May for many a summer. A beautifying touch has been given to the oiled-silk bathing cap; a necessity for the woman who would be careful of her hair. The new caps are made of gay silk shaped like a Tam O'Shanter and are very *chic* looking.

*Table Talk*, August 1899

BATHING SUITS.

THE selection of a bathing suit demands quite as much thought and consideration as the choice of any other article of clothing. It is an absolutely erroneous idea that anything will do for this purpose, if only it conforms with the regulations of some " Beach" or "Grove," and it is equally erroneous to assert that all bathing suits must of necessity be unbecoming and hideous. Undoubtedly the figure that comes before the mind's eye at the mention of this costume is that of a visibly two legged creature incased in voluminous knickerbockers covered with a shapeless sack-like garment, belted loosely somewhere under the arms, and surmounted by a conical lid of straw coming well down over the ears and upturned in front— truly a fitting bride for the old man of the sea!

Deb Salisbury

However, there is neither excuse nor necessity for this appearance. A bathing suit can be and should be a thing of beauty. If its material is suitable, its cut stylish, and its fit perfect, a woman need fear neither open nor covert criticism. Neither need she feel that she is breaking all the canons of modesty if she lingers for an instant on the beach on her way to or—which is more important—from the water. A bathing suit may be fully as decent and modest as the average bicycle suit, and is, as a matter of fact, vastly more modest and decent than the average evening gown, or the up to date street gown that must be lifted from the ground with both hands and, in the process, be so drawn that every movement of every muscle is revealed.

Before a bathing suit is selected certain questions should be answered. Where, when, and for what purpose is it to be worn? On the sands or in the sea? For dabbling in the edge of the surf or for long distance swims, straight out past all warning buoys, out beyond all restraining ropes? And is sport, real sport, to be sacrificed to complexion?

Material is the first thing to be decided upon. The bathing suit already described is, of course, made of flannel. For ages and generations flannel has been considered the only proper material for bathing suits, and yet of all manufactured cloths, excepting perhaps cotton, flannel is the most unsuitable. It is heavier when dry, it absorbs more water, it is soggier when wet, than any other known material. It shrinks so that after a few dips into salt water it is absolutely shapeless; it fades so that no matter what its color has been it becomes a dingy, brownish green; and, last and most important of all, when it is wet it clings to the figure, revealing every curve and line. Serge, another old time favorite, is almost as bad and for the same reasons.

An excellent material is a thin, light weight mohair or alpaca. This has so little wool in its composition that it absorbs practically no water, and therefore gains little or nothing in weight; it never loses its wiry qualities, but stands out well from the figure, and in dark blue or black it holds its color. But the most satisfactory suit is of knitted wool, or silk and wool, or even mercerized cotton. A combination suit of blouse waist and tights of this material with an alpaca skirt is an absolutely perfect swimming costume. The waist should be pleated in front and, possibly, bloused a little. Otherwise it should be close fitting. The objections to the flannel do not apply to this knitted woolen suit, for in it there is no superfluous material to hold the water, and if it is made by a reputable firm the yarn is shrunk in salt water before it is woven.

French models for bathing suits are almost invariably without a skirt, having instead a tunic-like coat that comes half way to the knees. There is neither grace nor comeliness in this garment, however, and it should be ruthlessly condemned in this country. In France, where the bathing machines are rolled out into the water, and the bather has simply to step from the threshold of her room into the opaque covering of the sea, these suits are excellent, for they leave the legs free and untrammeled, and, as every swimmer knows, it is the leg motion that counts, the arms being little more than rudders to make and keep direction.

Deb Salisbury

On our bathing beaches the houses are well back from the sea; there is always more or less of a walk with more or less publicity about it, and a skirt is absolutely essential for comfort—mental comfort, that is. So a bathing suit must consist of a waist, a skirt, and tights, or knickerbockers with stockings. The waist should always be fastened to the knickers or tights, so that in any or every catastrophe of wind or wave there need be no anguish of mind over apparent and visible discrepancies.

The prettiest waist is bloused, with pleated fronts and a plain back. It may be open at the throat and finished with a square sailor collar, or it may be brought high and close about the neck. Square necks or open Vs. any infringements upon the décolletage of evening bodices are emphatically out of place on bathing costumes, and, as in every other thing in life, unseemliness is equivalent to ugliness. The sleeves may be either long or short according to the taste of the wearer and according also to her desire to protect her arms.

If the suit is made of alpaca, it is wiser to have the sleeves short, because the weight of the material on the arms is considerable, and unnecessary weight means unnecessary danger. In the knitted suits this point need not be considered, inasmuch as the sleeves cling close to the arms, and it is quite possible to nave them come well down over the hands without adding perceptibly to the weight. If the sleeves are short they should be lined or faced with oil silk. This will prevent the disagreeable chafing this is so frequently caused by the rough, wet fabric. In fresh water bathing, however, this precaution is not necessary, because it is the brine that cuts into the skin.

The skirt should come just a little below the knees and must be very scant. In ordinary surf bathing this will not hamper the movements at all, and for long distance swims it is a simple matter to pin the hem in front up to the belt. In addition to the button that fastens this skirt in the back, there should be two more buttons, either on the sides or near the front, to keep the band, which of necessity is loose, from slipping up or down. These buttons, by the way, should be the old fashioned white china affairs, this being the only substance that will surely withstand the action of salt water.

If knickerbockers are worn, they must also be scant, but tights are so much superior in every way to these shapeless garments that when they have been tried once the knickers are sure to be discarded. Stockings and stocking supporters are necessary adjuncts to knickers, and it matters not in what way these articles are worn, they are bound to be unsatisfactory. Elastic loses its essential quality after one or two immersions in salt water; the buckles and clasps of the suspender garter are sure to rust no matter what their material. The band garter around the leg can never be depended upon; if it is loose enough to be comfortable, it is of no possible use, while if it is tight enough to hold, it is almost sure to cause bather's cramp. When tights are worn the stockings are, of course, woven on them. Garters are therefore unnecessary. Neither is there any possibility of a wide, yawning crevasse between the overhanging knickerbockers and the slouching stockings, or, worse still, a harlequin vision of one white leg and one black.

Then, if the knickers are loose enough to permit absolute freedom of motion, they must of necessity be clumsy, they must have superfluous material that will hold water and drag the swimmer back and down, and they will assuredly add some half dozen inches to her circumference. The

A FRENCH SUIT MADE WITH FULL BLOOMERS INSTEAD OF THE HAMPERING SKIRT.

tights, on the other hand, are like a second skin. They create no extra bulk, and yet every muscle has free play; there is no material to sag or bag, and yet nowhere is the garment tight or binding.

There has heretofore been one good and valid objection to these woven tights, and that is that the feet were cut out, and that no matter how carefully they were darned that part of the garment was used up long before the rest. But that objection has now been overcome. Extra feet may be obtained, or even extra soles or heels, and it requires no skill and very little patience to put them on. If bathing shoes are worn, the stockings will not wear out so readily, and for inshore pebbly beaches these canvas slippers are very comfortable. They are, of course, shaped like moccasins, and are not especially attractive in appearance, but they save the feet from sharp little pebbles or shells and from the slimy little jelly-fishes that are foolish enough to seek their fortunes on the sands. For swimming these shoes are impracticable, because they are exceedingly heavy and hold the water.

The decoration of a bathing suit not only seems but is quite absurd. It is in simplicity alone that this sort of garment can gain style, in simplicity and a closes adherence to suitability. Mohair or cotton braid of white or some contrasting color is the only trimming that is ever permissible, and either one of these will add more or less weight to the suit; they are sure to shrink differently from the material on which they are sewed, and until this material is unusually well dyed its color will undoubtedly run into them. A wide white canvas belt adds to the appearance of a black or dark blue suit, but, in reality, it should be the only line to break the severity of the costume.

Bathing corsets seem an absurd anomaly, and for the swimmer they are quite impossible, because of all forms of exercise swimming demands the freest, most untrammeled muscles; but for the mere dabbler in the surf, for the aquatic maiden who clings to the life rope, these unboned flannel corsets are, while perhaps not advisable, quite permissible. If a woman has a heavy figure, if the rolls and billow of flesh are a weary, sagging weight, a corset is almost essential and never more so than when she is liable to be tossed about by discourteous, irreverent waves. The corset must be loose, there must be no attempt to create a "figure" with it, but it will quite do away with the pillowy appearance that is no often seen on bathing beaches, that is so ludicrous to the well corseted onlooker, that is so dispiriting and uncomfortable to its unfortunate possessor.

Hair dressers and wig makers are fond of asserting that sea bathing is good for the hair, but this can only be put down to one of two reasons. Either they are grossly ignorant on the subject or else they are desirous of creating a demand for their wares, because nothing is much more injurious to the hair that a protracted season of sea bathing; that is to say, unless it is water. The hair is a sort of physical barometer. It indicates disease, losing its color and luster quickly and responding readily to any tonic influence. Sea bathing undoubtedly does tone the entire system, and of course the hair receives its share of vigor, but this general benefit is slight in comparison with the local injury to the tresses themselves.

If, every day, after the bath, they could be thoroughly rinsed in fresh water and well dried, the injurious results would be modified, but this is impossible. Even summer days are too short to devote a couple of hours to drying the hair, and in every climate there are innumerable days when there is no sunshine and when of necessity it must be left in a damp and cloggy state.

Deb Salisbury

On calm days, in smooth water, it is perhaps possible to hold the head out of the water and keep the hair fairly dry. but the ocean is apt to be rough in its treatment of intruders, and if the hair is to be kept really dry it must be covered with some material that is impervious to water.

An oilskin or rubber bag held in place by means of a tight elastic may not sound alluring, but it is absolutely to be relied upon. And then, it is not intended for show. It need not be a baggy mop cap. It should, in fact, be small and fit close, so that it will not increase the size of the head, and over it should be worn a silk handkerchief drawn close in at the back of the head and tied in a bow in front. The cap and handkerchief may be the only head coverings, but if old Sol's kisses are liable to be transformed by the alchemy of the sea into black or yellow blotches, a wide brimmed hat may be fastened to the cap with tiny buttons and elastic loop. For real swimming a hat is abominably in the way, but then to the real swimmer freckles and sunburn seem infinitesimal trifles compared with the joy of the sport, and she knows, too, that lemon juice and cream are easy and efficacious remedies.

If a woman is not averse to the use of powder, a liberal application of cold cream dusted over with ordinary baby powder will render the use of a shade hat quite unnecessary: that is, for an ordinary half hour bath on days when the thermometer can content itself in the eighties. When it wanders up into the nineties or demands three figures to express its feelings, some sort of wide brimmed hat or vizored cap is necessary. This is also essential if the sea bath is to be prolonged for hours, dashes into the sea alternating with siestas on the sand, unless complexion is such a minor detail that it is not given the slightest consideration.

On the other hand, if complexion is the most important thing in a woman's life, if her clear pink and white skin is the one complete joy of her existence, and if at the same time she longs for a refreshing plunge into the sea.it is quite possible for her to wear a swimming mask. In France and England these masks are sold as regular additions to swimming outfits, but at American watering places they are rarely seen.

They are made of thin chamois skin fitted over the nose, with holes for the eyes and mouth, and are drawn up over the forehead and around over the ears and the nape of the neck. They are uncanny objects, however, and if a woman encased in one of them could only meet herself in the water she would undoubtedly decide that it would be preferable to be moderately ugly for a long time than to be so frightfully and fiendishly hideous for even a little short half hour. Except for the hair and the skin the salt water will prove most beneficial. It will be a tonic for tired eyes, and even when it is swallowed the disagreeable effects will only be momentary.

The foregoing suggestions apply to the bathing suits that are to be worn into the water. If they are to appear only on the sands, or if the summer girl who wears them intends to venture only knee deep into the white sea suds, she can allow herself greater latitude in material and decoration. The most charming material for her to select would be the new heavy weight cotton canvas. It comes in good solid colors and pretty mixed effects that will stand the bleaching processes of the sun and the hot, dry sand. Somewhat more daring combinations of colors may be permitted the suits which will not be exposed much to the fading, shrinking influence of salt water. Brilliant belts, collars, ties, and cuffs may brighten even demure and conventional blue and black alpaca. In cut and design she should follow to a certain extent the directions given to her more daring sisters, but the accessories of her costume may be as picturesque as she pleases.

And it is perhaps fortunate that on every summer beach there should be a few of these maidens who are willing to obey the old nursery rhyme and hang their clothes on a hickory limb but not go near the water. They are the joy of those who watch the animated scene from piazzas and piers; they are the inspiration of many a poster artist and many a newspaper illustrator. They certainly add color and brilliancy to the scene, and if the fun of sitting on the sands in a swagger they must remember that there are bathing suit does seem a bit insipid to compensations in the realization of a the rollicking crowds in the breakers, picturesque ideal.

*The Puritan*, July 1899

Apropos of clothes under one aspect, there has been quite a new departure in the matter of bathing-dresses at most of the smart Continental seaside-places this summer.

At Trouville and Ostend, where the gay world does much foregather, lovely woman has been disporting herself by the no means sad sea waves in black alpaca bathing-costumes, frogged and vandyked with white mohair braid, white bathing-shoes, and white crinoline bathing-bonnets.

The blouses this year were in most cases made quite long, almost entirely hiding the knickerbockers, a departure by means of which some modesty and much grace have distinctly been achieved.

Many women who are content to take their sea-baths without swimming have worn straw hats, simply tied under the chin, which have been found very practical and protective from the sun's rays, while for those others who do not approve of doing things by halves, waterproof foulard caps of much variety and jauntiness have been evolved, those worn *en marmotte* being much the prettiest.

The smartest of peignoirs have been also used when entering and leaving the water – molleton, which is light, soft, and warm, being in first favour. Various coloured plaids have also been used, and these, edged round the collar with fringes to match, have made a capital finish to other fascinating seaside adjuncts. A white serge dress should also be taken in a seaside trousseau. It is always smart and serviceable. High boots of white doeskin and a white Manilla-straw sailor-hat are also necessary to complete these fresh and charming altogethers.

*The English Illustrated Magazine*, September 1899

# 1900

## BATHING GOWNS AND WRAPS.

THE increasing popularity amongst English people of the dressing tent pitched on the sands when on bathing intent, in place of the stuffy uncomfortable machine, whose owners tyrannised over us for so long, accounts in great measure for that vast improvement in bathing toilettes now so noticeable this side the Channel as well as on the more cosmopolitan of our compatriots at French watering places, the reason of course being that the tent is of necessity some distance from the water, to reach which one has to run the gauntlet of countless critics, instead of being at once immersed as when the machine was drawn right out. No longer, therefore, is the average woman content with a shapeless sack of serge (which, passing in quick rotation all its days from one unknown wearer to another, remained always in that same uncanny stage of sticky dampness peculiar to the hired bathing dress), and a hideously unbecoming cap, which the casual observer mistook for the sponge bag. Rather does she give her best energies to the achievement of a dress whose charm and little individual touches shall mark her out from the crowd, and this is completed by

### a coquettish cap

of soft bright red silk, or pretty floral mackintosh made up as a dainty tarn o' shanter with classic sandals trimly laced round the ankles by interlacing ribbons, and lastly, a long cloak in which to run down the sands to the water's edge. The most noticeable thing about these modern bathing dresses, apart from their increased elegance of cut and finish, is the lengthened skirt, for it is to this that erstwhile scanty tunic has grown – and the adoption of the boned Swiss belt, lightly boned it is true, but still unmistakably a species of corset, in place of the straight unstiffened narrow band, which hitherto has been universal in this connection, and much too reminiscent it was (when round that "too too solid flesh" of middle age) of the "roly poly pudding" of our nursery days. For the gown itself the materials mostly used are serge and stockinette, in red, white, black, and blue, and a pretty cream woollen corduroy, though there are several fancy materials checked, spotted, and sprigged, which have found purchasers for this purpose, and at Ostend, satin is used not only for facings and pipings, but for the dress itself, but it is not likely to commend itself to English maids and matrons for such a purpose. Drill, nankeen, and galatea, however, have always a certain following over here. The material chosen, there are several

### new styles

available for the making thereof, apart from the difference in the skirts, many of which even display flat stitched pleats, while full loose trousers reaching nearly to the ankle are an integral part of many of this season's suits, but are not nearly so smart and workmanlike, at any rate, for swimming in, as the short knickers trimly banded below the knee. Then, though the sailor collar, with a bodice cut open to display a vest, is immensely worn, some very charming gowns have been made with a yoke, from which depends a full belted bodice and tunic or skirt. This, in that rather coarse, strong make of cream-coloured serge (which neither shrinks nor hardens like most of the soft fine makes) is particularly chic, trimmed with wide cream braid, and the wearer's monogram on the vest in silks, and, if she be a brunette, a dark red silk sash and handkerchief cap twisted round the head. For

### the bathing wrap

a wide choice of materials and colours offer themselves, while for the shape, the military cloak reaching to the heels, banded at the waist and displaying the regulation service collar, is new and eminently smart and adaptable to the bathing wrap. If this style be chosen, a thick red or dark blue blanketing flannel suggests itself as a good material for the purpose, or, if one of the picturesque cloaks with a monk's hood, sling sleeves and girdle, be preferred, Turkish towelling can be had for it in a variety of colours, including mauve and green either plain or patterned with white. Bolton sheeting, Turkey twill, and pirle-finished serge are are [sic] all used, too, very successfully.

### For the head

there is a choice of caps as indicated above, and also the mob cap, the flower-girl shape – flat, like a plate, with a button in the centre – and the charming Breton one, and some girls follow the Frenchwoman's example and wear a rustic hat when bathing of either rush or sunburnt straw, with plenty of shade, and tied down over the ears. Writing of hats reminds me that for yachting women there are some most attractive caps of the true nautical style, but in white or coloured linen to match the gown, the crown loose with a trimming of gold galon and a peak, but to essay these caps successfully one needs to be thoroughly well turned out in every respect, as the effect of such a cap worn with an unsuitable dress is common and bad form. The prettiest hats, after all, for either seaside or country remain those big picturesque Leghorns and burnt straws, simply trimmed with roses and black velvet, and these, as was prophesied when "She Stoops to Conquer" resurrected them this Spring, have been immensely worn everywhere, and there is really nothing better, as they are so shady, a merit the sailor cannot claim, and the reason, perhaps, that it is rather at a discount this season. However it has always a certain following and the newest are of nutmeg straw, with a double brim – and only a feather weight in spite of this.

   *Golf Illustrated*, July 27, 1900

## A Rare Lot of Bathing Suits

They're unusually good or we would not feel justified in calling your attention to them. And it's not the fact of their goodness alone, but the moderate prices we've been able to put on them, that will interest the surf lover. The fit, the material, the colorings, each appeal to a critical eye.

### Men's Bathing Suits.

Wool, 2 pieces or combination ... ... ... ... ... ... ... ... ... ...  $2.00
Jersey Wool, plain black... ... ... ... ... ... ... ... ... ...... ... ... 3.00
Jersey Knitted Suits, ankle length trunks, long sleeves  ... 4.50
Jersey Wool, fancy stripes... ... ... ... ... ... ... ... ... ... ... ... 4.00

### Women's Bathing Suits.

Plain or trimmed Black Mohair,   $2.50 to $10.00
Black or Blue Flannel ... ... ... ... ... 3.50 to  5.00
Misses' Black Mohair ... ... ... ... ... 2.25 to  3.50
Misses' Flannel Suits ... ... ... ... ... 3.00 to  4.00
Bathing Caps... ... ... ... ... ... ... ... 15c. to  1.50
*The Land of Sunshine*, July 1900

# 1901

The summer girl who contemplates hieing herself away for a month or two by the sad sea waves, is of course much interested in the question of bathing suits.

One naturally hesitates to trust the fashioning of such a thing to the perhaps unfamiliar fingers of one's dressmaker, for fear that it may emerge from those fingers an article so completely wanting in beauty and correctness to be entirely unavailable.

But milady on the bathing dress intent may find a very pretty assortment of these articles of apparel – or is it perhaps, un-apparel – at L. S. Ayres, the only establishment, in the city by the way, that features the bathing dress, and may satisfy herself of their attractiveness and correctness in advance – one of the desirable qualifications of ready-to-wear garments. Combinations of blue and white predominate in this showing. One or two of black and white, or glowing scarlet offer a contrast, but the overwhelming majority show the traditional blue and white in their make-up. And it is undeniable that for seaside wear nothing seems so attractive and appropriate as the eternal blue and white.

The time-honored flannel has been altogether discarded for a Turkish mohair brilliantine, a far more satisfactory fabric. The flannel, when water-soaked became heavy and almost unmanageable, and beside acquired an exaggerated and altogether undesirable cling. The brilliantine on the contrary is light in weight, does not absorb water and has nothing of the clinging vine in its composition and for these reasons is far preferable to the earlier fabric.

One of the prettiest dresses in the collection is of a warm blue, a happy medium between navy and royal, the skirt, belt, and sailor collar trimmed with bands of white Sicilian mohair, a quality somewhat heavier than the Turkish mohair, on which are applied narrower stitched bands of the blue. A white tie of mohair finishes the exceedingly pretty little suit. Another, almost as pretty, has for decoration innumerable rows of the tiniest white mohair braid imaginable, completely covering the broad hem, the belt, and the square sailor collar, giving a delightfully chic and jaunty effect. The prices of the bathing dresses range from four dollars to twelve, the range including a considerable variation in elaboration and in quality of material.

*The Indiana Weekly*, June 29, 1901

## BATHING SUITS

The old standard materials for bathing suits have not been much improved upon this season, and flannels, serges, brilliantines, and silks still constitute the most used and the most desirable goods. Perhaps, for general utility, brilliantines are specially to be recommended. They are not so heavy, when wet, as flannels, will not shrink so much as serge, nor cling so closely as silk. Of course, before making up a costume, the goods, of whatever kind selected, must be thoroughly shrunken; and even then it is advisable to leave the waistband loose, as it will inevitably shrink a little from the daily wettings. The bands around arms and knees are best finished with a firm elastic, and, for decoration, cotton braids are preferable to woolen, as they shrink less.

There is also very slight variation in the cut of bathing suits this summer. The most satisfactory style of garment is made in two pieces, the blouse and knickerbockers in one piece, with a short skirt. This should not fall lower than the knees, or it will be apt to get in the way of the hands in swimming. Sleeves are curtailed to a short puff, reaching about one-third the distance between shoulder and elbow.

For a woman with good neck and arms, the low-cut bathing suit is undeniably more picturesque; this style is not much worn, however, because of the sunburn and tan which inevitably follow its use.

If corsets are worn under the suit, hose-supporters are fastened to them, but they are usually dispensed with, the hose-supporters being fastened to a belt. Hose should match the suit in color. A fancy of the season is bright Scotch striped hose, and a cap of plaid or stripes in salt-waterproof silk. This silk is something new, and makes a welcome change from the yellow, oiled silk, covered with a handkerchief, which has hitherto been chiefly used. This silk is made up in coquettish sun-bonnets, which perform the double duty of protecting face and neck from the blistering rays of the sun and making a very becoming addition to the suit. It is also made up in small caps, which are lined with oilskin, with the silk draped over them, turban-style, the ends tied in a large bow in front.

A charming costume can be made up in red brilliantine, trimmed with white braid, red hose, low, white canvas shoes, a white canvas belt, and a dainty sun-bonnet of this waterproof silk, in red and white plaid.

*Pearson's Magazine*, June 1901

NOW that so many of us will be enjoying sea bathing, our thoughts naturally turn to the subject of bathing dresses, and the subjoined illustration shows two charmingly pretty dresses for lady and child. The lady's swimming costume or bathing dress looks remarkably pretty in pink Viyella, and may be edged with white or red braid if desired. The blouse part has a Russian basque falling just below the hips, sailor collar, and short sleeves. It fastens down the front with buttons, being shaped somewhat at the waist, and the broad band is loosely fastened round the waist. For this garment about 3 3/4 yards of Viyella, 31 inches wide, are required. This material is most suitable for bathing dresses, as while having all the advantages of a thin flannel, it does not shrink at all, and retains its colour even after daily immersion in the briny. The colours are very dainty, and may be had either plain or striped in various ways, in pale blue, pink, mauve, pale green, scarlet, &c., and all of these colours combined with white in various designs. The knickers are set into a broad-shaped band fastening on each hip; a little band is drawn in at the bottom of the legs, tying with a tape to the requisite size, and fastening loosely below the knee. To make the knickers requires 3 1/2 yards of Viyella, so that the total quantity required is about 7 1/4 yards for a medium-sized figure. Pattern of this dress may be had from the office of WOMANHOOD, post-free 1s. 7d. for lady's size; 1s. 1d. for the child's size, cut to measure.

*Womanhood*, July 1901

On the beach the wonderful display of bathing suits at once strikes the eye. There are suits of silk, satin, mohair and, what seems exceedingly popular this summer, of a Japanese crepe material which seems well adapted for the purpose. One of the most noticeable features this season is the fit of these costumes; and this point must receive great consideration if one wishes to make a smart appearance. Short linen corsets are necessary to obtain the desired effect. The blouse, if cut on correct lines, will have the long-waisted straight front. While black will be worn to some extent, the white suit is undoubtedly the season's choice. Our friend being, of course, strictly up to date, appears in a fetching suit of white mohair, trimmed with bright blue strapped with white. The skirt is tucked to within ten inches of the hem, then flares gracefully around the bottom. The blouse is tucked and finished with a sailor collar and broad upturned cuffs. The entire effect is attractive and the suit bears comparison with the many stunning garments on exhibition.

*Good Housekeeping*, July 1901

OUTING ATTIRE. [for men]

Speaking of bathing suits, I hear that in the higher priced garments there are few loud color effects shown. Plain black or blue mohairs, with Roman stripes near the border in brighter colors, predominate. One of the swellest suits imaginable is of gray, with a border of black.

*American Wool and Cotton Reporter*, July 25, 1901

A word anent [sic] bathing suits. Why cannot a man wear a fairly decent garment when bathing, instead of the sleeveless, almost backless, garment that is now so generally affected? If a man cannot swim with a sleeve that covers his shoulder, he should give up bathing in company that includes women.

Etiquette for All Occasions, 1901

The great watering places where Parisians transport themselves during July and August are parade grounds of fashion. In July there is a week of racing at Dieppe, in August a fortnight at Trouville. This kind of sport appeals in general more than golf and bicycling and tennis, although all are practised along the Normandy and Brittany coast. Trouville, Dieppe and Dinard are the most fashionable watering places in Prance. In the north all Frenchwomen swim well. They wear bathing suits of flannel or serge, made in two pieces, with a skirt above the knees; they do not wear stockings, nor do they cover their bathing caps with the pretty colored scarfs which make other beaches so gay. They do on the other hand, however, cover themselves with long *peignoirs* of rough towelling which they drop only at the water's edge. There is very little coquetry among even the fashionable Frenchwomen with regard to the morning swim. Their costumes out of the water sufficiently compensate. They experiment with every remarkable combination, always keeping within the limits of good taste.

*The Delineator*, August 1901

Lady Constance Mackenzie, who is a handsome young girl still in her teens, is a particularly daring and graceful swimmer, and usually dives in with a quaint little cry; often she appears in a wonderful scale bathing-gown, a veritable mermaid's dress, at other times she dons a stockingette costume just relieved by the tartan of her clan.

*Cassell's Magazine*, October 1901

# Bibliography

191st Annual Report of the Town Officers of Brookline, Massachusetts, 1897

Acting Charades, or Deeds Not Words, a Christmas Game.  Brothers Mayhew. London: D. Boque, 1850

*The Almanack of the Month: a View Everything and Everybody*, October 1846

*American Home Magazine*, July 1897

*American Wool and Cotton Reporter*, July 25, 1901

*The Anglo-American Magazine*, May 1854

*The Anglo-American Magazine*, July 1854

Annual Report of the Commissioner of Patents for the Year 1869. 41st Congress, House of Representatives.
    Washington: Government Printing Office, 1871

*Appletons' Journal*, August 14, 1869

*Appleton's Journal*, July 31, 1875

The Art of Swimming in the Eton Style. "Sergeant" Leahy. London: Macmillan & Co., 1875

*Arthur's Home Magazine*, July, 1859

*Arthur's Home Magazine*, July 1867

*Arthur's Home Magazine*, July 1877

*Arthur's Home Magazine*, May 1881

*Arthur's Home Magazine*, August 1882

*Arthur's Home Magazine*, November 1886

*The Atlantic Monthly*, October 1866

*The Badminton Magazine of Sports and Pastimes*, August 1898

*The Bazaar, The Exchange and Mart*, July 11, 1881

*The Bazaar, The Exchange and Mart*, July 20, 1881

*The Bazaar, The Exchange and Mart*, August 15, 1881

Bazar Glove-Fitting Patterns, James McCall, Kramer & Co. Pattern Catalog, 1879

Belgium as She is.  H. R. Addison. Brussels and Leipsig: C. Muquardt, 1843

*Belgravia: An Illustrated London Magazine*, Holiday Number, 1876

Bentley's Miscellany.  Richard Bentley. London: Richard Bentley, 1856

*Brooklyn Magazine*, August 1885

*Bow Bells*, July 3, 1872

*Bow Bells*, September 17, 1873

The Boy Travellers in Central Europe: Adventures of Two Youths through France, Switzerland, and Austria.
    Thomas W. Knox. New York: Harper & Brothers, 1893

The Boy's Treasury of Sports, Pastimes, and Recreations.  Samuel Williams. Boston: D. Bogue, 1844

The Boy's Treasury of Sports, Pastimes, and Recreations.  Williams and Gilbert. Boston: John P. Hill, 1847

Cassell's Household Guide, Volume II, 1869

*Cassell's Family Magazine*, October 1885

*Cassell's Family Magazine*, Autumn 1886

*Cassell's Family Magazine*, October 1887

*Cassell's Magazine*, Summer 1894

*Cassell's Magazine*, October 1901

*Chambers' Edinburgh Journal*, May 4, 1850

*Chambers' Edinburgh Journal*, November 23, 1850

*Chamber's Journal of Popular Literature*, October 17, 1863

Children's Fancy Work: A Guide to Amusement and Occupation for Children.  Unknown. London: Ward,
    Lock and Co., 1882

The Children's Magazine and Missionary Repository.  J. F. Winks. Boston: Simpkin, Marshall, and Co.,
    1848

*The Clothier and Furnisher*, July 1887

*The Clothier and Furnisher*, February 1894

*The Clothier and Furnisher*, May 1894

*The Clothier and Furnisher*, June 1889

The Code of Health and Longevity.  John Sinclair. London: Sherwood, Gilbert & Piper, 1844

A Complete Descriptive Guide of Long Branch, N.J.  J. H. Schenck. New York: Trow & Smith Book
    Manufacturing Company, 1868

A Complete Dictionary of Dry Goods. George S. Cole. Chicago: 1892

*Cornhill Magazine*, November 1896

*The Cosmopolitan*, June 1895

*The Cosmopolitan*, July 1895

*The Cosmopolitan*, August 1895

*The Cottage Hearth*, August 1885

*Country Gentleman's Magazine*, July 1868

*Country Life Illustrated*, August 18, 1898

*Current Literature*, November 1889

The Daily Governess; or Self-Dependence. Mrs. Gordon Smythies. London: Hurst and Blackett, 1861

Dashes of American Humour. Henry Howard Paul. London: Piper Brothers and Co., 1852

Decorum: A Practical Treatise on Etiquette and Dress of the Best American Society. S. L. Louis. New York: Union Publishing House, 1883

*The Delineator*, June 1894

*The Delineator*, August 1901

*Demorest's Monthly Magazine*, July 1879

*Demorest's Monthly Magazine*, August 1879

*The Deseret Weekly*, August 12, 1893

*Domestic Monthly*, June 1881

An Encyclopædia of Domestic Economy. Thomas Webster. New York: Harper & Brothers, 1845

*The English Illustrated Magazine*, September 1899

Etiquette for All Occasions. Mrs. Burton Kingsland. New York: The Platt & Peck Co., 1901

*Every Saturday: A Journal of Choice Reading*, August 25, 1866

*The Exchange and Mart*, August 16, 1871

*Family Friend*, August 1866

Fitzherbert: or, Lovers and Fortune-Hunters. Unknown. London: Saunders and Otley, 1838

*Frank Leslie's Illustrated Weekly*, July 6, 1893

*Frank Leslie's Lady's Magazine*, July 1879

*Frank Leslie's New Family Magazine*, August 1858

*Frank Leslie's New Family Magazine*, August 1859

*Frank Leslie's Popular Monthly*, August 1895

*Fraser's Magazine*, February, 1860

Girl's Own Outdoor Book, ed. by C. Peters, London: The Religious Tract Society, 1889

*Godey's Lady's Book*, August 1857

*Godey's Lady's Book*, July 1867

*Godey's Lady's Book*, July 1868

*Godey's Lady's Book*, September 1879

*Godey's Magazine*, August 1894

*Golf Illustrated*, July 27, 1900

*Good Health*, June 1869

*Good Housekeeping*, August 3, 1889

*Good Housekeeping*, July 1899

*Good Housekeeping*, July 1901

*Graham's Magazine*, August 1855

Grandmamma's Pockets. Mrs. S. C Hall. Edinburgh: William and Robert Chambers, 1849

Greenwood Leaves: a Collection of Sketches and Letters. Grace Greenwood. Boston: Ticknor, Reed, and Fields, 1850

The Guide to Knowledge. Unknown. London: Orlando Hodgson, 1837

Hand-book for European Tourists: through Belgium, Holland, the Rhine, Germany, Switzerland, Italy, and France. Francis Coghlan. London: H. Hughes, 1845

Hand-book for Travellers in France. Unknown editor. London: John Murray, 1847

The Hand-book of Bathing. Unknown. London: William S. Orr & Co., 1841

*Harper's Bazar*, July 25, 1874

*Harper's Bazar*, July 25, 1874, Supplement

*Harper's Bazar*, July 9, 1887

*Harper's Magazine*, November 1852

*Harper's New Monthly Magazine*, June 1858

*Harper's New Monthly Magazine*, September 1876

Hastings Considered as a Resort for Invalid. James Mackness. London: John Churchill, 1842

Health for the Million. Unknown author. London: W. Kent & Co., 1858

*The Herald of Health and Journal of Physical Culture*, June 1866

Hester Stanley at St. Marks. Harriet Prescott Spofford. Boston: Roberts Brothers, 1882

Hogg's Instructor. James Hogg. Edinburgh: James Hogg, 1851

Home and Health and Home Economics: A Cyclopedia of Facts and Hints For All Departments of Home Life, Health, and Domestic Economy. C. H. Fowler and W. H de Puy. New York: Phillips & Hunt, 1880

Home Dressmaking, 1892

*Household Words*, July 16, 1881

*Household Words*, August 13, 1881

*Household Words*, July 5, 1884

*Household Words*, July 26, 1884

How to Make Home Happy: or, Hints and Cautions for All. William Jones. London: David Bogue, 1857

*The Illustrated American*, September 20, 1890

*The Illustrated American*, June 25, 1892

*The Illustrated American*, August 15, 1891

*The Illustrated London Magazine*, August, 1854

*The Illustrated London News*, Supplement August 16 1856

*The Indiana Weekly*, June 29, 1901

*The Knickerbocker: Or, New-York Monthly Magazine*, January 1856

*The Knickerbocker: Or, New-York Monthly Magazine*, October 1859

*The Lancet*, January 1858

The Ladies' and Gentlemen's Etiquette: A Complete Manual of the Manners and Dress of American Society. Mrs. E. Be. Duffey. Philadelphia: Porter and Coates, 1877

*The Ladies' Companion and Monthly Magazine*, August 1852

*The Ladies Companion and Monthly Magazine*, 1858

*The Ladies' Friend*, June 1869

*The Ladies' Home Journal*, September 1888

*The Ladies' Home Journal*, August 1892

*The Ladies' Home Journal*, September 1898

*The Ladies' Repository*, August 1865

The Ladies Treasury for 1882: A Household Magazine. Mrs. Warren. London: Bemrose and Sons, 1882

The Ladies' Work-Table Book. Unknown. London: H. G. Clarke & Co., 1843

*The Land of Sunshine*, July 1900

*Le Follet*, September 1865

Letts's Illustrated Household Magazine, London: Letts, Son & Co., 1883

Letts's Illustrated Household Magazine, London: Letts, Son & Co., 1884

*Life*, August 1, 1889

*Life*, August 10, 1893

*The Life-Boat*, November 1, 1879

*The Literary World*, September 5, 1879

*Littell's Living Age*, November 2, 1850

*Littell's Living Age*, January 17, 1857

*Littell's Living Age*, September 25, 1869

*London Society*, June 1864

*London and Paris Ladies' Magazine of Fashion*, July 1882

Manners, Culture and Dress of the Best American Society. Richard A. Wells. Springfield, Mass: King, Richardson & Co., 1891

*The Magazine of Domestic Economy*, February 1838

The Master's Service, A Practical Guide for Girls. Lady Brabazon et al. London: The Religious Tract Society, 1883

*The Metropolitan*, October 1837

Miscellaneous Writings of F. W. P. Greenwood, D. D. F. W. P. Greenwood. Boston: Charles C. Little and James Brown, 1846

*Mother's Journal*, August 1869

*Munsey's Magazine*, July 1892

*Myra's Threepenny Journal*, April 1, 1882

*Myra's Threepenny Journal*, July 1, 1882

*Myra's Threepenny Journal*, August 1, 1882

*National Magazine*, August 1896

New York as it is, in 1837. Unknown. New York: J. Disturnell, 1837

North America. Anthony Trollope. Leipzig: Bernhard Tauchnitz, 1862

The Old Log Schoolhouse. Alexander Clark. Philadelphia: J. W. Daughaday, 1864

*Once a Week*, August 3, 1867

Our Deportment: Or, The Manners, Conduct, and Dress of the Most Refined Society. John H. Young. Detroit, Mich.: F. B. Dickerson & Co., 1882

*Our Country Home*, July 1888

Parisian Sights and French Principles, seen through American Spectacles. James Jackson Jarves. New York: Harper & Brothers, 1855

*Pearson's Magazine*, June 1901

Pebbles from the Sea-shore; Or, Lizzie's First Gleanings. A Father. Philadelphia: Geo. S. Appleton, 1851

*The Penny Magazine of the Society for the Diffusion of Useful Knowledge,* August 31, 1837

*The Penny Magazine of the Society for the Diffusion of Useful Knowledge,* November 29, 1845

*The People's Journal,* July 4, 1846

*Peterson's Magazine,* July 1869

*Peterson's Magazine,* August 1870

*Peterson's Magazine,* July 1871

*Peterson's Magazine,* July 1873

*Peterson's Magazine,* August 1876

*Peterson's Magazine,* August 1879

*Peterson's Magazine,* July 1880

*Peterson's Magazine,* August 1882

*Peterson's Magazine,* July 1883

*Peterson's Magazine,* July 1884

*Peterson's Magazine,* August 1884

*Peterson's Magazine,* August 1887

*Peterson's Magazine,* July 1888

*Peterson's Magazine,* July 1889

*Peterson's Magazine,* August 1889

*The Photographic News*, August 15, 1884

Picturesque Excursions. Arthur Freeling. London: Ackermann & Co., 1842

The Popular Encyclopedia; or Conversations Lexicon. Volume VI. Unknown editor. London: Blackie and Son, 1862

*Printers' Ink*, June 22, 1898

*Publishers' Weekly*, June 14, 1879

*Puck*, September 5, 1888

Punch, or the London Charivari. Unknown. London: Published for the Proprietors, 1842

*Puritan*, July 1899

Random Rambles. Louise Chandler Moulton. Boston: Roberts Brothers, 1881

San Francisco Municipal Reports for the Year 1871-1872, Ending June 30, 1872. Board of Supervisors. San Francisco: Cosmopolitan Printing Company, 1872

*The Saturday Review*, August 30, 1856

*The Saturday Review*, September 5, 1863

The Science of Swimming, as Taught and Practiced in Civilized and Savage Nations; with Particular Instructions to Learners. Experienced Swimmer. New York: Fowlers and Wells, 1849

Sea-Air and Sea-Bathing for Children and Invalids: Their Properties, Uses, & Mode of Employment. Mons[r]. Le Docteur Brochard, trans. William Strange. London: Longman, Green, Longman, Roberts, & Green, 1865

Sea-Bathing: Its Use and Abuse. Ghislani Durant. New York: Albert Cogswell, 1878

Sketches, by Boz. Charles Dickens. Paris: Baudry's European Library, 1839

*Smith's Illustrated Pattern Bazar*, Spring, 1873

Southwold, and its Vicinity, Ancient and Modern. Robert Wake. Yarmouth: F. Skill, 1839

*The Spectator*, September 26, 1863

*The Spectator*, August 11, 1894

Studies in the Psychology of Sex. Havelock Ellis. Philadelphia: F. A. Davis Company, 1900

A Summer Amongst the Bocages and the Vines. Louisa Stuart Costello. London: Richard Bentley, 1840

*Sylvia's Home Journal*, June 1879

*Table Talk*, August 1892

*Table Talk*, July 1899

*Table Talk*, August 1899

*Tinsley's Magazine*, August 1867

The Tourists Companion and Guide to Coney Island, Fort Hamilton, Bath Beach, Sheepshead Bay, Rockaway Beach and Far Rockaway. J. Perkins Tracy. New York: Austin Publishing Co., 1887

The Tourist's Guide, or Pencillings in England and on the Continent. John Henry Sherburne. Philadelphia: G. B. Zieber & Co., 1847
Transatlantic Tracings; or, Sketches of Persons and Scenes in America. J. R. Dix. London: W. Tweedie, 1853
The Traveller's Classical Guide Through France. M. Richard. Paris: Maison, 1840
*Truth*, August 25, 1881
*Truth*, July 24, 1890
*Truth*, August 18, 1898
*The Union Magazine*, December 1848
*The United States Democratic Review*, February 1848
*The United Service Journal, and Naval and Military Magazine*, August 1837
A Vacation Tour in the United States and Canada. Charles Richard Weld. London: Longman, Brown, Green, and Longmans, 1855
The Visitor's Guide to the Watering Places. Unknown. London: W. Strange, 1841
*Warehousemen and Drapers' Trade Journal*, August 5, 1876
*Warehousemen and Drapers' Trade Journal*, July 29, 1876
The Western World: or, Travels in the United States in 1846-47. Alex. Mackay. Philadelphia: Lea & Blanchard, 1849
The What-not; or Ladies' Handy-Book. Unknown. London: Kent & Co., 1861
*Womanhood*, July 1901
The Workwoman's Guide. A Lady. London: Simpkin, Marshall, and Co., 1838

## About the Editor

I'm the owner of the Mantua-Maker Historical Sewing Patterns, established in 1994. My costuming career began early – making dresses for my sister's dolls. I discovered costuming at the BayCon masquerade, a science fiction convention held in 1985, and soon thereafter fell in love with historical costuming. After many years of collecting historical clothing terms, I decided to assemble and share them with other costume historians.

*Five Rivers Publishing*, based in Canada, published my first non-fiction work, *Elephant's Breath & London Smoke: Historic Colour Names, Definitions & Uses* in 2009.

My second non-fiction work, *Fabric à la Romantic Regency: A Glossary of Fabrics from Original Sources, 1795 – 1836* is available on Createspace, Smashwords, and on Etsy. It was published in 2013.

Although I grew up in Northern California, I've lived in England and Colorado, and currently reside in sunny Central Texas. I've been a receptionist, a waitress, a computer programmer, a warranty clerk, a real estate assistant, an inept archer, a costume maker and a dressmaker.

### Connect with Me Online:
www.mantua-maker.com
www.etsy.com/shop/MantuaMakerPatterns

Published by
The Mantua-Maker Historical Sewing Patterns
Abbott, Texas